Calgary

SPIRIT OF THE WEST

Calgary

SPIRIT OF THE WEST

A History by
Hugh A. Dempsey

GLENBOW
and
FIFTH HOUSE PUBLISHERS

Front cover painting, *Downtown Calgary,* by Douglas Stephens, courtesy Glenbow-Alberta Institute, with permission of Shirley Stephens Begg

Cover design by John Luckhurst/GDL

The publisher gratefully acknowledges the support received from The Canada Council and Heritage Canada.

Printed and bound in Canada by D.W. Friesen & Sons
94 95 96 97 98 / 5 4 3 2 1

Canadian Cataloguing in Publication Data
Dempsey, Hugh A., 1929-

Calgary: spirit of the west

Includes bibliographical references and index.
ISBN 1-895618-49-5 (bound)
ISBN 1-895618-53-3 (pbk.)

1. Calgary (Alta.) - History. I. Title.
FC3697.4.D45 1994   971.23'38   C94-920097-2
F1079.5.C35D45 1994

Fifth House Ltd.
620 Duchess Street
Saskatoon, SK, Canada
S7K 0R1

CONTENTS

Preface — 1

IN THE BEGINNING
A Pristine Land — 3
The Mystery of Fort La Jonquiere — 5
Peace Treaty at Nose Hill — 8

WHISKEY AND BIBLES
First Intrusions — 11
The Whiskey Merchants — 12
The Pious Mavericks — 15
First Family of Calgary — 19

COMING OF THE REDCOATS
A Fort in the Wilderness — 23
The Policeman, the Girl, and the Stove — 25
What's in a Name? — 30
The Sarcees Find a Home — 32

GROWING PAINS
An End to Isolation — 37
Arrival of the Railway — 38
Patriots and Renegades — 41
Jerry Travis and the Whiskey Ring — 45
Fire and Sandstone — 53
Gunfighters and Killers — 56

A CITY IS BORN
Waiting for the Boom — 61
When Calgary Became a City — 65
The Ranchmen's Club — 68
The Terrible Floods — 71

A NEW CENTURY

Optimism – 75

A Capital Idea – 78

The Hundred Thousand Club – 81

The Privately Owned Centre Street Bridge – 89

The Birth of Chinatown – 93

Women of Calgary – 97

WAR AND ITS AFTERMATH

Prelude to Battle – 103

Calgary Goes to War – 104

One Big Union – 109

Bob Edwards and Prohibition – 112

The Twenties that Didn't Roar – 114

HUNGRY THIRTIES AND OFF TO WAR AGAIN

Depression and War – 119

Riots of the Unemployed – 120

Another War – 125

ANOTHER BOOM

Into a New Era – 131

A Gridiron Spectacle – 133

Finding the Lost Fort – 137

The Incredible Seventies – 139

DOWNSIZING

The Uneasy Eighties – 145

A Bunch of Pinheads – 146

Old Neighbours – 151

Into the Twenty-first Century – 154

Notes – 156

Index – 160

PREFACE

Whatever else Calgary's history might have been, it was never dull. It had booms and busts, villains and heroes, and moments of greatness and ignominy. It was populated by men and women who were unabashed optimists, shameless boosters, and those who genuinely cared about the welfare of others.

This book looks at these people and events through words and pictures. It consists of a running series of stories in chronological sequence which highlight some of the events of the various epochs in the city's history. It is not intended to be a comprehensive reference work nor does it try to include a multitude of statistics and facts to monitor the city's growth. Instead, it focuses on the stories that reflect the spirit of Calgary—its brashness, optimism, and its resilience.

The formal history of Calgary already has been covered in Grant MacEwan's *Calgary Cavalcade,* Tom Ward's *Cowtown,* Max Foran's *Calgary, Canada's Frontier Metropolis,* Leishman McNeill's *Tales of the Old Town,* and the various writings of Jack Peach. In addition, the 1975 Century Calgary Historical Series produced booklets on such diverse topics as mayors, churches, band music, police, and municipal affairs. Other authors have written about sports, the fire department, and various municipal services.

The voyage of discovery which led to the writing of this book revealed some interesting data about Calgary. For one thing, historians have said that the Canadian West was never really "wild," not like the American West. In fact, Calgary had its moments in the early 1880s when it seemed to be very much a wild western town. It had a corrupt chief of police, illegal bars, open prostitution, a "hangin' judge," and even a laughable one-sided gunfight.

The persistent theme running through Calgary's history is one of optimism. This is not a modern phenomenon—although it is one of the city's strongest features today. Just look at the city's economic roller coaster ride: it went from a boom in 1883 to a bust a year later. It had a spurt of activity during the Riel Rebellion of 1885 then went into the doldrums when the railway failed to bring the expected rush of settlers. It had another economic boom in 1890 with the start of the Calgary & Edmonton Railway but this was followed by the recession of the 1890s. Laurier's Liberals brought the country's economy back to life after 1896 and Calgary rode the crest of a rising boom through to 1914. It crashed again during the First World War, never completely recovered in the 1920s, then hit its low ebb during the Hungry Thirties. The Second World War and the 1947 discovery of oil led to Calgary's biggest boom in history, but this too began to slip in 1981 and plummeted six years later.

During these periods of booms and busts, Calgary never lost its optimism or its entrepreneurial spirit. This was especially true during tough times. It achieved city status and built some of its finest sandstone buildings during the 1890s recession; it almost went broke in the Hungry Thirties helping the unemployed; and it sponsored the world-class Winter Olympics at the outset of its worst recession in years.

The preparation of this book was made possible with the help of a number of people and institutions. I wish to thank the Glenbow Museum for its support and particularly Lindsay Moir and Catherine Myhr in the Library, Doug Cass in the Archives, Donna Livingstone in Publications & Research, Ron Marsh and staff in Photography, and Anthony Cooney in Glenbow Enterprises. Appreciation also is expressed to Kate O'Rourke and others in the National Archives of Canada, to the RCMP Archives, Provincial Archives of Alberta, City of Calgary Archives, and all the others who had information and advice to offer. And I wish to give special thanks to my wife, Pauline, for her unfailing support to a husband who at times seems to get swallowed up in his computer.

IN THE BEGINNING

A PRISTINE LAND

IN THE BEGINNING, THE LAND BETWEEN THE BOW AND ELBOW RIVERS

WAS ONE OF PRISTINE BEAUTY. WHEN THE FIRST EUROPEAN SETTLERS ARRIVED

IN THE 1870S, THEY REMARKED ON THE CRYSTAL CLEAR WATERS, THE GRASSY VALLEY

ENCLOSED BY HIGH HILLS WITH A FEW COTTONWOODS AND WILLOWS FLANKING THE RIVER BANKS.

IN THE BACKGROUND—REMARKABLY CLOSE AT TIMES—WAS THE UNBROKEN RIDGE OF THE

ROCKY MOUNTAINS. IT WAS LIKE AN IMPENETRABLE BARRIER WHICH

DOMINATED THE WESTERN HORIZON.

In winter, chinook winds rolled down through the foothills, bathing the area in its warm caresses, melting the snow and banishing it to the dry brown soil. In summer, a rich carpet of grass provided nourishment for the thousands of buffalo, elk, and other animals which grazed along the edge of the foothills.

This scene had remained unchanged for centuries. Buffalo in large thundering herds followed trails down to the water to drink. Deer and elk stood nervously nearby, watching for grizzly bears and prairie wolves. Overhead, a hawk circled in a cloudless sky of azure blue, while in the trees, a band of crows carried on a noisy conversation.

Into the scene of tranquil beauty came Calgary's first inhabitants, the native peoples. No one will ever know which tribe first gazed upon the forks of the two rivers. Does one accept the finding of archaeologists who claim that the first peoples came across the Bering Strait about 12,000 years ago? Or should one listen to native elders who say that their ancestors didn't come from anywhere, that they were created right here?

There is a story told by the Blackfoot[1] about the creation of the land which occurred after a great flood. And lest anyone think this is simply an adaptation of the Old Testament, it must be pointed out that as early as 1809—fully thirty years before the first missionary arrived in the West—fur trader Alexander Henry heard this Indian story of the flood being told at his trading post on the North Saskatchewan River.

In the Blackfoot tale, a trickster/creator named Napi, or Old Man, was floating on a raft with four animals after the flood. At Napi's request, each creature dived into the water to search the depths, but only the muskrat was strong enough to bring some earth to the surface. Napi took the mud, rolled it in his hands, and it began to grow until it formed a huge land mass. Napi then began a trek northward on this new land, creating prairie grass, rivers, and mountains. Along the way, he also made animals, sometimes experimenting until he got it right. For example, he made the delicate antelope in the mountains but found it could not survive in the rugged terrain so he led it onto the open plains where it happily bounded away beyond the horizon. On another occasion, he made a sturdy bighorn sheep but it was clumsy and awkward on the plains so he took it to the mountains where it was comfortable on the craggy peaks.

Napi did much of his creation work in what is now southern Alberta. The names of Oldman River, Tongue Creek, and the big glacial erratic from which Okotoks gets its name all originated from Napi's adventures.

When the land was complete, Napi made the first woman, then she went away to create more women. Napi, meanwhile, began to make men. He taught them how to hunt but discovered he had made another mistake. When he created buffalo, he made them as meat eaters and they began to hunt the first natives and devour them. This was the opposite of what Napi intended, so he changed the buffalo into grass eaters and the natives into hunters.

Finally, the men and the women were brought together at a buffalo jump west of Cayley—now known as the Old Woman's Buffalo Jump—and the first marriages took place. Then Napi realized that his usefulness was at an end, so he turned himself into a pine tree.

From an archaeological viewpoint, there are many signs of ancient human occupation in the immediate Calgary area. More than a hundred sites, including buffalo jumps, tipi rings, camp sites, butchering sites, and cairns have been recorded. One of the most interesting of these was found in 1968 on 17th Avenue near 7th Street SW when excavating for the Mona Lisa Art Gallery. Buffalo bones and stone butchering tools were discov-

ered about nine feet below the surface, indicating that hunters had been butchering at this site more than 8,000 years ago.

Points or arrowheads of a similar age have been excavated at a site in Hawkwood while other artifacts have been found in Parkdale, Point Mackay, Bow Bottom, Strathcona Park, and at other locations. On Nose Hill alone some forty-two pre-contact sites have been recorded, with another forty-six at Fish Creek Park. All these sites point to the fact that Calgary was an important location for early native peoples. It offered one of the best river crossings for many miles and provided an excellent shelter for winter camps. In summer, the surrounding hills and western breezes provided relief from heat and the myriad of mosquitoes, black flies, and other unwelcome pests.

Later, when trading posts were opened at Edmonton and Rocky Mountain House in the 1790s, the site of Calgary was the regular fording place for bands going north from the plains. Twice a year, in the spring and fall, the Blackfoot loaded their travois and packhorses with buffalo robes, dried meat, and furs and made the ten-day journey to the fort. They bought knives, axes, kettles, powder, shot, and other necessities, then returned to the plains and foothills south of the Bow River.

From these travels developed the Blackfoot Trail, a

THE UNSPOILED BEAUTY OF THE NORTHERN PLAINS WAS RECAPTURED IN THIS 1922 SKETCH BY C.M. RUSSELL. (AMON CARTER MUSEUM, 1961.318)

THE MYSTERY OF FORT LA JONQUIERE

In 1911, the *Albertan* carried a story in its tenth anniversary special issue that in 1751, French explorers had established a fort at Calgary "right on the site of the present North West Mounted Police barracks at the junction of the Bow and the Elbow rivers."[1] This was startling news and, if true, the fort would have been the first European structure in what is now Alberta.

Certainly, French explorers had been active in the West in the mid-1700s and their work had been monumental. In 1731, Pierre La Verendrye had received a monopoly over the fur trade west of Lake Superior. Much of this area was unknown territory to the Europeans so he immediately launched a series of expeditions into the interior. Trading posts were built in the Winnipeg region and from there La Verendrye learned of two big rivers which flowed from the west. One, called *Riviere de l'Ouest,* was the Missouri, while the other, *Riviere Blanche,* was the Saskatchewan. La Verendrye was convinced that one of these would lead to the legendary "Western Sea" which had been sought by explorers for generations.

La Verendrye's two sons, Louis-Joseph and Francois, made an epic voyage of discovery to the south-west of Lake Winnipeg in 1742-43 which took them through the present states of North Dakota and South Dakota and as far as the "shining mountains"—likely the Big Horn range in Wyoming.

La Verendrye then decided to explore the Saskatchewan but he died before the plans could be effected. So the governor of New France appointed Jacques LeGardeur de St. Pierre in 1750 to continue the explorations. When he came west, St. Pierre's goal was to find a route to the Western Sea. He established his headquarters at a fort near the present Dauphin, Manitoba, and sent his lieutenant, Boucher de Niverville, to explore the Saskatchewan River system. He was given instructions to build a post 300 leagues above a fort which already existed on the lower waters of the river, probably in the area of the present The Pas, Manitoba. From their explorations, they hoped to find westward flowing rivers which would lead them to the Western Sea.

Niverville was caught in a terrible blizzard and almost

well-known route which is commemorated in the naming of one of Calgary's major thoroughfares.

Pat Bad Eagle, a Peigan elder, recalled: "When people in our camp went to trade, we went to where Fort Macleod now stands and went north to Tongue Creek and the river at Okotoks. We always kept in the open. We went on to Calgary and farther north we passed through the pines and Peace Hills to Edmonton. When we travelled, the leader of the warrior society went in front; one of the main warriors was in the rear. We always did this when we got into enemy country."[2]

When surveyor John Nelson passed through the area in 1880, the Blackfoot Trail was a well-marked route. North of Calgary, it forked near Rosebud Creek, one branch leading to Rocky Mountain House and the other to Edmonton.

So from time immemorial, the site of Calgary was important as a river crossing and camp site. Yet it was not the site of a trading post until the latter part of the nineteenth century . . . or was it?

starved as he made the difficult overland trip to the Saskatchewan. He was so fatigued by the time he got to the trading post that he became ill and was unable to continue the voyage. However, in May of 1751 he decided that he could wait no longer so he "sent off ten men in two canoes, who ascended the river Paskoya [Saskatchewan] as far as the Rocky Mountain, where they made a fort, which I named fort Lajonquiere [in honour of the Marquis de La Jonquiere, the governor of New France], and a considerable store of provisions, in expectation of the arrival of M. de Niverville."[2] No journals, maps or other documents which would pinpoint the exact location of this fort appear to have survived.

In November, St. Pierre visited Niverville, who was still sick at his fort on the lower Saskatchewan River. Then the trader learned of a tragic incident at Fort La Jonquiere which caused him to abandon his plans of exploration. As he explained in a letter to his superiors:

This is the result of the treason. The Assinipoels [Stoneys] going to where the French were newly established at the Rocky Mountains, found the Yhatchelini [strangers or enemies] there to the number of forty to forty-five [dwellings] . . . The Assinipoels, seeing that they were much more numerous than the others, slaughtered them, and no mention is made of a single person saved, except a few women and children whom they carried off as prisoners. This unfortunate event totally deranged my plans, and compelled me, most unwillingly, to abandon them.[3]

This slaughter would undoubtedly have led to further hostilities and because the attack had taken place at Fort La Jonquiere, the French would have been seen as allies of the Stoneys. The Yhatchelini tribe was never identified. The term is a Cree one and could have been used to describe any enemy, such as the Blackfoot, Sarcee, or Beaver Indians.

St. Pierre was further frustrated when the men at Fort La Jonquiere and local Indians told some fascinating stories about the unknown country towards the Western Sea. One Indian said that a great distance to the west north-west was a trading post whose occupants were neither English nor French. They were located at the mouth of a large river and had their storehouse on an island. These men—perhaps Spaniards or Russians—wanted beaver skins and were willing to trade knives, lances, horses, and saddles for them. St. Pierre could never find out if the story was true or if it was just a wild tale.

These brief references to Fort La Jonquiere set off a flurry of controversy among twentieth-century historians regarding the location of the elusive fort, even as to whether it was on the North Saskatchewan or South Saskatchewan river system.

Surveyor J. B. Tyrrell believed that Niverville's men would have stayed in the north, along the edge of the woodlands and among friendly Crees, rather than venturing out onto the barren prairies among the unknown Blackfoot. In fact, Tyrrell did not think that the men penetrated any farther west than the present Nipawin, Saskatchewan. On the other hand, historian W. J. Eccles hypothesizes that the expedition actually did come within sight of the mountains and that the later Rocky Mountain House may have been built at the site of La Jonquiere.

Lawrence Burpee did not agree. In his major study, *In Search of the Western Sea,* Burpee believed that Niverville's men would have taken the southern route because they did not know the source of the other stream and were afraid they might end up on the shores of Hudson Bay among the British. As evidence, there is St. Pierre's statement:

> I had only to fear landing at Hudson's Bay, which I had fully determined to avoid by turning to the West, in order to find the sources of the Missouri River, in the hope that they would lead me to some rivers having their course in the part to which I sought to penetrate.[4]

However, if they had travelled up the South Saskatchewan 300 leagues—about 750 miles—it would have brought them only to the Medicine Hat area and not as far west as Calgary. In fact, 300 leagues on either the North or South Saskatchewan would not have been enough to bring Niverville's men within sight of the Rocky Mountains.

Historians Elliott Coues, Louis Masson, Harold Innes, A.G. Morice, and Archibald McRae all believed that Fort La Jonquiere was on the southern stream and Masson in 1889 was one of the first to claim that it was located at Calgary. Georges Dugas ventured even farther west in his calculations. He stated that "the older voyageurs, who know the country and the Indian traditions, state that it was much nearer the Mountains ... It is said that when an Indian passes that spot he casts a stone on it."[5]

Other pieces of evidence were presented to support a South Saskatchewan location for Fort La Jonquiere. One was a claim that the Bow and Belly rivers were actually corruptions of the French terms *beau* and *belle,* indicating that the streams had been named by French explorers. However, very little research was required to prove that the Bow River is a translation of the Blackfoot term *Namuh'tai,* which means "bow river" or "weapon river," and the Belly River was named by the Blackfoot because it passes near the Belly Buttes, a ridge that looks like a buffalo on its side with its belly exposed.

The relationship of Fort La Jonquiere to Calgary ultimately proved to be tenuous at best. The whole idea originated in the mind of a stately gentleman named Ephrem Brisebois, commanding officer of the Mounted Police who built Fort Calgary in 1875. When F Troop arrived at the confluence of the Bow and Elbow rivers, Brisebois saw the ruins of a trading post and, recalling the exploits of early French explorers, he assumed it was Fort La Jonquiere. He immediately wrote to Benjamin Sulte, a Quebec historian who was writing an eight-volume work, *Histoire des Canadiens-Français,* and he obligingly made reference to the discovery.

However, it turned out that Brisebois was mistaken. What he probably saw was not a 125-year-old ruin but the remains of an American whiskey fort destroyed only two years earlier. Cecil Denny, who was second in command of F Troop, described the destruction of the fort:

> They [the traders] had been attacked by Blackfeet their horses run off and one of their number killed and several wounded. Mr. Davis who was trading whisky a few miles above, had loaned them horses and they had all gone south. The Indians sacked the stores and burnt them to the ground.[6]

But like other legends, the story of Fort La Jonquiere being at Calgary refused to die. Historians frequently referred to Sulte's notation in his history of French-Canada and others repeated Brisebois's comments as if they were proven facts. In 1930, for example, when the federal Department of the Interior published a list of historic trading posts, it stated that "Capt. Brisebois of the Royal North-West Mounted Police founded a post called Fort Brisebois which grew into the city of Calgary. Capt.

Brisebois stated that he had found traces of old fort Jonquiere on the spot."[7]

When the Calgary *Albertan* published its account in 1911 it stated that "beyond doubt" Fort La Jonquiere was built at Calgary.[8] But not everyone was willing to accept the story. Pioneer missionary John McDougall immediately wrote to the newspaper and utterly rejected the idea. He said that the Indians knew about all the trading posts which had been built and abandoned in the region. They were aware of the various sites of Fort Edmonton, Peigan Post, and Chesterfield House but "after 50 years of understanding their language and sojourning with them, and studying their traditions and history, I never heard a word of any 'house' or fort near where Calgary is situate."[9] McDougall also insisted that any fort would have left chimney mounds and disturbed soil which could still be seen a century later.

But in spite of evidence to the contrary, Fort La Jonquiere has lived on as part of Calgary's tradition. Perhaps because no one has ever found the actual remains of the fort anywhere else and no new evidence has come to light, Calgary is thought to be as good a place as any. The *Calgary Herald* in 1936 and 1955 raised the possibility that the fort was here and the *Albertan* brought up the suggestion in 1947. It's a nice thought, but it probably isn't so.

PEACE TREATY AT NOSE HILL

From the times of the earliest explorers, the site of Calgary had been Blackfoot country. Even by the late 1800s, the Stoneys seldom camped any closer than Cochrane while the Sarcees were farther north near Rocky Mountain House and Buffalo Lake. Of the three Blackfoot tribes, the Peigans had claimed the Calgary area until about the 1830s then gradually moved south to the Missouri River. Sometimes the Bloods wintered at the Bow and Elbow but most often it was the Blackfoot tribe, the people who today call themselves the Siksika Nation, who claimed the area.

Because the Blackfoot were the most northerly of the three tribes, they were frequently at war with the Crees.

Both tribes were well armed so the fighting was often disastrous. Cree war parties waylaid their enemies on their way to the trading posts and the Blackfoot responded by attacking Cree camps. This fighting reached its peak in the 1860s after the Crees had killed a Blackfoot chief en route to Fort Edmonton. The tribe immediately retaliated and any peace-making efforts by the Hudson's Bay Company were in vain.

By the spring of 1869, some of the Cree elders had become so tired of war that they decided to put a stop to it. Accordingly, an expedition was organized by Broken Arm, or *Maskipitoon,* a respected leader who had come under the influence of Methodist missionaries and had been baptized by them four years earlier. He was known to the Blackfoot as Young Man Chief, or *Manikapi'na.*

A ten-man party travelled south to the Bow River, hoping to meet some friendly chiefs like Crowfoot or Three Suns. Instead, they stumbled onto the camp of Many Swans, the most intractable of the three head chiefs of the tribe.

Many Swans, or *Akoi'mukai,*[1] had become a chief in 1858 when he took over from his older brother. Traveller William F. Butler described him as "a man of colossal size and savage disposition, crafty and treacherous."[2] The Blackfoot considered him to be one of their greatest leaders. He was a generous man who kept valuable buffalo-running horses to loan to the poor people to hunt. But he was a man who showed no diplomacy, sympathy, or mercy when dealing with an enemy or anyone who opposed him.

When Broken Arm and his party found Many Swans' camp, they dressed in their best clothes, hid their horses in a coulee, and went to a nearby hill. There they raised a Union Jack and sat with a Bible, pipe, and tobacco, and waited to be discovered. This was a traditional way of making contact with an enemy.

As soon as Many Swans saw them, his only thought was to kill them. He approached them on horseback, holding his hands in the universal sign for peace and suggested that both sides go into the discussions unarmed. As soon as the Crees had agreed and put aside their guns, Many Swans said to his warriors, "Go ahead! Shoot and kill them!" The Blackfoot dashed among the unarmed peacemakers and in a few minutes all of them were dead, scalped, and their bodies dragged triumphantly back to camp.

Later that month, the Crees near Battle River learned that Broken Arm and his peace delegation had been slain but they had none of the gory details. The result, of course, was more warfare and by the end of summer almost a hundred Blackfoot had been slain.

During the winter of 1869-70, a smallpox epidemic swept over the plains, killing more than 600 of the tribe. The Crees, less affected by disease, saw it as an excellent time to attack their weakened foes. In the early autumn of 1870 some 800 Cree and Assiniboine warriors struck a small encampment of Bloods on the St. Mary River, but they were unaware that a huge village of Peigans was located a short distance upstream. Within a short time, the better-armed Peigans counterattacked and the raid became a slaughter. According to participant Jerry Potts, "You could fire with your eyes shut and would be sure to kill a Cree."[3] Exact casualties are unknown, but between two and three hundred Crees and forty Blackfoot died that day.

The Blackfoot spent the winter of 1870-71 recovering from the smallpox epidemic. Like other chiefs, Many Swans seems to have been chastened by the devastation caused by the virulent disease and seemed less inclined to go to war. With the havoc created in their lives, the chief needed to concentrate on his followers, to feed them and to protect them; intertribal fighting seemed less important.

In the spring of 1871, Many Swans was camped on the plains below Nose Hill within the present limits of Calgary when a messenger arrived from the Hudson's Bay Company at Edmonton, encouraging the Blackfoot to bring their furs and provisions to them rather than to the Americans at Fort Whoop-Up. He also brought a proposal for peace from the Cree Indians. Many Swans agreed to trade with the British so a small party left Nose Hill late in July and arrived at Fort Edmonton on August 3 where they were treated royally by the Hudson's Bay factor.

Two days later, Father Albert Lacombe arrived and gave Many Swans some tobacco which the Crees had sent as a peace offering. Many Swans still had no love for his enemies but he knew that times had changed. In addition, his wife, Many Buffalo Stones Woman or *Akai'niskimyaki,* had become an outspoken proponent of peace. She was his senior wife and because of her position, she had the privilege of freely expressing her opinion. She convinced her husband that they should make a treaty and offered to take the message personally to the enemy camps.

When his followers asked Many Swans why he would let a woman make the dangerous trip, he replied, "If we went it would be taken as a sign of war, but they will let her go into their camp and deliver the message."[4]

While the rest of the trading party went back to Nose Hill, Many Buffalo Stones Woman set out alone for the Cree camps on the Battle River. She carried a frame of crossed sticks with tobacco, eagle plumes, and sweetgrass tied to its centre to show that she was a messenger of peace. The Crees welcomed her, for they too were tired of war and their leader, Sweetgrass[5], had been pressing his people to make a treaty with their Blackfoot enemies.

She presented the tobacco to Sweetgrass, who accepted it, filled his pipe and passed it to all the chiefs in his camp. Many Buffalo Stones Woman explained that she was there to lead them to the treaty site at Nose Hill and a few days later a Cree delegation set out with her for the Bow River.

Meanwhile, Many Swans made plans for the forthcoming treaty. Soon the scattered lodges were assembled in a huge circle with four tipis pitched in the centre. Each was occupied by one of the warrior societies, the protectors of the camp. The chief also sent the men out hunting so there would be plenty of fresh meat for their guests.

When Many Buffalo Stones Woman, Sweetgrass, and the other Cree chiefs arrived they marched in a procession, one holding a Union Jack and another a frame of crossed sticks with sweetgrass, plumes, and tobacco. A few yards behind them came the rest of the Crees in an orderly line.

They were welcomed by Many Swans and his followers, and the Cree chiefs were taken into the four society lodges where, in formal ceremony, they smoked a pipe of peace and the treaty was concluded.

After two days of feasting and visiting, a camp crier announced that on the following morning they would be moving to the Rosebud River, thirty miles to the northeast. There, after another two days of feasting, Many Swans told his followers, "Tomorrow I'm going to put up a big dance for the visitors." He pitched his tipi in the centre of the circle, tied four horses in front of it, and loaded them with gifts. When the crowds had gathered, the chief began handing out weasel-tail suits, shields, drums, and other presents.

The Crees were pleased and one of their leaders cried out, "Now we know the Blackfoot are the greatest of all the four tribes—the Blackfoot, Blood, Peigan, and Sarcee—and Many Swans is the greatest chief of all of you."[6]

But then a Blackfoot orator through his incessant bragging, wrecked the feeling of comradeship which had been created over the previous week. Perhaps he was a relative of Many Swans who could not resist talking about his leader, or perhaps he was someone who loved to gossip or taunt his enemy. Whatever the reason, he was not satisfied to simply tell the Crees that the Blackfoot chief was a great leader.

"Many Swans is our head chief," he cried aloud, "because he is the one who fooled *Manikapi'na.*"

The Crees listened intently to the orator. They knew that he had spoken the Blackfoot name of their great chief, Broken Arm. The orator went on to describe in detail how Many Swans had tricked the peace party into giving up their guns under the Union Jack, how he told his men to slaughter them, and how they performed a great victory dance to celebrate the event. Sweetgrass and the others were appalled; this was the first time they had been told how their leader had died.

The visitors were angry but quiet for the rest of the day and left the following morning. Along the way north, they talked about revenge, but no one was willing to break the pact of peace. Then one of the chiefs commented that during the ceremonies, Many Swans had fallen from his horse and had been badly bruised; perhaps his weakness left him vulnerable. When they reached their camps on the Battle River, the chiefs had decided what they should do. Even Sweetgrass, the peacemaker and convert to Christianity, agreed when the others sent for the most powerful medicine man in the tribe.

Using songs, incantations, and secrets known only to himself, the medicine man put a curse on Many Swans. The Crees believed he sent spirit messengers to fill the chief's body with pain and that he would suffer great agony until he died.

According to the Blackfoot, the medicine man's attack struck Many Swans in his joints—first in his arms, then his legs, and finally throughout his whole body. The Blackfoot recognized the presence of "Cree medicine," a power which often was greater than anything their own medicine men could combat. Many Buffalo Stones Woman sought out the three best medicine men in the Blackfoot tribe but they were unable to help and that autumn, Many Swans died. Some people said the fall from the horse had killed him. The fur traders claimed he had died of tuberculosis. But his followers were convinced that the Crees had gained their revenge for the killing of Broken Arm.

Yet the peace treaty which had taken place within the shadow of Nose Hill survived the death of Many Swans. A few small skirmishes took place over the next few years, but the days of pitched battles and destruction of entire villages were virtually over. Yet Many Buffalo Stones Woman must have wondered about the strange turn of events as she watched her grandchildren playing in the peaceful camp. She had helped to stop the war between the two tribes but she had lost her husband in the process. The price of peace had been a high one indeed.

WHISKEY AND BIBLES

FIRST INTRUSIONS

CONTRARY TO WHAT MANY PEOPLE THINK, THE NORTH-WEST MOUNTED POLICE WERE

NOT THE FIRST WHITE PEOPLE TO SETTLE AT CALGARY. IN FACT, THEY WEREN'T EVEN THE SECOND OR

THIRD TO ARRIVE; THEY WERE THE FOURTH. THE FIRST WERE THE AMERICAN WHISKEY TRADERS, FOLLOWED

BY MISSIONARIES, AND THEN BY AN EARLY FARMER/TRADER/PROSPECTOR WITH HIS CONSIDERABLE

FAMILY. ALL THIS HAPPENED IN THE THREE YEARS IMMEDIATELY PRIOR TO THE ARRIVAL OF THE

MOUNTED POLICE IN 1875.

The whiskey trading era on the Canadian prairies began in 1869 when authorities in Montana Territory began to crack down on the sale of illicit liquor. Two enterprising merchants from Sun River—John J. Healy and Alfred B. Hamilton—realized that if they could cross the 49th parallel into "British possessions," they would be beyond the reach of the local sheriff. At the same time, they were aware that there was no effective law enforcement on the southern Canadian prairies. The transfer of the West—or Rupert's Land—from Great Britain to the newly formed Dominion of Canada was underway, but the closest law officers were a thousand miles away at Red River.

Accordingly, Healy and Hamilton went north in the spring of 1869 and built a small trading post at the junction of the Belly and St. Mary rivers, just west of the present city of Lethbridge. Naming it Fort Hamilton, they had an active winter trade with the Blackfoot tribes, taking buffalo robes and furs in exchange for whiskey, repeating rifles, and other items. When their wagons rolled back to Sun River in the following spring, Healy and Hamilton had made a profit of more than $50,000.

In 1870, a crew of wood cutters and carpenters returned to the site of Fort Hamilton (the first one had accidentally burned down when the wagons were leaving) and proceeded to build a large fortress. It was complete with blockhouses, catwalks, cannon, and an internal defence system in the event they were overrun by Indians. This post, dubbed Fort Whoop-Up, became the granddaddy of all the whiskey forts and shacks that sprang up on the Canadian prairies during the next two or three years.

Trading establishments were built at Standoff, Slideout, Kipp, Robber's Roost, Pine Coulee, Blackfoot Crossing, Highwood River, Waterton Lakes, and at a number of other locations. The main stock in trade was whiskey and its effect on the Indians was disastrous. As Chief Crowfoot commented a short time later:

The whiskey brought among us by the Traders is fast killing us off and we are powerless before the evil. [We are] totally unable to resist the temptation to drink when brought in contact with the white man's water. We are also unable to pitch anywhere that the Trader cannot follow us. Our horses, Buffalo robes and other articles of trade go for whiskey, a large number of our people have killed one another and perished in various ways under the influence.[1]

At least two of these American whiskey trading posts were built within the immediate vicinity of Calgary between 1871 and 1875—Elbow River Post and Berry's Post. The first was a sub-post of Fort Whoop-Up while the other was an independent operation which lasted for only a few months. Like other such forts, they experienced Indian attacks and violence as they peddled the poisonous whiskey. And some of it *was* poisonous. In addition to raw alcohol, burnt sugar, and molasses, the mixture often contained blackstrap chewing tobacco, red ink, castile soap, and even copper sulphate.

To give some idea of the disastrous effects of the trade, an estimated seventy Blood Indians died near Calgary during the winter of 1872-73 from the direct effects of the whiskey trade. Some froze to death, others died in violent quarrels, and some were killed by the poisonous effects of the rotgut whiskey.

While the soul-destroying whiskey traders arrived in this area from the south, the soul-savers came from the north. First were the Oblates headed by a newly ordained priest, Constantine Scollen, who had been a brother and school teacher at St. Albert. His first mission, Our Lady of Peace, was in the Springbank district, just west of Calgary. Erection of the rude shelter had started late in 1872 but was not ready for occupancy until the spring.

The Methodists were not far behind. In April of 1873, the father and son team of George and John McDougall chose a site for a mission at Morleyville, about thirty miles west of Calgary. Construction work started in the fall and the mission was occupied before winter. Later, both the Oblates and Methodists moved closer to the confluence of the Bow and Elbow rivers, locating in what is now the heart of Calgary.

Also during the summer of 1873, former gold prospector Sam Livingston built a small trading post and started a farm not far from the Oblate mission. A year later, he moved closer to the site of Calgary, farming in the area now flooded by the Glenmore Reservoir.

So from 1871 to 1875, the area within a day's travel of Calgary was home to some fascinating people— whiskey traders, priests, buffalo hunters, and a resolute brood who would become Calgary's first family.

THE WHISKEY MERCHANTS

Although a number of men were involved in the American liquor trade near Calgary, two stand out because of their later careers. One went on to become a prominent hotelman while the other was elected Alberta's first Member of Parliament.

When Fort Whoop-Up proved to be a bonanza for Hamilton and Healy, they decided to construct another post on the Bow River where it could serve the Blackfoot tribe.[1] In the spring of 1871, they hired a man named Henry Alfred "Fred" Kanouse to take charge. He was born in Illinois and had come west after the Civil War as a clerk for the American Fur Company. In 1869 he had joined the firm of Carrol & Steell in Fort Benton, Montana Territory, but was lured away to the Canadian whiskey trade. At the time of his hiring, Kanouse was the sheriff of Choteau county and his father was a respected lawyer in Fort Benton. The elder Kanouse never approved of his son's illicit activities and reportedly died "of a broken heart over the misadventures of son Fred."[2]

Young Kanouse took a leave of absence from his lawman's position and set out in the spring of 1871 with a party of three other Montanans and an Indian woman—probably one of his many native wives. Well stocked with whiskey, rifles, and regular trade goods,

AMERICAN WHISKEY TRADERS USED BULL TEAMS TO HAUL FREIGHT FROM FORT BENTON TO SOUTHERN ALBERTA. THIS "BULL TRAIN" WAS PHOTOGRAPHED WHILE EN ROUTE FROM MONTANA IN THE 1870S. (HOOK VIEW COMPANY, 517)

they travelled to the Elbow River, within the present limits of Calgary, and here Kanouse built a small fort. It was on the north side of the river, about three miles upstream from the Bow. This would likely be in the present Elbow Park district.[3]

The fort was about twenty by forty feet with ten-foot walls. Adjoining it to the north was a yard of similar dimensions, palisaded with ten-foot cottonwood poles. The fort had only two doors and no windows. One door led into the courtyard while the other permitted the Indians access to the trading room. Inside were four rooms—a trading room, a store, fur storage room, and living quarters. The trading room ran along the front of the store and was only seven or eight feet wide. This is as far as the Indians were allowed to go. They could see into the store but they had to pass their buffalo robes through a wicket and receive their whiskey or trade goods the same way. The wicket was equipped with a trap door which could be closed quickly in an emergency.

The fort had a sod roof but if any Indians tried to attack from that quarter, the traders simply fired their Winchesters at random into the ceiling. They called it "lighting the candles."

Late in the 1871 trading season, the fort was visited by a band of Bloods under the leadership of White Eagle. During the bartering, one of the men of the fort became involved in an argument with an Indian and "buffaloed" him with the butt of his revolver. The enraged Bloods carried their injured comrade to their camp across the Elbow River but returned a short time later. Kanouse went to parley with them but the Indians opened fire, killing his comrade and wounding Kanouse in the arm. Returning the fire, Kanouse killed White Eagle then rushed to the safety of the fort.

Once behind the palisades, Kanouse and another trader, as well as the Indian woman, resolutely fought off the attackers. A third trader, a man named Fisher, turned out to be a coward; he fled to the storeroom, dug a shallow trench, and lay huddled there during the entire fight.

The Bloods surrounded the fort for three days but then called for a temporary truce so they could haul away their dead. In the interval, Kanouse gave a Blackfoot Indian $50 in trade goods to hurry down to Spitzee Post—a whiskey fort on the Highwood River—to seek help. A short time later, Dave Akers and Liver-Eating Johnston[4] arrived with a party of men and the fight was over. Although shot just below the shoulder, Kanouse was not seriously wounded and stayed at the fort until spring.

This was not the only violent incident along the Elbow River that season. A man named Dick Berry, who had heard of Kanouse's success, organized a trading party and planned to build a post nearby. However, as soon as they started building, they were attacked by a party of Blood Indians and moved upstream to a safer location. However, the Bloods found them again and one of their leaders, Old Woman's Child, ambushed Berry while the rest of the war party ran off the horses. The remaining traders, fearing for their lives, hastily buried their leader, borrowed horses from Kanouse, and left the country. As soon as they were gone, the Bloods burned the fort to the ground.

Meanwhile, in the spring of 1872, Kanouse and his party abandoned their trading post and set out for Whoop-Up and then on to Montana with their wagons of buffalo robes. They had crossed the American line and were about fifteen miles from the Marias River when Kanouse got into an argument with another trader, Jim Nabors, and killed him. The local newspaper sarcastically reported a few weeks later that Kanouse "is sheriff of Choteau county, and has not up to present been arrested."[5]

Kanouse came back to the Canadian prairies with Healy and Hamilton but he was kept at Fort Whoop-Up while another man was sent to replace him at the Elbow River. In 1874, after the North-West Mounted Police arrived, Kanouse became one of the first residents of Fort Macleod where he ran a rooming house which eventually became the Waldorf Hotel. After the turn of the century he opened another hotel in the Crowsnest Pass before retiring to the state of Washington.

In 1912, Kanouse was brought back to Calgary as a guest at the first Calgary Stampede. He arranged to build a replica of a trading post and spoke in glowing terms about "wonderful" men who had taken part in the trade.

"The public of the present day are laboring under a misapprehension concerning the old traders," he sanctimoniously proclaimed. "A sort of stigma is attached to

FRED KANOUSE WAS THE FIRST MERCHANT TO LOCATE AT THE FUTURE SITE OF CALGARY, OPENING A TRADING POST THERE IN 1871. HE WAS A VIOLENT MAN WHO WAS INVOLVED IN AT LEAST TWO FIGHTS WITH INDIANS AT HIS FORT ON THE ELBOW RIVER. (GLENBOW, NA-31-1)

them. But let me tell you emphatically that the traders of those days were not 'whiskey traders' in the sense it is now understood."[6] He then went on to explain how they used whiskey only because the Hudson's Bay Company sold rum. He didn't mention the fact that the Bay had given up the practice many years before the dark days of the 1870s. He also claimed that he never knew of an Indian coming in for whiskey alone even though eyewitnesses stated otherwise. His stories were a pack of lies but they sounded good in 1912 when people enjoyed this sanitized version of how Calgary began.

But let's get back to the 1870s.

When the trading season of 1872-73 arrived, Healy and Hamilton needed another man to take charge of the post at Calgary. Possibly Kanouse had been too violent and had created unnecessary confrontations with the Indians. To replace him, the partners chose Donald Watson Davis, a man who had been in their employ since 1870. Davis was born in Vermont and had served in the Civil War. He then joined the regular army and was sent to Montana Territory where he saw the profits to be made in the Indian trade. As soon as he took his discharge he became a trader for Healy and Hamilton.

Healy commented that "Davis was my trader . . . and was out with teams trading and establishing winter trading stations. One was on the Elbow, near the present site of Calgary . . . He was my best man."[7]

Davis, with a crew of four white traders and a black interpreter, left Whoop-Up late in 1872 with a supply of whiskey and trade goods. The fort at Calgary had become dilapidated during its summer abandonment but it was soon repaired and turned into a small fortress. When the winter snows began to fly, the Indians came to the fort from their camps along the Bow and south from the foothills; unlike his predecessor, Davis got along well with them, although there were occasions when the liquor resulted in violence.

The following spring, when writing to his parents in Vermont, Davis commented:

DONALD W. DAVIS WAS A WHISKEY TRADER AT CALGARY IN 1872-73. AFTER THE ARRIVAL OF THE MOUNTED POLICE, HE BECAME THE CANADIAN AGENT FOR I.G. BAKER & CO. IN 1887 HE WAS ELECTED THE FIRST MEMBER OF PARLIAMENT FOR ALBERTA AND ENDED HIS CAREER AS A CUSTOMS OFFICER IN THE YUKON. (GLENBOW, NA-32-1)

My work is not without danger as it is trading with Indians altho I have never been hurt or scared yet had to kill 2 last winter in act of stealing horses.[8]

Another view of D.W. Davis and the whiskey trade was offered by Donald Graham, a young traveller who had come down from Fort Edmonton and spent a month at the Elbow River fort in the spring of 1873. He observed that an orderly society existed in the north where the Hudson's Bay Company was in control, but the south was cursed with "whiskey traders, wolfers and American influence—chaos, in fact."[9]

He noted that when Indians entered the trading room, they would pass a small empty keg and a buffalo robe through the wicket. A half gallon of whiskey was poured into the keg and the next person took his place in line. During one trade, Graham saw eighteen buffalo robes cross the counter and nine gallons of whiskey poured into the kegs. The results were predictable. That winter, scores of Indians died violently, mostly from drunken quarrels. The Many Children band of the Blood tribe, for example, was reduced from twenty-eight lodges to only two lodges because of intratribal fighting. The survivors had to seek refuge with a neighbouring tribe.

D. W. Davis' wife was a Blood woman named Revenge Walker. She was a sister of Red Crow, the head chief, so the tribe became regular customers. Red Crow himself regularly came to the fort for whiskey and killed his own brother in a drunken argument.

Yet Davis could be compassionate when circumstances permitted. On one occasion, a young Indian came to the fort with two serious wounds. His thumb and wrist had been split open by a knife thrust and there was a bullet wound through the point of his shoulder. He refused medical attention but as he rode away from the fort, there was a gunshot and puff of smoke in the distance. A short time later, the Indian rode back with a bullet wound in his chest.

Davis and his crew immediately took the man inside, dressed his wounds and put him to bed. He stayed there for several weeks, Davis' wife caring for him until he had recovered. He later showed his appreciation by presenting the trader with a horse.

As soon as the winter trade was over, the Elbow River post was abandoned. More than 2,000 buffalo robes were loaded into wagons and the remaining trade goods removed. There is no indication whether the fort reopened for the winter of 1873-74 but it is unlikely.

When the North-West Mounted Police came west in 1874, Healy and Hamilton fled from Canada but D.W. Davis remained, becoming Canadian manager for I.G. Baker & Co. of St. Louis. This was a major merchandising firm which quickly shifted its allegiance from whiskey traders to Mounted Policemen. Ironically, when the decision was made to establish a police outpost on the Elbow River, Davis was sent there with an I.G. Baker crew to undertake much of the construction work. Thus he was back in the Calgary area where two years earlier he had been one of the whiskey traders that the police had come west to suppress.

In the next couple of years, Davis built stores for I.G. Baker in Calgary, Fort Macleod, and Fort Walsh. He became a prosperous businessman, fulfilling contracts for the Mounted Police and the Indian Department, and establishing his own ranch near Fort Macleod. In line with his new status, he also abandoned his Indian wife and married a white woman.

In 1887, when the District of Alberta was given the right to elect its first Member of Parliament, Davis was a Conservative candidate. With financial backing from his American bosses, he campaigned the best way he knew how. According to the Mounted Police, "When he went north to canvass his constituents in the Edmonton section of Alberta, he took with him a sleigh load of carcasses of hogs, and each carcass contained bladders full of whiskey."[10]

Davis won the election, served two terms in Ottawa, and in 1896 he was appointed Collector of Customs for the Yukon. There he met his old boss, John J. Healy, who was running a trading and transportation company. Davis remained in the Yukon for the rest of his life, dying there in 1906.

In the passing years, both Fred Kanouse and D.W.

Davis had gained respectability, but their years of whiskey trading meant that Calgary's earliest beginnings were founded in murder, violence, and tragedy.

THE PIOUS MAVERICKS

While the whiskey traders were dealing in death and havoc, there were others who came to the Calgary area with bibles and blessings. Among them were three remarkable men who were attached to the Catholic mission in the years before the arrival of the Mounted Police. One thought he was the Pope, another named himself after the Holy Trinity, and the third was a British-hating Irishman. They were quite a combination; however, their eccentricities were more than offset by their dedication and their remarkable achievements.

In the fall of 1872, Bishop Vital Grandin received a request from Chief Crowfoot for help in protecting his

FATHER ALBERT LACOMBE WAS A BELOVED AND RESPECTED OBLATE MISSIONARY TO THE BLACKFOOT. IN LATER YEARS HE WAS PARISH PRIEST AT CALGARY AND ESTABLISHED THE LACOMBE HOME. (GLENBOW, NA-60-7)

people from the temptations of the whiskey trade. Grandin responded by agreeing to establish a mission in the Bow River area—the first in southern Alberta. Even before it was built, he named it *Notre Dame de la Paix,* Our Lady of Peace.

The idea of building the mission was immediately taken up by Alexis Cardinal, a Metis buffalo hunter who had dedicated himself to the church. Born near Lac La Biche, Cardinal had worked for the Hudson's Bay Company and had married his childhood sweetheart from his home area. However, in 1853, she deserted him and ran off with a Cree named The Hawk. To make matters worse, the man was a Protestant.

Cardinal, a devout Catholic, offered his services to the church with the idea of eventually becoming a brother or priest. However, from the beginning, his behaviour was sufficiently erratic that he spent most of his time as a servant to Father Lacombe. Methodist missionary John McDougall commented that, "This man was religiously crazy. At times he was an ordinary priest, self-ordained and set apart specially; at other times he was the Pope himself; and sometimes he told the people that he was greater than the Pope of Rome. When he could, he dressed as a priest."[1] At the same time, McDougall praised him for being a good-hearted man and an excellent hunter.

When Father Lacombe was transferred to eastern Canada to raise money for the missions, Cardinal considered himself to be the new "Apostle of the Blackfeet."[2] Without any direction from the church, he travelled to the Bow River late in the fall of 1872 and began construction of a log cabin about twenty-five miles up the Elbow River in the present Springbank district. It was a crude log building about fifteen feet long with no floor, a clay and stone chimney, bark-covered roof, windows covered with canvas sacks, and a door made of rawhide stretched on a frame. In short, it was a Metis wintering shelter which would normally be abandoned in the spring. In

WHILE THE CATHOLICS WERE BUILDING A MISSION ON THE ELBOW RIVER IN 1873, THE METHODISTS UNDER THE REV. JOHN MCDOUGALL, SEEN HERE, WERE LOCATING MORLEYVILLE MISSION AMONG THE STONEY INDIANS FARTHER WEST. AFTER THE POLICE ARRIVED TWO YEARS LATER, MCDOUGALL BUILT A SMALL CHURCH NEAR THE FORT. (GLENBOW, NA-28-1)

this instance, however, Cardinal intended to offer it to the Oblates to be the seat of the Roman Catholic Church in southern Alberta.

The building was likely used by Cardinal over the winter as a base for buffalo hunting. Then, in the summer of 1873, it was inspected and accepted as a church by Constantine Scollen, the second unusual man to occupy the mission.

Scollen was born in Fermanagh, Ireland, and joined the Oblate Order as a brother. He was teaching in Dublin when he responded to an appeal from Bishop A. A. Taché for missionaries. He went to St. Albert in 1862 where he was virtually the only English-speaking missionary among the Oblates and thus he was a valuable addition to the staff. He taught school at Fort Edmonton, learned to speak Cree and French, and used his free time to study for the priesthood.

One of his most outstanding achievements was to help prepare a French-Cree dictionary. Entitled *Dictionnaire et Grammaire de la Langue des Cris* it was published under the authorship of Father Lacombe but should have been credited to both Lacombe and Scollen. According to Father Emile Tardif, when Scollen went out with a crew to chop wood he would use the opportunity to study their language. "Whenever they were resting," said Tardif, "he would ask the Metis the meanings of words. He would write these on chips of wood and at the end of the day he would gather them all up and take them to the mission. Then he would sort them out and copy them into a book."[3] The chips were used for kindling wood the next day.

By the late 1860s Scollen was so proficient in languages that he was given the task of teaching Cree and English to newly arrived missionaries. As a scholar, he was also useful to the bishop for writing letters in English and acting as bursar to the mission.

When Crowfoot asked for a missionary, Father Lacombe was away, so the long-delayed ordination of Constantine Scollen was rushed through. It took place on Easter Sunday, 1873, and the priest was immediately dispatched to the Elbow River.

Scollen was an intelligent, dynamic, and outspoken man. As the only Irishman among the French-speaking missionary Oblates, he sometimes experienced discrimination but his anger and hatred were pointed only in one direction—to the British. Methodist missionary John McDougall described him as "an Irishman of the intense sort to whom Britain was 'Nazareth'—no good could possibly come out of her."[4] By inference, this hatred extended to the Canadian government, particularly to the Indian Department and the politicians and bureaucrats who formulated policies relating to the West in general and Indians in particular.

Scollen's views are best expressed in a poem which he wrote while he was at Our Lady of Peace mission, probably in the late 1870s. Untitled, it tells about his love for Ireland and contains such anti-British phrases as, "May tyranny's chain fall from thee," "Thy sons from beneath foreign skies/ Shall stand in proud battle array," and "The soil whereon our forefathers fell/ Shall be bought with brave blood as of old."[5]

When Scollen arrived at Our Lady of Peace mission in the spring of 1873, he arranged with Cardinal to have a leanto added to the shack to serve as a dormitory and chapel. He then returned to St. Albert to prepare for the winter. The bishop decided that although he had been ordained, Scollen's studies were not complete. Accordingly, Father Vital Fourmond was chosen to go along with him to give theology lessons over the winter while at the same time the teacher could receive instruction in the Cree language. Also selected for the caravan was Louis Daze, a Metis hunter whose brother was a priest in Ottawa.

When Father Hippolyte Leduc learned that the Methodists were also planning to locate a mission on the Bow River, he took immediate action to get there first. As he stated:

> I felt very sad to think that . . . a Protestant minister was to settle on that same Bow River only a few kilometres away from the place we had taken. Were we to see ourselves preceded by heresy? . . . I decided to send F. Scollen away immediately . . . The day after the departure of our missionaries for Bow River, the Wesleyan minister started to chase them, not very happy, I think, to see himself preceded so unexpected by the Catholic priests.[6]

Scollen and his party arrived at Our Lady of Peace in November of 1873 and found a band of Bloods already camped by the mission. They were under the leadership of Rainy Chief, one of the two head chiefs of the tribe. On Christmas day, the first Indian child was baptized. He was the two-year-old son of Dog Pound and was given the name of Vital Constantin.

The first winter in the cabin was cold and long but the buffalo were plentiful. The local Indians made too many visits to the nearby whiskey traders and were annoyed at the presence of Americans who were hunting and poisoning wolves but otherwise the winter was without incident. However, one can imagine the hardship suffered by the clergy in a rude shack far from the comforts of St. Albert.

In the spring of 1874, Father Fourmond returned to St. Albert while Scollen coursed the plains, ministering to Blackfoot and Cree Indians. He almost drowned while trying to cross the Bow River near Calgary and lost all his baggage and supplies. Four days later, with the help of his dog, he managed to kill a buffalo calf but the meat lasted for only a couple of days and they were starving again. Then his guide deserted him and it took the priest two arduous days to locate the Blood camp of Rainy Chief where he spent the next month.

Rainy Chief was an interesting man. While most Blackfoot leaders ignored the missionaries, he welcomed them and embraced their teachings. However, one might wonder how the leader actually interpreted Christianity if these comments by a Blackfoot elder are any criteria:

> Rainy Chief had great power. He followed the white man's religion. He was able to do like Father Lacombe—write something on a piece of paper and let it fly up in the air. Then another piece of paper with writing on it would fall from the sky in answer. But Rainy Chief always had to wait longer for his reply than Father Lacombe.[7]

Father Scollen was back at Our Lady of Peace mission in the fall of 1874, this time with Father Etienne Bonald

FATHER CONSTANTINE SCOLLEN WAS THE FIRST PRIEST TO OCCUPY OUR LADY OF PEACE MISSION AT CALGARY. SHORTLY AFTER THE MOUNTED POLICE ARRIVED IN 1875, THE MISSION WAS MOVED FROM THE SPRINGBANK AREA TO A SITE IN THE PRESENT MISSION DISTRICT. AN IRISHMAN, SCOLLEN HAD NO LOVE FOR THE ENGLISH (OR CANADIANS) AND FINALLY LEFT FOR THE UNITED STATES AFTER GIVING MORAL SUPPORT TO THE CREES DURING THE TROUBLES OF 1885. (GLENBOW, NA-3022-2)

who needed a winter of instruction in English and Cree. Louis Daze and Alexis Cardinal were also there and they were joined by another adherent to the Oblates, a man named Jean L'Heureux. Of the three religious mavericks—Alexis Cardinal who thought he was the Pope, Father Scollen with his Fenian tendencies, and Jean L'Heureux—the latter was probably the most interesting.

He was born in Quebec and had studied for the priesthood. However, he was expelled either for theft or because he was found to be a homosexual. He came west and in 1862 he tried to become an Oblate but was caught in the act of sodomy and sent away. He joined a band of Blackfoot, donned a cassock, and passed himself off as a priest. He convinced the Jesuits in Montana that he was legitimate and later that year he built a mission for them near Chief Mountain.

For the next thirty years, L'Heureux lived with the Blackfoot and became a close confidant of Chief Crowfoot. He took the name of Three Persons, *Nio'kskatapi,* after the Holy Trinity of the Father, the Son, and the Holy Spirit, and gained considerable influence among the Blackfoot tribes. He usually wore a cassock, celebrated mass, and performed marriages and baptisms. Generally, the fur traders and missionaries despised him, or at least distrusted him, largely because of his sexual preferences and his allegiance to the Blackfoot. However, both the Hudson's Bay Company and the Oblates made use of him because of his influence. He was paid to bring the Indians to trade at Edmonton and Rocky Mountain House, and was used as an interpreter by the priests when they went among the Blackfoot.

In 1870, L'Heureux helped establish peace between the Blackfoot and the American army and generally worked on behalf of the Indians. He also had literary and scholarly aspirations, drawing a map of Blackfoot country, preparing a Blackfoot-English dictionary, and writing a number of articles on the geography and antiquities of the area.

The priests referred to Cardinal and L'Heureux as catechists, although they had no official standing in the church. But to reinforce the illusion that they were indeed part of the clergy, both men wore skull caps and priestly cassocks of checkered cotton. "With these," commented an historian, "and their pipes in their mouths

any lack of rubrical perfection was compensated by enthusiasm."[8] On one occasion, a priest recalled Cardinal going into a Blackfoot camp and preaching to them in Cree. Although the Indians could not understand a word he said, he boasted that he was the most powerful preacher in the region, even more powerful than the bishop.

The winter of 1874-75 turned out badly for the missionaries. Not only was the weather severe, but the buffalo did not come close to the mission. In December, Louis Daze accompanied a band of Indians who were going hunting near the present city of Calgary. While they were out on the plains, seven of the horses strayed and Daze went alone on foot to look for them. While he was away, a blizzard struck and he wandered in the storm until he finally froze to death. His body was discovered two weeks later only twelve miles from the mission and possibly within the present limits of Calgary.

During that same winter, the missionaries learned that the North-West Mounted Police had arrived in the West and had built a fort about a hundred miles south on the Oldman River. In February of 1875, Scollen made a winter trip to Fort Macleod where a police surgeon described him as "a jolly kind of man" and a person who "frequently gives the Indians a good drubbing, going at them with his fists."[9]

During another visit to the police in the spring of 1875, Scollen learned that they planned to build an outpost at the junction of the Bow and Elbow rivers. Accordingly, in July he sent Alexis Cardinal to the forks to construct a new mission. The site was near the present 9th Avenue and 6th Street SE. The new building was crude, about nine feet square, and beside it was a tent to provide added space.

When the North-West Mounted Police arrived in August, Scollen discovered that his shack was too close to the new fort so he sent Cardinal a mile upstream along the Elbow to construct a third mission. This one was much more impressive—eighteen by twenty feet in size. A Mounted Policeman who visited it in 1876 described it as follows:

The hut is divided into two portions, the inner and smaller one being floored and the floor dug down about a foot below the line of the ground. The roof has a great slant, evidently intended to represent as nearly as possible a Gothic roof. Two little windows about 6 x 10 inches square on either side let in all the light. At one end he has a covered place that he has built into an altar & a small porcelain image of the Virgin & the child Jesus surmount this. A cook stove warms the place & a board resting on two old nail kegs forms a rude bench for his small congregation.[10]

The mission was finished by November and the old building was given to the Mounted Police to use as an interpreter's house.

As a result of these moves, the Oblates became the first civilian residents of what is now downtown Calgary. It was a humble beginning but the small building on the Elbow River—located at the site of the present Holy Cross Hospital nurses' residence—grew into the village of Rouleauville and later became the Mission district of Calgary.

As for the three strange characters—Cardinal, Scollen, and L'Heureux—none of them stayed around Calgary for the rest of their lives. Upon Father Lacombe's return from his European and eastern travels, Cardinal again became his companion. He helped build a mission at Fort Macleod in 1880 and then continued his pioneering work north of Edmonton.

Father Scollen stayed at Our Lady of Peace mission until 1882 during which time he frequently railed against the Canadian government. He was a witness at Treaty Seven in 1877 and two years later he was convinced it had been a poor deal for the Indians. In 1881, he wrote to Father Lacombe telling him that "for many years I have found myself at war, fighting all alone against enemies too strong for me."[11]

Working out of St. Albert, Scollen was sent to help establish a mission among the Crees at Hobbema. He was there in 1885 when the North-West Uprising erupted and remained with the Indians during the period of anxiety and danger. However, according to an officer of the Hudson's Bay Company, Scollen's sympathies were entirely with the rebels. As he stated:

There is no doubt in my own mind that the Revd. Father was a great sympathizer of the rebellion and

would have taken part in it openly if he thought that it had a shadow of a successful termination.[12]

After the arrival of Canadian troops, Scollen became involved in a dispute with his bishop and abandoned his station. He spent a short time in Winnipeg, then moved to the United States, away from British influences, and served in a number of churches. He wanted to return to Ireland probably to take up the struggle for independence but he never made it. He finally passed away in Ohio in 1902.

As for Jean L'Heureux, he spent only one winter at Our Lady of Peace mission, then went back to live with the Blackfoot. However, he continued to wear a cassock, perform marriages and baptisms, and do all the things he had done before he came to Calgary. In 1877, he was Chief Crowfoot's personal interpreter at Treaty Seven, and two years later he became an interpreter for the Department of Indian Affairs. He remained in that role for the next twelve years, then was a recluse near Pincher Creek. He spent his last days in the Lacombe Home at Midnapore on the outskirts of Calgary, dying there in 1919.

But Our Lady of Peace and the Blackfoot missions were left in good hands. Father Doucet, who had come in 1875, stayed for the next sixty-two years, retiring to St. Albert in 1936. The three remarkable misfits who established the mission had done their job well.

FIRST FAMILY OF CALGARY

By the time the Mounted Police arrived in the summer of 1875, a pioneer farmer had already started to till the land along the Elbow River. In fact, when the police came to the site of Calgary, this man was observing their actions from a high hill to the west. He was Sam Livingston, a prospector/trader/farmer who at that moment had been looking over the country with a spyglass. From his vantage point he saw a lone rider coming towards the Bow and Elbow rivers—an advance scout for the police. A short time later, the main party arrived, threading their way south along the base of Nose Hill towards the river crossing.

Livingston had been in the area for two years and in

the spring, when he learned that the Mounted Police were coming, he had located a homestead five miles up the Elbow River, in an area now under the waters of the Glenmore Reservoir. With his wife and five children, his family became the first settlers in what is now Calgary.

Samuel Henry Livingston was born in Blessington, Ireland, in 1831 and had migrated to the United States when he was sixteen. When the gold rush to California began in 1849, he was among the thousands of prospectors to flood the area. He may not have found much gold but he did learn how to prospect and moved northward as more discoveries were made. He took part in gold rushes in Oregon and Montana, then went to northern British Columbia to the Cariboo gold fields.

About 1862 he travelled east from British Columbia with three companions until they were out of the mountains, then prospected around Great Slave Lake and Lake Athabasca. When he found no signs of gold, he went south through Fort Edmonton to the Wild Horse diggings near the present Fort Steele, B.C. While there, he heard that gold had been found on the North Saskatchewan, so with a party of miners, including James Gibbons, John Healy, Joe Kipp, and Charlie Thomas, he crossed the mountains onto the prairies. As Gibbons recalled:

> We travelled by way of the Kicking Horse Pass and Banff and washed our shirts in the Bow River just below where the CPR hotel now stands. We endeavoured to go across country from Banff to Rocky Mountain House, but . . . we got lost in the snow in the mountains. After quite a struggle we got back to Banff and following the Bow down we came to where Calgary now stands, where we split up.[1]

SAM LIVINGSTON HAD BEEN A GOLD PROSPECTOR AND TRADER BEFORE SETTLING NEAR CALGARY IN 1874. WITH HIS LARGE FAMILY, HE BECAME THE AREA'S FIRST FARMER AND AN AVID PROMOTER OF AGRICULTURE. (GLENBOW, NA-3162-1)

Gibbons and Livingston went north to Rocky Mountain House and downstream to the Methodist mission at Victoria Post. Livingston then began to freight for the Methodists and during this time he met a young Metis girl, Jane Mary Howse. She was from a prominent family; her father was employed at the local Hudson's Bay Company post while her grandfather, Joseph Howse, had established Henry House near the present Jasper, Alberta. Sam and Jane were married in 1864 and Livingston tried to settle down, farming near Victoria mission until 1871. However, the enterprise failed so he decided to try his hand as a free trader and to return to freighting.

In 1873, Livingston observed with interest when the Rev. John McDougall and his brother David left Victoria to open a Methodist mission and trading post among the Stoneys on the upper waters of the Bow River. Next spring, Livingston heard that David had done so well that the Hudson's Bay Company planned to go there too. Seeing the potential of trading near the protection of the Methodists, Livingston decided to join them and do some trading on his own. He bought an assortment of trade goods, loaded his wife and four children on one of the Red River carts he had been using for freighting, and set out for the south.

When he got to the mission, Livingston discovered that it was located almost entirely within Stoney territory which would be dominated by David McDougall and the Hudson's Bay. In scouting the country, he discovered the Catholic mission on the upper waters of the Elbow in the present Springbank district and immediately chose it as a trading site. It was just west of the present city and had the advantage of being central to the Blackfoot, close to a mission station, and away from his competitors. The

McDougalls were twenty-five miles west while three or four American whiskey forts were located downstream.

"We needed more than a one-room pole shanty," recalled Livingston's daughter, "so we decided to build a two-room log cabin. One half could be a place to trade and the other half a place to live."[2] As soon as it was built, Livingston knew he had chosen well. The Blackfoot flocked to his post while even a few Stoneys came from the west. Yet the site was not without its dangers. In December 1874, he explained his problems to a friend in Winnipeg. His letter, later printed in the Toronto *Globe,* was probably the first communication from the Calgary area ever to appear in print. Livingston addressed it from "Elbow River" and sent it east via Fort Macleod and the United States.

"I got to this place all right," he began, "and I cannot complain of my success."[3] He then went on to tell about the arrival of the North-West Mounted Police at Fort Macleod.

You have heard ere this I presume that the police are stationed at Belly River. We have heard of them through the Indians . . . They have in a great measure squashed the whiskey trade in their vicinity, but in these parts there is plenty of it at every trading post . . . In a distance of forty miles from here, down Bow River, there are four posts where the Indians say they buy whiskey, and they have brought some to this place, and were drunk all one night . . . I have just received news of the death of some of them in the storm . . . through being drunk. Notwithstanding they are still heading for the whiskey shops with their furs. Some of them are destitute of horses, blankets, and guns—all gone for whiskey.

Livingston heard that the police were not coming to the Bow River that fall and was afraid that the whiskey traders would turn the Indians against them. He continues:

There are a large number of Blackfeet here under some petty chiefs—the meanest Indians I ever knew. There is nothing but fear that can keep the Blackfeet at peace. The sooner the Dominion Government knows this the safer it will be for the white settlers. The Blackfeet are the perpetrators of most of the murders and robberies which have taken place.

At the same time, Livingston felt some sympathy for these Indians in view of the rapidly changing conditions. "If the government does not do a great deal for the Blackfeet," he wrote, "they are doomed to destruction. They are not like the Crees and other tribes on whom civi-

THIS IS A VIEW OF THE LIVINGSTON FARM IN THE 1880S. THE FOUR TEAMS AT RIGHT PROVIDE THE HORSE-POWER FOR THE SEPARATOR. THE THRESHED GRAIN WAS STORED IN SACKS, SOME OF WHICH ARE SEEN ON THE LEFT. SAM LIVINGSTON'S FARM DISAPPEARED UNDER THE BACKWATERS OF THE GLENMORE RESERVOIR ABOUT 1932. THE MAIN HOUSE WAS ULTIMATELY MOVED AND IS NOW IN HERITAGE PARK. (GLENBOW, NA-3981-1)

lization have been creeping slowly. On the Blackfeet it will fall like a bombshell."

The winter of 1874-75 was a profitable one for Livingston, partly because of his location and because of the quality of goods he handled. At the beginning of the season, the Hudson's Bay trader complained that "Livingstone is selling fancy stuff that puts us in the background."[4] He carried shawls, woollens and other items which were in great demand.

By the spring of 1875, rumours were rife that the Mounted Police would soon be coming to the Bow River. Ever since he was married, Livingston had wanted to be a farmer. He had tried his luck in the north but the markets simply didn't exist. Now, with the impending arrival of the Mounted Police, he realized that settlement wouldn't be far behind and that the fertile valley along the lower waters of the Elbow River offered both good farm land and the protection of the police.

With this view in mind, when the Catholics moved to the junction of the two streams, Livingston gave up his trading post and chose a site about four miles upstream from them. Here he built a log cabin and moved his wife and five children—Jane, Nellie, George, Hugh, and John—to the new location. They constituted the first family of Calgary. They planted a garden and later sold fresh vegetables to the Mounted Police.

As one of the first farmers in the district, Livingston was held up as an example of the agricultural potential of the Calgary area. He didn't mind; in fact, he became an enthusiastic booster himself. In 1881, he was visited by the Marquis of Lorne, Canada's governor general, and served him meat and vegetables from his farm. Reporters accompanying the vice-regal party were impressed with the agricultural future of the region. In 1883, a new settler noticed him on the streets of Calgary and when asked his identity, he was told, "That man with long hair and critical blue eyes is Sam Livingston, the noted pioneer farmer of Alberta who is considered a little over eloquent about the agricultural possibilities of this country."[5]

Two years later, a promotional booklet described him as "a warm-hearted pioneer, whose latch-string always hangs out for the virtuous wayfarer."[6] As years passed, Livingston was one of Calgary's greatest champions. An eternal optimist, he was the first farmer in the district to plant fruit trees and imported the first threshing machine, mower, and rake. In 1885, he went to Ontario with an exhibition of vegetables to promote Calgary at Toronto Agricultural Fair.

Livingston went on to raise a large family of eight boys and six girls. He was always one of Calgary's most respected pioneers and when he died in 1897 he was mourned by the entire district. His wife, Jane Mary, continued to work the farm with her children until her death in 1919. The second Livingston house, built about 1883, now sits at Heritage Park. As for the farm, it is deep beneath the waters of the Glenmore Reservoir.

COMING OF THE REDCOATS

A FORT IN THE WILDERNESS

ALMOST TEN MONTHS AFTER THE NORTH-WEST MOUNTED POLICE ARRIVED IN
BLACKFOOT COUNTRY IN 1874, THEY FINALLY MOVED NORTH TO SUPPRESS THE WHISKEY TRAFFIC ON THE
BOW RIVER. F TROOP UNDER INSPECTOR EPHREM BRISEBOIS WAS INSTRUCTED TO GO UP TO THE RED DEER
RIVER TO MEET MAJOR-GENERAL EDWARD SELBY-SMYTH, COMMANDER OF CANADA'S MILITIA, WHO WAS
MAKING AN OFFICIAL TOUR OF THE WEST, AND THEN GO TO THE BOW RIVER TO ESTABLISH A FORT.
SELBY-SMYTH'S TRIP HAD BEEN NECESSARY BECAUSE EASTERN CANADA HAD BEEN BUZZING WITH RUMOURS
THAT THE MOUNTED POLICE WERE DISPIRITED AND NEAR MUTINY AND THAT THE WHOLE EXPEDITION
HAD BEEN A FAILURE. THE OPPOSITION PRESS HAD CARRIED NUMEROUS ARTICLES, SOME FROM
DISAFFECTED MEMBERS OF THE FORCE, COMPLAINING OF THE CONDITIONS.

By the time Selby-Smyth met F Troop at the Red Deer River, he knew that the police had experienced gruelling conditions but their efforts to bring law and order to the West had been a great success.

After seeing the major-general on his way, Brisebois took his fifty men and wagons south to the Bow River. They crossed just above its junction with the Elbow, Cpl. George King claiming the honour of being the first Mounted Policeman to set foot on the site of the future city. There Brisebois met Father Doucet and set up camp between the two rivers.

Someone—the person was never identified—had already been to the locale and indicated the place where the fort should be built by marking it with a buffalo robe and sticks. This was about a mile up the Elbow River. I.G. Baker & Co., contractors for the job, had based their estimates of $2,476 on that spot and its proximity to a good stand of timber. However, Brisebois decided that the fort should be closer to the forks and picked out his own location. Later, I.G. Baker tried to collect an addi-

tional thousand dollars for the extra work involved in bringing the logs downstream, but with no success.

Construction was undertaken by a crew of Metis and Americans from Fort Macleod supervised by D.W. Davis, Canadian manager for the Baker company. In a relatively short time, the contractors had erected a fort about 150 feet square. It consisted of men's quarters on the west side, shops and storerooms on the east, officers' quarters and guardhouse on the south, and stables on the north. All doors and windows faced into the square and the backs of the buildings formed the perimeter of the fort. The spaces between the buildings were enclosed by palisades and bastions erected by the police. The roofs were sod, and stone fireplaces were the main source of heat.

The fort was made of vertical log construction, a poor way to put up permanent buildings but it was fast and cheap. Horizontal logs could have been squared, dovetailed, and made virtually airtight. But the vertical logs apparently were not squared, the chinking constantly fell out, and the buildings were cold and draughty. All in all, it was a quickly and badly constructed fort, providing little protection from either the weather (which proved to be a real hazard) or Indians (who weren't). One might guess that the Americans cut corners because of the changed location, but perhaps they were also irritated that their huge profits from whiskey trading had come to an end.

In any case, the police were stuck with a badly built fort that leaked in summer and had snow drifting between the cracks in winter. Perhaps the police themselves saw the fort as a temporary one to be used only to suppress the whiskey trade. Certainly, the events which followed over the next seven years gave no indication that it had much of a future.

BY 1889, THE MOUNTED POLICE HAD A NEW BARRACKS IN CALGARY. HERE, SGTS. FORRESTER, WHITEHEAD, SIDE-BOTHAM, STILLMAN, AND BAGLEY DINE ON RABBIT PIE IN THE SERGEANTS' MESS WHILE CST. BLACK STANDS READY TO SERVE THEM. (GLENBOW, NA-3173-14)

When the fort was completed a small community arose in the surrounding area. I.G. Baker & Co. built a trading post immediately to the south, while near them was the store of T.C. Power & Brother, and a billiard hall operated by Harry "Kamoose" Taylor. Just west of the fort, near the present Langevin Bridge, the McDougalls put a small shack to be used for Methodist services when they visited from Morleyville. It also served David McDougall from time to time as a trading post. East, across the Elbow River from the fort, the Hudson's Bay Company put up a store and dwelling house.

When news of the fort's establishment was spread, a number of Metis came from Edmonton in their Red River carts and built cabins near the Catholic mission. The men expected to find work as hunters, freighters,

and messengers and their village became one of the focal points for the social life of the community. Families such as the Roselles, Mallettes, Munroes, and Fayants became the first settlers of Calgary village. That Christmas, 1875, was a memorable one. As Mounted Policeman Cecil Denny commented:

> I returned to Bow River on Christmas night, and found a Christmas dinner in full swing. It was given by the non-commissioned officers, and all civilians of the village were invited. Every one had a good time, and a dance followed in the Taylor billiard hall. The ladies, who attended in numbers, were the half-breed belles, well dressed and some very, very good looking.[1]

Denny knew about the girls first-hand, for during his stay at Calgary he bedded down with a Metis girl who was reputed to be the niece of Sir Stafford Northcote, governor of the Hudson's Bay Company. Other policemen were more serious about their relationships. For example, Cpl. George King—who later became Calgary's first postmaster and its second mayor—married a Metis girl named Louise Munroe from the village.

For the first few years, Fort Calgary's main responsibilities seemed to be to keep peace among local Indians, watch over the increasing number of small-time ranchers, and act as a communications link between Edmonton and Fort Macleod. However, the fort's importance steadily waned because of its isolation. In 1875, it was manned by fifty-two men and officers but this number was reduced to thirty-seven in 1876, and to fourteen by 1879. In 1881, the entire fort was occupied by only three men—a non-commissioned officer and two constables.

The main variations in the daily routine during the late 1870s were the attendance of the police at the signing of Treaty Seven and coping with increasing starvation among the Blackfoot as the buffalo herds disappeared. In 1879, in response to the plea from Indians and missionaries, the Department of Indian Affairs assumed jurisdiction over the prairie tribes and started a supply farm just south of Calgary at Fish Creek. To accomplish this, the government bought the farm of John Glen, an early settler, at a location which is now well within the city's limits.

Another change occurred in 1880 when the federal government introduced regulations to encourage large-scale ranching. For a cent an acre a year, up to 100,000 acres of land could be leased for twenty-five years. One of the first companies to respond was the Cochrane Ranche Co. Ltd., which took a huge lease west of Calgary and placed its first cattle on the range late in 1881. More than 6,000 head were driven up from Montana, officially counted by the police at Calgary, then herded across the Bow River near the present Mewata Bridge en route to Big Hill Springs. Later, the Cochrane Ranche opened a butcher shop close to the I.G. Baker store in the flats south-west of the fort.

By this time, Calgary was just a tiny outpost where few demands were made on the two or three policemen stationed there. In 1882, for example, Constable A.R. Dyre described the opportunities for the avid sportsman:

> The fishing and shooting here are splendid, ducks and geese and prairie chicken hens so cheeky that they come and light on the building. As many as a dozen chickens have been shot inside the fort lately, and a daring young antelope came right behind the fort the other day ... The prairie wolves come around every night and serenade us with their unmusical voices and if we go to shoot at them they will suddenly convey themselves away like a streak of lightning.[2]

Reflecting the views of many Calgarians who would follow him in later years, Constable Dyre added that, "I like Calgary . . . as it is in a very pretty part of the country."[3] But then it was still a wilderness and would remain so until Sir John A. Macdonald's dream of a railway from sea to sea became a reality.

THE POLICEMAN, THE GIRL, AND THE STOVE

Ephrem Brisebois, the first commanding officer of Fort Calgary, was a courtly gentleman, well mannered, and possessing an Old World charm. He was a caring, compassionate man, concerned about the lofty problems of society and the welfare of the disadvantaged people around him. He was completely bilingual, vitally interested and active in Canadian politics, and faithful to the Catholic Church.

But he was no policeman. He may have been an officer in the North-West Mounted Police and the commander of F Troop which was sent to establish the fort, but he lacked the essential prerequisites necessary for a good policeman on the Canadian frontier. He also possessed enough arrogance, ego, and callousness to ultimately seal his fate. Brisebois's role in the history of Calgary, therefore, was one of failure.

He was born in 1850 in South Durham, Quebec, where his father was a hotel owner and a prominent member of the Conservative party. When Ephrem was seventeen, he was among 500 Quebecers who volunteered to go to Rome to fight to preserve the authority of the Pope. He stayed there for two years but was never in a battle; his unit served as guards and their only excitement was in chasing local bandits. When Rome fell in 1870, the Canadians were withdrawn and Brisebois returned to Quebec.

He had had a taste of military life but he lacked the proper connections for a commission in the British Army serving in Canada. However, his local Member of

THE EARLIEST KNOWN PICTURES OF CALGARY WERE TAKEN BY AN ITINERANT PHOTOGRAPHER, W. E. HOOK, IN 1878. BY THE TIME THE RAILWAY ARRIVED IN 1883, MOST OF THE ORIGINAL LOG BUILDINGS AT FORT CALGARY HAD BEEN REPLACED BY A LARGE BARRACKS. IN THIS VIEW OF THE FORT, SGT. JAMES BARWIS IS SEATED IN THE FOREGROUND WITH A BAND OF BLOOD INDIANS. BEHIND, LEFT TO RIGHT, ARE CST. R.W. FLETCHER, CST. T. CHRISTIE (ON HORSE), SAM LIVINGSTON, UNKNOWN, INSP. CECIL DENNY (IN CHAIR), CST. JOE BUTLIN (IN WAGON), CST. SCHOFIELD (WITH ROPE), AND UNKNOWN. (HOOK VIEW CO., 486)

Parliament, Christopher Dunkin, arranged for Ephrem to be appointed a compiling census clerk in Ottawa in 1872. In the following year, when the North-West Mounted Police were being organized, Sir Hector Langevin, leader of the Quebec wing of the Conservative party, and Louis Masson, a Member of Parliament, arranged for Brisebois to get a commission as a sub-inspector.

He spent the winter of 1873-74 as a recruiting officer in the Maritimes then accompanied the troops to Dufferin, Manitoba, the jumping-off place for the Great March. At first, Brisebois was second in command of B Troop but when his superior officer was discharged for disputing orders, Brisebois was promoted to full command.

On July 8, 1874, the Mounted Police set out for the West, following a route just north of the international boundary. The summer was one of the driest on record and the police suffered from heat, dust, and a lack of water. However, Brisebois apparently conducted himself very well for half way along in their journey he was promoted to the rank of full inspector. And when the Force reached the Sweetgrass Hills and needed help, Brisebois was one of the officers chosen to accompany Colonel Macleod to Fort Benton, Montana.

But that's where his good record seems to have ended. The Mounted Police reached the site of Fort Macleod in September and shortly afterwards B Troop was taken away from Brisebois. "There was so much crime and misconduct," reported Colonel Macleod, "that I had to remove him therefrom . . . He is inclined to be insubordinate and to make difficulties about trifles."[1]

The next spring, Brisebois was assigned the task of establishing an outpost on the Bow River near its junction with the Elbow. Several whiskey traders had been working in the area and the presence of the police was needed to discourage them. The troop left the Oldman River early in August and after meeting Sir E. Selby-Smyth, commander of the Canada Militia, at the Red Deer River, they reached the Elbow River. A short time later, crews from I. G. Baker & Company arrived from Fort Macleod and proceeded to build the fort. The policemen had the task of erecting the palisades and blockhouses.

GEORGE CLIFT KING WAS GIVEN CREDIT FOR BEING THE FIRST MOUNTED POLICEMAN TO CROSS THE BOW RIVER AND STAND ON THE PRESENT SITE OF FORT CALGARY. AFTER HE LEFT THE FORCE HE BECAME POSTMASTER AND SERVED AS MAYOR OF THE TOWN IN 1886-87. (GLENBOW, NA-1198-1)

The contractors and police went some distance up the Elbow, cut sixteen-foot logs, and floated them down the river to the site. With these timbers the contractors erected the stables, men's quarters, and other buildings. In the meantime, the fifty men of F Troop lived in tents or built crude log shacks which were to serve as their accommodation until the fort was finished in December.

The winter turned out to be one of the coldest on record. The snows came early and stayed. Blizzards racked the area and temperatures of minus 40 C. were recorded. Although the men had come in August, the last of the logs which they were to cut for the palisades were not ready until November and work was carried on through the bitterly cold weather. The policemen had to dig trenches four feet deep in the frozen ground and erect walls and bastions twelve feet high.

Many of them were poorly dressed for the work. Some had never received an issue of winter clothing while others had uniforms that were almost worn out. Many lacked warm gloves. The men wanted to buy buffalo coats and mittens from the traders—even at their outrageous prices—but some of them hadn't been paid for months. For example, Constables Clyde, Fraser, Griffiths, Antrobus, Robinson, Marlin, and King were last paid when they set out from Manitoba in the summer of 1874.

George King described the conditions they experienced as they completed the fort:

The weather was so severe that the men could not stand it to remain outside and work for more than an hour at a time. Then they would go inside to get warm and in this way the work went on, the men working an hour in the cold and then remaining inside two hours to thaw out.[2]

These kind of conditions required the leadership of a stern disciplinarian. He might sympathize with the plight of his men and try to ease their suffering as much as possible but he had to see that order was maintained and that the work was done. "Things were in such an unsettled state," recalled King, "that they had to post sentries night and day, as they did not know what attitude the Indians might take. There were thousands of the red men in the country and they could easily have annihilated the small force of police had they so wished."[3]

Brisebois turned out to be neither an understanding officer nor a strict disciplinarian. The first problem occurred when Constable Shead left his sentry duty and went inside to warm himself. He was caught by an N.C.O. but when he appeared before Brisebois he received only a mild punishment. He pleaded ignorance and thought he could leave his post any time he needed to thaw out.

A short time later Constable James Pell was riding in the bitter cold without gloves but when he asked the N.C.O. for permission to go inside to warm his fingers, he was refused. However, he ignored the order and went to the barracks anyway. When he was charged with leaving the stables without permission, Brisebois again refused to support his N.C.O. Instead, he said that Pell had "a very good character" and by implication the N.C.O. was guilty of withholding his permission.[4]

The third incident occurred when Constable J.S. Perrault drove into the fort with his team and took them to the stables. He was almost frozen and half an hour behind the others who had stabled their animals and had been dismissed. Perrault unhitched his team and left the stables without permission. When he was ordered back from the men's quarters he refused, complaining about the cold and wanting time to get warm. He was placed under arrest for leaving before being dismissed and then for direct disobedience in refusing to go back when ordered. Again, Brisebois took the side of the constable, claiming that the man hadn't really disobeyed an order but had simply been slow in responding to it. Like the others, Perrault was given a light sentence.

In each instance, Brisebois may have been justifiably sympathetic to his men but in doing so he was undermining the authority of his non-commissioned officers and turning a blind eye to military discipline. Rather than gaining the trust and affection of his men, he was telling them that they could interpret the regulations any way they wished and he would support them rather than their immediate superiors. This, of course, was exactly the opposite to what the men needed. They wanted someone who was a tough and forceful leader.

But Brisebois had other things on his mind. During the month of December, before the fort was finished and while the whole country was in a deep freeze, he was pondering the problems of the Blackfoot Indians. He became convinced that the destruction of the buffalo would be a catastrophe to the tribes and that action should be taken to control hunting. He devised his own set of regulations and sent two Metis scouts, Piskan Munro and E. Berard, to the Blackfoot camps to tell the Indians to kill only enough buffalo for food.

When the traders heard about the order, they were incensed, for they were looking for a good business in buffalo robes over the winter. "This will come hard on the Indians," commented a Hudson's Bay trader, "...and this will be a drawback to our Trade."[5]

Brisebois also sent a copy of his draft regulations to the Hon. David Mills, Minister of the Interior in Ottawa, suggesting that they be enforced throughout the West. He said that anyone killing a buffalo cow or calf in the spring should be fined five dollars and that the same fine be levied in winter against anyone killing more than their own needs. He also suggested the banning of buffalo empoundments and that there be a fine of $100 levied against any trader who employed Indians to hunt buffalo for their hides. "Unless this is done," wrote Brisebois, "the Buffalo will disappear in less than ten years. Those Indians will then be in a starving condition and entirely dependent upon the Canadian Government for subsistence."[6]

He was right, of course, in trying to take this action but at the same time he seemed to be ignoring the serious

INSPECTOR EPHREM BRISEBOIS WAS THE OFFICER IN CHARGE OF F TROOP WHEN THE MOUNTED POLICE FORT WAS BUILT IN 1875. HAD HE BEEN A MORE FORCE-FUL LEADER, THE FORT MAY HAVE RETAINED THE NAME HE GAVE IT: FORT BRISEBOIS. HOWEVER, THE OFFICER LOST CONTROL OF HIS MEN DURING THE SEVERE WINTER OF 1875-76 AND RESIGNED FROM THE FORCE THE FOLLOWING SUMMER. (GLENBOW, NA-828-1) problems within his own fort. The weather remained bitterly cold, morale was low, and yet Brisebois seemed to remain aloof from the troubles. As a French-speaking officer and a strong Catholic, he gravitated to the local Catholic mission and to the Metis village that surrounded it. This resulted in two actions on his part which brought relations between him and his men close to the breaking point.

The first was to engage in an illicit relationship with one of the Metis girls and install her in his officer's quarters. Brisebois was a virile twenty-five-year-old so perhaps his action was understandable, but under the circumstances the added warmth of a girl under his buffalo robes would not have endeared him to his men, who were freezing—and alone—in their crude barracks.

Then Brisebois added insult to injury when he appropriated the only sheet iron stove in the fort. Initially it had been placed in the men's quarters both for cooking and heating purposes. Everyone else had to make do with the stone fireplaces which had proven to be less than perfect; they were smoky and sent much of the heat up the chimney.

Presumably Brisebois's new paramour had lived in a well-constructed Metis home where she could cook her meals on a decent stove. But whatever the reason, Brisebois ordered that the men's stove be ensconced in his own quarters. Now he had all the heat—from his buffalo robes, the iron stove, and the dark-eyed girl.

It would take only one more incident to cause a complete breakdown between the officer and his men,

and this Brisebois was quick to provide. While constables were still struggling with the palisades and becoming frost-bitten in the bitter December weather, the commanding officer detailed three men to build log cabins for the fort's two Metis interpreters, Munro and Berard. The three constables refused. Brisebois then ordered his N.C.O.s to place the men under arrest. They refused. At that point, the entire F Troop mutinied and stopped work. According to a local trader:

> The whole are now their own Bosses, waiting for Col Macleod's arrival to set things straight. The Men have sent a list of Charges agst. the Captain . . . some of them crushing ones.[7]

And to make sure their grievances weren't buried and forgotten, the constables and N.C.O.s gave a copy to Methodist missionary George McDougall who promptly sent it to Sir Selby-Smyth, head of Canada's militia in Ottawa. In addition, Constable H.E. Griffiths sent a copy to his father who forwarded it to his Member of Parliament.

Once the grievances were prepared, two constables and a corporal volunteered to take them to Fort Macleod despite the terrible weather. When they arrived, half frozen, they were immediately placed under arrest and put in the guardhouse. However, after the circumstances were explained, no charges were laid pending a review of the situation on the Bow River.

Although the grievances were directed to Colonel

THE PARADE SQUARE
INSIDE FORT CALGARY
IN 1878. (GLENBOW,
NA-659-16)

Macleod, the responsibility for acting upon them fell to Colonel A.G. Irvine, for on January 1, 1876, Macleod had resigned and had been appointed stipendiary magistrate, while Irvine had become the new Assistant Commissioner. However, Irvine was still new to the position so he asked Macleod to accompany him.

The officers wanted to leave immediately but a succession of blizzards prevented them from going until the second week in January. When they arrived at the Bow River they found matters had settled down somewhat but that "the state of the Troop has been bordering on mutiny for some time & the Col. will find his hands full endeavouring to sift the matter & get at the truth."[8]

Accompanying Irvine was the paymaster who gave out more than six thousand dollars in cash thus resolving one of the men's complaints. The surgeon in the party, Richard Nevitt, found the men in surprisingly good health.

Irvine heard the evidence from Brisebois, N.C.O.s, and constables and had no doubt where to place the blame. "I consider Inspector Brisebois utterly unfit to command them," he reported. "It is to be regretted that such a fine Troop should be commanded by one who is perfectly ignorant of the duties of commanding. I consider Inspector Brisebois unfit for the position he holds."[9]

Brisebois responded to the charges by requesting four months' leave of absence to look after some private business in Quebec. In fact, he probably wanted to go directly to Ottawa to seek political support for his tenuous position. Irvine, realizing that Brisebois had been a political appointee who had been backed by strong Quebec interests, refused the request. In the summer of 1876, when he was finally given the leave he was so thoroughly alienated from the Force that he submitted his resignation and returned to eastern Canada.

In retrospect, Brisebois was probably a good officer but he was either unwilling or unable to control his men during the critical stormy winter months of 1875. They were poorly clothed, unpaid, living in crude barracks, and performing arduous work in terrible weather. The conditions were not of Brisebois's making. It was not his inefficiency which had caused the men to remain unpaid and without adequate winter clothing;

those had been the blunders of the Ottawa bureaucrats. Neither could he be blamed for the quality of the barracks, the plans and costs for which had been approved by his superiors.

The fault of the young officer was in not controlling his men despite these shortcomings. He should have been firm and led by example. Instead, he looked after his own comforts and was lenient when he should have been harsh.

The later career of Inspector Brisebois attests to the man's capabilities. On his return to Quebec he threw himself into political campaigning on behalf of the Conservatives. In the federal election of 1877 he played a major role in the defeat of Wilfrid Laurier who was running in Brisebois's home constituency of Drummond-Arthabaska. For his services Brisebois was appointed Registrar of Land Titles for the federal district of Little Saskatchewan and when that area was incorporated into the province of Manitoba, he became an employee of the provincial government.

His headquarters were at Minnedosa, Manitoba, and during that time he was one of only two French-Canadian families in the district. He proved to be an efficient registrar and he and his new wife, Adele, were among the most popular couples in town. A local newspaper commented that "the people of Minnedosa hold the Major in high esteem."[10]

At the outbreak of the North-West Rebellion in 1885, Brisebois was appointed a brigade major in the 65th Mount Royal Rifles, organized a home guard, then recruited men for the Winnipeg Light Infantry. Ordered to Edmonton, he passed through the town of Calgary—his first visit since his ignominious departure—and continued on to Edmonton where he had charge of the local military district. At the conclusion of the rebellion, he returned to Minnedosa where he was given a hero's welcome. Commented a local newspaper:

He was met at the station by a detachment of the Home Guards and many of his friends who welcomed him and escorted him from the depot, and on passing up Main Street, he was saluted by the shrill notes of the mill whistles. At the armoury he addressed a few words to the men of the Home Guard who gave three hearty cheers for the gallant major.[11]

Four years later, in 1889, a change of government occurred in Manitoba and the Minnedosa land office was abolished. Brisebois and his wife sold their house and were in the process of moving to St. Boniface when, on February 13, 1890, Ephrem suddenly died of a heart attack. He was thirty-nine years old.

Upon his death, the *Montreal Gazette* commented:

> He was a most sincere and devoted Conservative . . . Personally he was of polished and courtly manner; was dignified without appearing to condescend. He was loyal to a degree towards his Queen, and to all who needed his assistance his purse was as open as his heart was full of sympathy for those of all nations or religions or politics.[12]

One can speculate what might have happened if the winter of 1875-76 had not been so severe; if there had been more than one iron stove and one less Metis girl; and if the men had been paid and warmly dressed. Calgary's history may have been quite different from the one we know today.

WHAT'S IN A NAME?

Obviously, Inspector Brisebois's questionable actions affected the naming of the Mounted Police fort. In 1874-75 three Mounted Police forts had been built on the southern prairies but the Bow River post was the only one not named after its founder. Fort Macleod honoured its officer in charge, James F. Macleod, and Fort Walsh was named after its commanding officer, James M. Walsh. The third was Fort Calgary.

Like other officers who had established outposts, Brisebois began calling the fort after himself, although his superiors referred to it as Bow River Post. Brisebois's poor reputation in the eyes of his superiors meant that no serious consideration was given to officially adopting the name of Fort Brisebois. When Commissioner A.G. Irvine arrived at the fort early in 1876, he immediately countermanded an order that all communications from

the post should be addressed from Fort Brisebois. Suspecting that the man would not be in their service much longer, Irvine did not want to be stuck with the embarrassment of having a fort named for a discredited officer. Instead, on the advice of Colonel Macleod, he tentatively renamed it Fort Calgary, pending approval from Ottawa.

In February, 1876, Assistant Commissioner A.G. Irvine penned a now famous—but not altogether honest—letter to Hewitt Bernard, the Deputy Minister of Justice in Ottawa:

> As we now have a Post or Fort at the Bow River it would be well if it was known by some name. I visited the Post about a fortnight ago with Colonel Macleod and when we were there Inspector BriseBois (who is in command of the station) issued an order without consulting either Col. Macleod or myself, stating that all public documents sent out from this Fort were to be headed Fort Brisebois.[1]

The implication by Irvine is not entirely correct. Brisebois had been using the name since December, and on January 1, a local trader began using Fort Brisebois as his address. Also, when the Mounted Police party arrived at the post from Fort Macleod, surgeon R.B. Nevitt wrote a letter to his sweetheart from "Fort Brisebois at the junction of the Bow and Elbow Rivers."[2] It is clear, then, that Brisebois had already adopted the name before Colonel Irvine arrived. The assistant commissioner's letter continues:

> I of course cancelled the order at once, as in the first place Inspector BriseBois had no authority to issue such an order and in the second place the Fort was not built by Inspector Brisebois' Troop & neither the Troop or the people about there wish the place to be called BriseBois.

Here again, Irvine was being less than honest with his superiors. It was splitting hairs to say that Brisebois's troop had not built the fort. While it is true the work was done by civilian contractors, Brisebois and his troop had to oversee the construction and to build the palisades and bastions. Also, the fact that the Catholic mission,

ASSISTANT COMMISSIONER ACHESON G. IRVINE RECOMMENDED THE NAME OF FORT CALGARY, WHICH HAD BEEN SUGGESTED TO HIM BY COLONEL MACLEOD. (GLENBOW, NA-23-3)

Hudson's Bay Company, and an independent trader had begun using the name Fort Brisebois would belie the statement that no one wanted it. The letter then concludes:

Colonel Macleod has suggested the name of Calgary which I believe in Scotch means clear running water, a very appropriate name I think. Should the Minister be pleased to approve of this name I will issue an order to that effect.

It is apparent that Irvine did not want to give the real reason for renaming the fort, i.e. that Inspector Brisebois was on his way out. So, with a few half-truths and a recommendation from a highly respected former officer, the name of Fort Brisebois was gently but firmly pushed aside and replaced with Fort Calgary.

In April, Brisebois was chastised for continuing to use the name of Fort Brisebois. However, he argued that the Fort Calgary name had not yet been sanctioned and he would continue to use Brisebois until an official notice came through. By this time Sir Edward Blake, the Minister of Justice, was probably aware of the problems at the outpost. However, in view of Brisebois's strong political connections in Quebec, he refused to take sides but diplomatically replied that he would "not interfere with the choice of the name."[3] On the basis of that spineless comment, Commissioner Irvine issued an order to all Mounted Police posts on May 19, 1876, that the name of Fort Calgary had been adopted.

Had the recommendation not been accepted in Ottawa, it is quite possible that today the city's major summer event would be the Brisebois Stampede while in winter everyone would cheer for the Brisebois Flames.

That directive ended the argument of Fort Brisebois versus Fort Calgary but other debates arose over the years. One was the correct spelling. Some suggested that the post had been called Fort Calgarry but that it was later shortened to Calgary. This is not true. However, part of the confusion might be explained by the fact that Inspector Brisebois, the first time he used the distasteful title, deliberately or accidentally misspelled it as "Calgarry."

Cecil Denny, who was second in command at the fort, was present when the discussion of a name took place between Irvine and Macleod. In fact, Denny claims to have been a party to the decision. He commented that Calgary "was never spelled with two r's as often stated . . . I having been one of three who decided on the name in February 1876."[4]

Spelling variations sometimes occurred in official reports and private correspondence—including one letter addressed from "Fort Kill-garry"—but "Calgary" was the only correct use of the term.

At one time there was also a question as to whether Colonel Macleod chose the name because of Calgary on the Isle of Mull or Calgary on the Isle of Skye, both in the Western Isles of Scotland. At first, Skye was the favoured choice because that is the location of Dunvegan Castle, ancestral home of the Macleod clan. Colonel Macleod had been born in Drynoch, Isle of Skye, in 1836. However, later evidence indicated that the Isle of Mull was actually the source of Colonel Macleod's inspiration.

Calgary Castle, or Calgary House, on the Isle of Mull had been in the hands of the MacLean clan until 1855 when it had been acquired by Colonel John Hugh Munro MacKenzie. As the MacKenzies were relatives of Macleod's sister through marriage, he had occasion to visit the area and was entranced by its beauty.

"He loved these islands," said one of the MacKenzie descendants, "and when he came west in 1874 with the North West Mounted Police, decided to call your city Calgary after our home at Calgary House." She added that Macleod almost didn't make it back to Canada as he "fell in love with one of my grandmother's sisters, but she turned him down."[5]

A visitor to the Scottish Calgary described how it looked in the 1970s:

Calgary Bay today is a remote, beautiful place of white sands, black rocks, and heather-covered hills. The only buildings are Calgary House and two small cottages near the sea. The castle itself is a late Georgian-style mansion with gardens of eucalyptus trees and exotic plants.[6]

COL. JAMES F. MACLEOD WAS PROBABLY THE MOST RESPECTED AND INFLUENTIAL MEMBER OF THE ORIGINAL NORTH-WEST MOUNTED POLICE. HE ESTABLISHED FRIEND-LY RELATIONS WITH THE INDIANS AND WAS KNOWN AS A MAN WHO ALWAYS KEPT HIS WORD. WHEN HE LEFT THE FORCE, HE BECAME A MAGISTRATE AND JUS-TICE OF THE SUPREME COURT OF THE NORTH-WEST TERRITORIES. HE DIED IN CALGARY IN 1894. (GLENBOW, NA-1698-1)

The translation of the word "Calgary" has also been the subject of discussion and controversy for many years but everyone agrees that Colonel Macleod's version was wrong. The Gaelic terms for "clear running water" are *t-suthain shoilleir* or *uisge shoilleir,* neither of which bears any resemblance to "Calgary."

Some of the translations given for the Calgary location in Scotland were "Wood of the Garry," "Hut in the Thicket," "Rough Haven," and "Laughing Bay." In 1930, an opinion was sought from W.J. Watson, professor of Celtic Languages at Edinburgh University. He stated that both Calgarys—the ones in Mull and Skye—were pronounced *Calagearraidh* in Gaelic. He said the term was Norse meaning "Kali's Enclosed Field," and that Kali was a common Norse personal name.[7]

But his wasn't the last word. Later, another Scot suggested the term meant "water running through a gorge," or "willows beyond the border." Other suggestions were that it was derived from *Calgaradh,* meaning "cabbage garden," or from *Calagardh,* "broad bay," or from *Calagarie,* meaning "laughing bay."

In 1976, Andrew Young of Calgary tackled the problem. He learned that in 1675, the owner of Calgary Castle, Lauchlan M'Lean, had been arrested by the Earl of Argyll and at that time his home was shown as *Calligourie.* An early tax record for the castle spelled it *Calligory.* From this information and an examination of the area around Calgary Bay, Young offered another translation. He stated:

> The original name in Gaelic was *Cala-ghearridh,* with the first part, *Cala,* meaning "harbour" or "bay," and the second part, *ghearridh,* meaning "preserved piece of pasture," "enclosed pasture," or "farm." Therefore, a translation of "Calgary" would be "preserved pasture at the harbour," or "bay farm."[8]

This may not be the last word on the subject but it is one which has been widely accepted.

Interestingly, the Indians have never had a problem with Calgary's name. The Blackfoot call it *Moki'nstsis,* or "Elbow." The same term is used by the Sarcees (*Kootsisa'w*), the Stoneys (*Wincheesh-pah*), and the Crees (*Otos-kwunee*).

When the Mounted Police first arrived in Calgary, the Blackfoot Indians were impressed by the number of buildings which were erected, not only at the fort but by the missionaries and traders. As a result, their first name for the community was "Elbow Many Houses." Then they gave separate names for each of its structures. The Mounted Police fort was called "Elbow Little House" and the Catholic mission was "Elbow Holy White Man's House." The Hudson's Bay Company store was called "Bear Child's House," after its manager, John Bunn, while the I.G. Baker store was "Tall Man's House," after its trader, D.W. Davis.

But perhaps the best name for Calgary was devised by the Slavey Indians of northern Alberta. They called it *Klincho-tinay-indihay,* which simply means "horse town."

THE SARCEES FIND A HOME

The presence of the Mounted Police, the Catholic mission, and the Hudson's Bay Company provided a convenient and friendly base for native wanderers. As soon as the fort was built, a colony of Metis settled near the mission while the Blackfoot and Sarcees found Calgary a handy place to trade. Of these wanderers, the Sarcees became the tribe most intimately associated with the growth of the area.

Today the Sarcee Indians—or Tsuu T'ina Nation— have a reserve on the outskirts of Calgary. Place-names

BULL HEAD WAS A GREAT LEADER OF THE SARCEE, OR TSUU T'INA PEOPLE. HE SIGNED TREATY SEVEN IN 1877 AND FOUGHT LONG AND HARD FOR A RESERVE ON THE WESTERN OUTSKIRTS OF CALGARY. HE DIED THERE IN 1911. (GLENBOW, NA-583-1)

such as Sarcee Trail, Weaselhead Bridge, and Crowchild Trail owe their origins to Calgary's western neighbours. Yet the location of the reserve was not a foregone conclusion; if the government had had its way, the Sarcees would be living out east somewhere in the Arrowwood district.

The Sarcees are a branch of the Beaver Indians of northern Alberta. They originally lived in the woodlands but by the late 1700s they were hunting along the North Saskatchewan River east of Edmonton. Then they became allied to the Blackfoot and drifted farther and farther south onto the Alberta plains. By the mid-19th century they were usually found in the vicinity of the Red Deer or Bow rivers but sometimes they joined Blood or Blackfoot hunting parties and could be found all the way south to the Missouri River.

In 1877, the Sarcees were one of the signers of Treaty Seven under their chief, Bull Head. The population at that time was about 450 persons. Bull Head had no strong feeling about a reserve, for as long as there were buffalo on the plains he had no intention of settling down. Accordingly, he had no objections when Crowfoot suggested that the Sarcees and Blackfoot share one big reserve near Blackfoot Crossing. Why should he object? The idea of actually staying in one place was utterly foreign to him and to most other Indians.

As a result, the government designated the Sarcee Reserve as a strip of land four miles wide "on the south side of the Bow River, commencing three miles above the Blackfoot Crossing and extending as far westerly as may be necessary."[1] That would encompass the present communities of Shouldice and Arrowwood. After the treaty was concluded, the Sarcees headed out to the plains to continue their old way of life, but within a year many of them were starving. The buffalo, their staff of life, had been virtually annihilated.

During the winter of 1878-79, most of the Sarcees camped near Fort Macleod but they were told they would have to move to their reserve if they expected to receive rations. They went north but when they got to Fort Calgary, they refused to go any further. Bull Head claimed an argument had arisen with the Blackfoot over the distribution of flour and there would probably be trouble if they camped side by side over the winter. Bull Head knew that conditions were so bad at Blackfoot Crossing that some of the Blackfoot were mere skeletons and their young men could be seen using wire snares to catch gophers for food.

For the rest of the winter the Sarcees stayed near Fort Calgary where the Mounted Police issued them with enough beef and flour to supplement what they got from hunting. From that experience, the Sarcees decided they liked the Elbow River area and wanted to stay. Not only could they hunt deer in the foothills, but there were odd jobs to be found in the village, and they felt safe with the Mounted Police close by.

In the summer of 1879, the newly appointed Indian commissioner, Edgar Dewdney, arrived at Fort Calgary with the intention of sending the Sarcees to their vacant reserve. He noted:

> With the Sarcee Chief I had some difficulty in convincing him to go to the Crossing. He says there is not a good feeling between his Indians & the Blackfoot & he fears trouble if he goes down.[2]

At first Dewdney tried to pressure the chief to move to the reserve if he expected to be fed but Bull Head said he would rather sell his horses for food, then go out on to the prairie and starve. Finally, he grudgingly agreed to go but only if the Sarcees were rationed separately from the Blackfoot and were not harassed by them. However, shortly after the Sarcees had reached the Crossing, trouble arose and the sounds of rifle shots echoed across the Bow River. Angrily, Bull Head pulled his people off the reserve and they were back to Fort Calgary for the winter of 1879-80.

Meanwhile, Dewdney hired a staff to issue rations at Blackfoot Crossing and opened a supply farm on Fish Creek just south of Calgary to grow grain and raise cattle. He allowed Bull Head to stay near the Mounted Police fort for the winter but only on the understanding that the Sarcees help out at the new government farm. By the spring of 1880, a number of Indians had been working steadily at the farm where they were "quiet and well disposed."[3] They also found Fish Creek to be an excellent wintering place.

However, when Indian Agent Norman Macleod (an older brother of Colonel Macleod) came to pay treaty money that summer, he insisted that the Sarcees go back to their reserve so that all men, women, and children could receive their five dollars. They finally agreed but by now Bull Head had decided that he wanted his reserve to be located at Fish Creek and when no action was taken, relations between the government and the tribe became strained. At the treaty payment there was

an argument about the number of persons in the tribe and Bull Head again complained about being paid and rationed with the Blackfoot. Finally, late in the summer the contractors failed to deliver the flour and beef on time and so the rations were temporarily suspended. Finding this to be the perfect excuse, Bull Head uprooted his entire clan and by November they were back at their favourite camping grounds on Fish Creek and demanding rations from the Mounted Police.

There were only four men stationed at Fort Calgary at that time—Sergeant Johnston and three constables—and they had neither cattle nor enough flour to feed 400 people. But the Sarcees were starving so their men descended upon the well-stocked Hudson's Bay and I.G. Baker stores and demanded food. They threatened the storekeepers, forced their way into the trading rooms, fired guns into the ceiling, and built a huge fire in front of the American store. Intimidated by this show of force, the police agreed to share their meagre supplies then sent a courier to Fort Macleod for help. Immediately, a detachment of thirty policemen under Inspector Cecil Denny and accompanied by Indian Agent Macleod rushed north to quell the "Sarcee war."

A council was held and Agent Macleod later reported to the Indian commissioner:

> They said they were starving and had determined to remain where they were and die, sooner than return to the Blackfoot Crossing. I told them that there was food for them at the Crossing, that I had no means of feeding them at Calgary, that your permission for them to remain at that place only lasted whilst Mr. Wright could find work for them at the Supply Farm, when you expected they would return to the Crossing . . . They remained obstinate and went away saying they would remain at the Elbow.[4]

When it was obvious that the Sarcees would not move to their reserve, the agent suggested they go to Fort Macleod where there were sufficient police to issue rations and keep them in line. Bull Head preferred Calgary but was told that if he stayed, his hungry people would receive no food. For three days, the tribe resisted but finally Bull Head agreed to go to Fort Macleod if his people were given transportation. Their horses were in poor condition so Denny arranged for Sam Livingston to supply some carts. Next morning, when the tribe still made no signs of being ready to move, Denny lost his patience:

> I therefore drew up the men with their rifles loaded, just on the outskirts of the camp, and I and Sgt. Lawder commenced to pull down the tents. The Indians swarmed out and were very nasty for a time, but cooled down at the sight of the armed party outside the camp, and presently began to pack up their goods.[5]

The hundred-mile trip proved to be a gruelling experience. The weather turned bitterly cold, the thermometer reaching 35 below with blowing snow. When they were about forty miles from their destination a blizzard struck which forced them to remain in camp for three days and when the food ran out, a messenger was dispatched to Fort Macleod for more. The Sarcees suffered terribly and Little Drum, a minor chief who had been ill, died during the winter ordeal. In all, it took the pitiful caravan eleven days to make the journey from Calgary to Fort Macleod. But they finally reached the friendly confines of the Oldman River where the Sarcees stayed and were issued rations until spring.

Meanwhile, Indian Department officials had grown weary of the "on again off again" Sarcee Reserve and demanded that the issue be settled. "Their dislike to the Blackfoot Crossing," Agent Macleod reported, "was having their reserve in common with the Blackfeet. This we overcame by showing them that they would be entirely independent of the Blackfeet, who would be asked to give up any right they might have to this land. The Bow River would form a decided boundary between them, and they would have an instructor of their own."[6]

Although not happy with the government's decision, Bull Head reluctantly agreed in the spring of 1881 to take his tribe to Blackfoot Crossing, provided that land would be broken and ready for seeding when they arrived. This the agent promised.

As the Sarcees marched northward to their reserve and their newly broken farms, it seemed as though the government had finally won its ongoing battle with the tribe. But while the Indians were on the trail, the Indian agent received an anxious message from the Crossing which wiped out all his careful planning. It stated that the contractor "has not ploughed any land for the Sarcees," and that "the Sarcees, if they can only find a little excuse, are liable to turn back, if everything that was promised them is not fulfilled."[7]

But here Bull Head proved that he was a wise leader who could turn defeat into a resounding victory. Instead of resorting to force or going back to Fort Macleod, the chief had someone write a petition for him which he sent to the authorities, outlining the details of the unfulfilled agreement. He went on to say that he wanted a reserve at Calgary eight miles above the mouth of Fish Creek where they would be far away from the big ranches. In that place, his starving people would not be tempted to steal cattle for food. Also, he said, at Fish Creek there would be no range cattle to knock down the fences around the farms they wanted to start.

The Indian commissioner, Edgar Dewdney, was obliged to meet with Bull Head that summer and in his annual report he stated:

> The Sarcees . . . got into trouble with Blackfoot Indians on their return from the south, the chief grievance being that the Blackfeet stole their crops. They met me at Fort Macleod and begged to be allowed to settle away from the Blackfeet; they assured me that unless they left there would be bloodshed. These Indians applied last year for the same thing, and asked to be located on Fish Creek, where they have already got out some timber and rails . . . I agreed to their removal to the point they selected.[8]

The two-year game of nerves between Bull Head and the government had finally come to an end. Bull Head had won.

The departure of the Sarcees from Blackfoot Crossing was typical of their relations with the Blackfoot. First they dug up the seed potatoes which had been planted for them and had a big feast. Then they destroyed all the fences they had erected so that the Blackfoot would not benefit by their labours.

And on that note, the Sarcees came to Calgary.

GROWING PAINS

AN END TO ISOLATION

EVER SINCE THE GOVERNMENT OF JOHN A. MACDONALD PROMISED TO BUILD A RAILWAY LINK
BETWEEN CENTRAL CANADA AND BRITISH COLUMBIA, PEOPLE WONDERED WHAT ROUTE IT WOULD TAKE.
DURING EXPLORATIONS IN THE EARLY 1870S, THE FAVOURED COURSE SEEMED TO AVOID THE OPEN PRAIRIES
AND PASS THROUGH THE EDMONTON REGION. HOWEVER, BY THE EARLY 1880S, AFTER THE CANADIAN PACIFIC
RAILWAY HAD BEEN RESTRUCTURED, THE MATTER OF COMPETITION FROM AMERICAN RAIL LINES
BECAME A CONSIDERATION. IF THE CPR TRACKS WERE TOO FAR NORTH, AMERICAN BRANCH LINES
COULD BE RUN INTO CANADA TO DRAIN OFF ALL THE BUSINESS FROM THE SOUTH. ACCORDINGLY, THE
DECISION WAS MADE TO FORGE STRAIGHT ACROSS THE PRAIRIES TO CONNECT WITH SUITABLE PASSES
THROUGH THE VARIOUS MOUNTAIN RANGES.

Finding the passes was the first problem. Major A.B. Rogers was given the task of locating a route over the Rockies and then across the formidable Selkirks. In 1881 his survey party reached Fort Calgary on July 4, just in time for some of the Americans to have a big celebration. Then, hung over, they left for the mountains and built a warehouse near the present Canmore. Meanwhile, Rogers and his nephew tried to cross the Selkirks from the west but were unsuccessful. Instead, he travelled south and reached the Bow River camp via Fort Steele.

On arrival, Rogers decided that the Kicking Horse Pass was better than Howse Pass, so the rest of the summer was spent in surveying lines for the railroad.

Meanwhile, surveyors were laying out a route across the prairies to Fort Calgary, and from there to join up with Rogers' survey. By the end of 1881, Charles Shaw and his team had surveyed as far west as the present city of Medicine Hat and decided to spend the winter at Fort Calgary. His crew travelled on the north side of the Bow River for several days until they came to a high hill which, as Shaw recalled, "we afterwards found was called Nose Hill and were delighted to see Calgary only a mile or so away, in a broad valley across the Bow River."[1]

Shaw managed to get the carts down the slope and crossed the river on the ice. He commented:

Calgary at that time consisted of I.G. Baker's trading post, a long log building; a small detachment of Mounted Police under Captain French; Major Walker, a retired Mounted Police officer who had settled at Calgary; Mr. Fraser of the Hudson's Bay Company, who had no supplies; a man named Butler [Butlin] and his wife; and Father Lacombe, whose mission was about a mile up the Elbow River."

After a winter at a depot which Major Rogers had built a year earlier, they headed back to Medicine Hat and completed the survey line to Calgary by late March, 1882.

By this time, the rails were already being laid across the prairies but still no route had been found through the Selkirks. The mountain surveyors were back the following year and in July 1882, Rogers finally found a way through the high peaks. He had discovered the perilous Rogers Pass. With that problem solved, construction crews came west across the prairies while others tried to complete the line through the rugged rock country north of the Great Lakes.

At the beginning of the railway surveys, there had been a question as to whether Calgary would live or die. If the line went through the area, the Mounted Police post would expand and a town would ultimately grow up around it. But if the CPR decided on another route, Fort Calgary would be closed and the land between the two rivers would again become part of the prairie landscape.

The fate of the outpost was decided early in 1882 when the government finally learned that the main line would indeed be passing through Calgary. Commissioner A.G. Irvine promptly complained that "the present buildings at Fort Calgary are utterly useless. As Calgary will become the Head Quarters of the District I would strongly recommend that permanent buildings be erected at once."[2]

His suggestion was approved and I.G. Baker again received the contract to undertake the construction work. Two or three of the original Fort Calgary buildings were saved but most of them were demolished. In their place half a dozen frame buildings were erected, all facing a barracks square some 400 by 250 feet in size. To the north were the stables and quartermaster stores; to the west were the officers' quarters; on the south the orderly room, guard room, and sergeant-major's quarters; and east the main barracks and mess room.

Calgary and its red-coated lawmen were ready and waiting for the onslaught of civilization.

ARRIVAL OF THE RAILWAY

A rail link with the East had been a dream of settlers since the arrival of Sam Livingston. By 1882, this dream was becoming a reality as construction workers steadily pushed the rail lines across the vast prairies. By the end of the year, the Canadian Pacific Railway had reached Medicine Hat and was scheduled to be at the foot of the Rockies by the following year.

Calgary was the only existing community along that part of the route, so speculators and merchants flocked there before the railway arrived. For example, George Jacques reached the fort in November, 1882, and commented optimistically, "It is expected that there will be a large city here. It is thought by some that it will grow as fast as Winnipeg."[1] In the spring of 1883—five months before the railway—he opened a watchmaker and jewellery shop and was ready for business. R.J. Ogburn came three months early and started a barber shop. A month later, John Cottingham found a ready business as a saddler and harnessmaker, and in June he was followed by Neil McLeod, a carpenter who built his own hotel, and Angus and Charles Sparrow who opened a meat market. Other entrepreneurs in the pre-railway village were ex-Mounted Policemen George King, Joe Butlin, T.H. Dunne, and James Carrol, and a few ex-whiskey traders like Lafayette French and Asa Samples. By early July, the village had eight hotels, three billiard halls, six laundries, ten stores, and a photographer—all in tents.

When the merchants came, most of them pitched tents on the east side of the Elbow River. At that time, almost the entire west side of the Elbow was reserved for Mounted Police grazing lands and no construction was permitted there. In February, 1883, Commissioner A.G. Irvine stated that the land they reserved

is known as the Calgary bottom, lying between the Bow and Elbow Rivers, on the South Side of the Bow and West of the Elbow. It extends up the Bow River from the junction to what is known as Shaganappe Point, a distance of about 3 1/2 miles in a direct line, and up the Elbow a distance of about 1 1/2 miles. The south-western side of the reserve is bounded by a well defined hill running from Shaganappe Point to a short distance above the R.C. Mission."[2]

CALGARY WAS A MOTLEY VILLAGE OF TENTS AND SHACKS ON THE EAST SIDE OF THE ELBOW RIVER WHEN THE RAILWAY ARRIVED IN 1883. THE SUBSTANTIAL LOG BUILDINGS IN THE BACKGROUND BELONG TO THE HUDSON'S BAY COMPANY. (GLENBOW, NA-1315-9)

A question arose as to where the new town would be located. On the east side of the Elbow, two parcels of land had been purchased by investors and lots were being sold to new arrivals. There was a strong feeling that this area—the present Inglewood—would become the centre of the town. The best of the two parcels was immediately adjacent to the Elbow River and had been claimed by a Metis freighter, Louis Roselle. However, as this area had originally been settled by the Hudson's Bay Company, the ownership was in question. Wesley Orr and W.C. Schreiber bought Roselle's claim but when they began to subdivide and sell lots, the land became tied up in litigation and new owners were unable to get deeds for the property. Farther east was the second parcel. Ex-Mounted Policeman Cecil Denny had subdivided it into the "Denny Estates" and sold a number of lots before disposing of his claim to rancher John Stewart and Mounted Police Commissioner A.G. Irvine for $10,000. This land was free and clear but was not in such a choice location as the Roselle claim.

Because of the uncertainty of the town's location and problems of ownership, new settlers preferred to live in tents or rough wooden structures until the railway arrived and matters were settled.

Meanwhile, the CPR construction work moved ever westward across the prairies. Contractors Langdon & Shephard pressed their men so hard that on one stretch between Medicine Hat and Calgary they established a world's record for laying steel. Their average had been six miles of track a day but on one section they laid an impressive nine miles, 300 feet of track. During construction, the surveyors laid out the line, followed by the grading crews. Then came the "front train" which was responsible for laying the track. It carried enough supplies for one mile of road—ties and rails for tracks, timber for bridges, and telegraph poles. It ventured to the end of the steel and unloaded the ties and timbers which were picked up by teams and wagons and dumped along the route. The rails were piled on a push car, laid in place manually by crews of labourers, and then the spike drivers did their work. By the time a mile of track was laid, the front train was back with another load.

As the rails approached Calgary, more and more merchants arrived on the work trains. Many of them were itinerants who pitched their tents at each new

townsite along the way and did a roaring business while construction was in progress. When the next town or station was designated, they struck their tents and followed. One of these was the Cheap Cash Store, operated by Repstein and Brothers, Winnipeg merchants. They had been following the route of the CPR all summer.

In later years, a number of people recalled arriving in Calgary just ahead of the railway. For example, T. B.

A CPR TRAIN, PULLED BY A WOOD-BURNING LOCOMOTIVE, STOPS AT THE CALGARY STATION IN 1884. (GLENBOW, NA-967-12)

Braden got off a work train at the end of the steel at the present town of Gleichen, then walked four miles to a railway camp. There was no room for him there so he slept on the prairie and next morning he had to go without breakfast because only the crews could eat at the cook tent. When he enquired about transportation to Calgary, he was directed to a man with a buckboard and team who was charging $25 per passenger, baggage extra. This was too expensive so he found another man willing to take him as far as the ferry at the Bow River, three miles east of Calgary, for $5. Braden recalled, "We got started about four o'clock in the afternoon and reached the ferry at six the next night, having spent a night on the prairie in a tent without blankets."[3]

From the Bow River, Braden picked up his bags and "after trudging along for some distance we came to a row of tents on the bank of the Elbow which we were informed was Calgary. The tents were all either saloons or restaurants, and we got a very fair meal in the Far West Hotel."[4] Braden then canvassed the embryo town about starting a newspaper and before the day was out he had a hundred subscribers, plenty of advertisements, and the *Calgary Herald's* future was assured.

The grading crews set up their camp on the east bank of the Elbow River and the spike drivers came on August 8, 1883. Three days later, the track layers passed through the tent village and brought the steel rails to the banks of the Elbow River. The front train immediately unloaded piles of timber and work was started on a bridge.

Meanwhile, the Elbow River marked the end of Langdon & Shephard's contract so its 400 graders, spike men, and track layers were paid off. There was a wild cel-

SOME OF CALGARY'S FIRST SETTLERS, SUITABLY DRESSED IN "WILD WEST" GARB, POSE IN FRONT OF SAMUEL SHAW'S RANCH HOUSE LATE IN 1883. (GLENBOW, NA-706-1)

ebration which lasted all day, even though it was a Sunday. There were foot races with bets running into the thousands of dollars. At least $5,000 changed hands on horse races; a wheel of fortune raked in hundreds of dollars; and the dozen or so prostitutes—both black and white—did a thriving business. According to one observer, "Whiskey flowed freely and the night was made hideous with yelling, screaming and blasphemy."[5]

Next morning, August 13, the bridge was finished and the first train entered the future downtown area of Calgary. But the jubilation lasted for only a short time before trouble broke out. As soon as the train was unloaded, the now-unemployed workers jumped on the flat cars and prepared to return to Winnipeg. The trainman ordered them off but the men, many of them hung

over, were in no mood to argue. The engineer-in-chief of the CPR, Herbert Holt, called the Mounted Police and, with rifles at the ready, they forced the men off the train.

A spokesman for the unemployed workers claimed that Langdon & Shephard had promised them free passes back to Winnipeg if they stayed on the job for three months. Holt replied that he would not honour the commitment as long as there was work to be done. North American Construction Company had the contract for building the railway west of Calgary and they were in urgent need of men. Until their requirements were met, no passes.

At the conclusion of the confrontation, Holt ordered the railway cars sent away empty and under guard. About a hundred men signed up with North American Construction but the remaining 300 refused to budge. They were "lying here idle, without any shelter day or night for some time"[6] until they engaged the services of a local lawyer, C.W. Peterson. After some negotiation, he succeeded in getting justice, and passes, for disillusioned and angry workers.

Meanwhile, there was considerable dissatisfaction and uneasiness among the settlers because Calgary still lacked an official townsite. As soon as the tracks were laid, a temporary station was located on Section 15 on the west side of the river, while nearby was the telegraph office. Then, amid cries of anger from some of the merchants, the post office was removed to the west side of the river. However, the CPR still had not surveyed a townsite and the land on the east side remained under litigation. Those living in tents hesitated putting up permanent buildings but as the winter of 1883-84 approached, a few more shacks began to appear. The promoters of the Denny Estates and the Roselle property tried to convince merchants that the east side would be the future Calgary but no one believed them. With the railway station and post office on Section 15, it would only be a matter of time before CPR land was surveyed.

Finally, in February, 1884, the CPR announced that it was ready to sell lots on Section 15. Applications were accepted and each person made his choice from a map of the new townsite. The first applicant was pioneer John Glen who took a corner lot on Centre Street and 9th Avenue, directly facing the CPR station. Herbert Holt, the CPR engineer-in-chief, took the entire north side of

8th Avenue between Centre Street and 1st Street East. Soon, most of the east side merchants, as well as I.G. Baker and the Hudson's Bay Company, had selected downtown lots. According to P. Turner Bone:

> The terms of sale were most reasonable: $300 for inside lots and $450 for a corner lot. One-third of the price was payable on signing the agreement for sale; and the balance in two annual instalments with interest at 6 per cent. The company further undertook to give a rebate of 50 per cent on all payments, provided a building was erected on the lots and occupied before a specified date in March.[7]

That sale spelled the end of the townsite question. As a local resident commented, the east side "got up suddenly one morning and moved itself westward across the Elbow—two hundred tar-papered shacks, half a hundred unpretentious wooden buildings, and a few log structures."[8]

During 1884, Calgary went through the pains of rapid growth as permanent buildings replaced the temporary tents and shacks. Merchants firmly believed that the railway would mean instant wealth for the community but it did not receive the influx of people that everyone expected. A visitor to the town in the autumn of that year commented that "Calgary's little boom" had collapsed but optimism was high.[9] Meanwhile, local boosters looked forward to the day when the rail link between the eastern provinces and the Pacific coast would be finished. Not until the formidable terrain north of the Great Lakes was spanned could the town expect a rush of settlers that would make everybody rich.

Meanwhile, Stephen Avenue was recognized as the main business section, while homesteaders and ranchers settled in the surrounding area. Soon it was possible to "drive twenty miles from Calgary without being out of sight of new settlements."[10]

By the summer, with an official census population of 428 (but 506 by local count), the community began to provide basic amenities and services. A private school was opened by J.W. Costello; Dr. Andrew Henderson started a medical practice; and lawyers such as James Lougheed, Henry Bleecker, and Fitzgerald Cochrane opened for business. In addition to the Catholics and

Methodists who were already there, the Presbyterians and Anglicans soon had churches under construction.

On November 12, 1884, a telegram was received by lumberman James Walker announcing that the North-West Territorial government had approved an application for Calgary to be incorporated as a town. An election was held in December and harnessmaker George Murdoch became the first mayor. With the first civic government came the inevitable by-laws, tax collector, and town police.

The town of Calgary was born.

DURING THE WINTER OF 1883-84, A NUMBER OF BUSINESSES MOVED ACROSS THE ELBOW RIVER TO THE NEW CALGARY TOWNSITE. MACKELVIE & GRAVES, G.L. FRASER, AND THE CALGARY HERALD (RIGHT), WERE LOCATED NEAR THE PRESENT CORNER OF 8TH AVENUE AND 1ST STREET EAST. (GLENBOW, NA-1931-1)

PATRIOTS AND RENEGADES

By 1884-85 there were a few clouds on Calgary's economic horizon. One was the huge grazing leases which had been given to ranching companies such as the Cochrane, Bar U, Oxley, and Walrond. These leases discouraged farming and made it difficult for the homesteader to find suitable land or for the squatter to get title to his holdings. While Calgary merchants appreciated the ranching trade, it was a business which employed relatively few people. Farming, on the other hand, could support thousands. The rancher-versus-homesteader was a thorny problem in southern Alberta.

Another difficulty was the unsettled state of the native population. Indians and Metis were complaining of the loss of the buffalo, starvation, and failure of the government to fulfil its promises of assistance. Generally, the townspeople of Calgary were unsympathetic. "Most people living up this way," commented a local resident, "are disgusted with the Government for keeping the Indians idle. They laugh at the humanitarian theory about the noble and generous red man. They say he is cruel, lazy, filthy, steals whenever he can, and won't work while the Government feeds him in idleness."[1]

As far as many merchants were concerned, the Indians were no longer important economically and should be confined to their reserves while the Metis settlements were too far away in the Edmonton and Battleford districts to be of any concern.

In the summer of 1884, Louis Riel returned from Montana and found support among the Metis of Batoche and Prince Albert as they sought a recognition of their land rights. By the spring of 1885, rumours of rebellion became commonplace as the government failed to respond to native appeals. Finally, on March 19, 1885, Riel formed a provisional government and occupied the village of Batoche. When his followers commandeered the guns and supplies of two local traders, a force of Mounted Police and volunteers was dispatched from Fort Carlton to arrest the ringleaders. They met a group of Metis near Duck Lake on March 26; in the ensuing fight ten police and volunteers were killed and another eleven wounded. This marked the beginning of the North-West Rebellion.[2]

When word of the Battle of Duck Lake reached Calgary, it caused uneasiness in some and fear in others. The town had three reserves within a sixty-mile radius, one being less than an hour's drive away. Of these, the Blackfoot was the source of most concern for with its allied tribes of Bloods and Peigans, its members could muster some 3,000 warriors. The fact that the Blackfoot were deadly foes of the insurgents made no difference; to many Calgarians an Indian was an Indian. Besides, the lack of sympathy which most Calgarians felt for the Indians was well known.

The day after the Duck Lake battle, the Mounted Police withdrew most of its contingent from Calgary and sent them towards the scene of action. They left only half

T. BLAND STRANGE, A RANCHER AND FORMER IMPERIAL OFFICER, WAS GIVEN COMMAND OF THE ALBERTA FIELD FORCE IN 1885. HE NOTED THAT "OF ALL THE COWARDLY RASCALS I EVER DEALT WITH, THE CALGARY PEOPLE ARE THE WORST. NO PATRIOTISM, NOTHING BUT TRYING TO CHEAT THE GOVERNMENT..." (GLENBOW, NA-1847-2)

a dozen men, most of them on the sick list. The reaction of Calgary mayor George Murdoch and his council was one of panic that they were being left unprotected. They immediately began to recruit a small army of special policemen to form a home guard and started a night patrol of the streets. One townsman commented, "I do not say that the steps taken by the town authorities were unnecessary, but I think they might have been taken and conducted without any display. To show fear when danger is remote is to invite attack."[3] The Indian agent on the Blackfoot Reserve agreed. "The people of Calgary are in a state of panic," he said, "and are doing the very thing calculated to raise a disturbance, viz: letting the Indians see that they are apprehensive of danger."[4]

Meanwhile, a retired army officer, T. Bland Strange, who owned a ranch near Gleichen, offered to form a militia corps of mounted riflemen. When he received permission from Ottawa, thirty-five of the Calgary home guard immediately applied for active service. This created a rift between Strange and Mayor Murdoch as the latter wanted to keep all the able-bodied men at home to protect the town. He claimed that after the mounted rifles left, the town was sure to be plundered and burned by Indians. When the frightened Murdoch was backed by his town council, Strange responded with the adage, "In the multitude of councillors was no wisdom found."[5]

At church services on Sunday, March 29, Methodist minister Joshua Dyke was trying to allay the fears of his flock when Archibald Grant came to the door and whispered to T.B. Braden, the usher. He in turn walked up the aisle and whispered to Richard Hardisty who picked up his hat and left the church. Within a few minutes twenty or thirty worried men had joined him. The rest of the congregation were so uneasy that the minister rushed through the rest of the sermon and pronounced the benediction.

When the women and children went outside, they learned that an Indian attack was said to be imminent. On Stephen Avenue, Roger & Grant's hardware store had been opened and frantic people were arming themselves with guns, revolvers, and axes. A telegram was dispatched to Ottawa saying that "a white man married to squaw came to Calgary and informed Major Walker that a large number Blackfeet would leave reserve this PM to attack the town."[6]

That evening the fear turned to terror when the telegraph operator at Langdon—about halfway to the Blackfoot Reserve—reported seeing large bodies of Indians just south of the railway travelling in the direction of Calgary. Mayor Murdoch and his crowd immediately sent an anxious telegram to the Minister of the Interior, "Blackfeet Indians moving in numbers toward Calgary."[7]

That night, Murdoch became the unofficial commanding officer of the fiasco. Women and children were herded into the Windsor Hotel and the building barricaded to withstand a siege. Groups of armed men were designated to patrol the streets. During the excitement, some men loaded their guns with the wrong ammunition; this included the chief of police, John Ingram, who noticed the mixup before any serious damage was done.

Also, liquor was freely available and as the night wore on, some of the guardians of the town became hopelessly drunk. It was a miracle that no one was killed. The town's saddlemaker, John Cottingham, said disgustedly, "Arms were placed in the hands of men and boys unfit for the duty assigned them . . . Some of our leading citizens were much the worse of liquor, those whom we looked to for advice, and had the Indian scare been real there would have been serious work done. I am familiar with the doings of the Mayor, Council and a few more of Calgary's drunken beauties."[8]

Some of the town's cooler and more sober heads decided to investigate the rumours. Cottingham rode through the night to Langdon and got the telegraph operator out of bed at 2 a.m. He learned that the man had no real information; he had simply seen some figures in the distance and couldn't say for sure what they were.

In the morning, a railway engine was commandeered and the missionary, Father Lacombe, was sent to the Blackfoot Reserve to find out if the threatened attack was real. When he got back later that day he reported the Indians quietly at work in their fields and surprised that anyone would think they would join the rebels. The whole "Blackfoot scare" had been nothing more than a frightened response to wild rumours and hysteria.

Now that an Indian attack was ruled out, some Calgarians started to worry about spies and rebel sympathizers. Homesteader Augustus Carney was marked as a "suspected Fenian [who] attempted to incite certain parties to tear up Volunteer Company service,"[9] while other people spoke darkly about men who were disloyal to the government. This fear seemed to have some credence when a number of homesteaders and farmers decided to capitalize on the unsettled times to press their demands. When a meeting was called on April 5 at John Glen's farm, five miles south of Calgary, a few townsmen unexpectedly appeared. Said a journalist, "They went to swell the numbers and to run the meeting."[10] Among them were Mayor Murdoch and town solicitor Henry Bleecker.

The farmers were openly hostile to the government because of the ill treatment they had received. Pioneer Sam Livingston said, "For the present I defend my claim as my neighbours do, behind my Winchester. Unless the land is all opened up for homestead entry all must either fight for our rights or leave the country."[11] These were strong words but they had nothing to do with the North-West Rebellion. John Glen, another respected old timer, was equally bitter about his inability to get legal title to his land.

When the farmers had finished speaking, the townsmen took over the meeting and used it as a means of embarrassing the government in Ottawa. When a list of resolutions was formulated, it was almost surely this group that added three demands which had nothing to do with the purpose of the meeting. One called for judicial reforms as already requested by the citizens of Calgary, and another insisted on representational government for the North-West Territory. The third, and most contentious, stated:

We are of the opinion that the halfbreeds of the North-West Territories are entitled to the same rights and privileges as have already been conceded to their brethren in Manitoba. And we most earnestly impress upon the Government the necessity of granting these privileges as the only way of removing the present discontent and of quieting the disturbances which have already unhappily arisen in these Territories.[12]

This was written at a time when Louis Riel had formed a provisional government, the police had been defeated at Duck Lake, the village of Frog Lake had been destroyed, the town of Battleford was under siege, and the government was yet to experience a victory. Little wonder that some eastern newspapers began to question the loyalty of Calgarians. The *Toronto Week* described them as "an ignorant, lawless set of rebels"[13] and before he left for

A POPULAR MEETING PLACE IN CALGARY DURING THE RIEL REBELLION WAS BOYNTON'S HALL (LARGE BUILDING, CENTRE). THIS VIEW IS LOOKING WEST ON STEPHEN (8TH) AVENUE FROM HARDISTY (3RD STREET EAST). (GLENBOW, NA-1075-14)

the front, General Strange commented that "of all the cowardly rascals I ever dealt with, the Calgary people are the worst. No patriotism, nothing but trying to cheat the government."[14] This stigma of Calgary's questionable loyalty remained throughout the rebellion and was refuelled later in the year when some townsmen gave a toast to Louis Riel shortly before his execution.

Calgary's days of military isolation came to an end on April 12 when more than 300 troops of the 65th Mount Royal Regiment arrived in town. Five days later the Winnipeg Light Infantry disembarked from the trains during a spring blizzard and a short time later the 9th Voltigeurs from Quebec came for local guard duty. Meanwhile, Mounted Police superintendent Sam Steele arrived from the mountains and formed a mounted corps known as Steele's Scouts while Major George Hatton organized the Alberta Mounted Rifles, both made up mostly of policemen and cowboys. Suddenly Calgary had become an army town.

The arrival of the troops was part of a strategy to launch a three-pronged attack on the rebel forces. Two columns would leave from rail points in Saskatchewan while the third, called the Alberta Field Force, would go north from Calgary then down the North Saskatchewan River to strike the rebels from the west. Meanwhile, Calgary would become a supply depot and military base to protect the area.

The town was quick to capitalize on its new status. Prices were raised on everything from oats to horses; contraband whiskey was even easier to get than it had been in the past; and twenty-five cents became the lowest coin in circulation. It was the era of "ripping off the soldiers."[15] One army man reported that "horses that sold at $60 on our arrival here are now worth from $120 to $130 . . . flour has gone up $5 a sack in four days."[16] During the next few weeks the three army units spent more than $73,000 in Calgary—a fortune considering that the town's annual budget was only $6,000.

While they were waiting to go north, the Montreal and Winnipeg troops drilled at the police barracks, went to the target range, and practised skirmishing with the enemy. After they left in two contingents, scouts and messengers constantly travelled back and forth carrying messages and telegrams. The guarding of Calgary and outlying points was left to the Quebec regiment under command of Colonel Guillaume Amyot who was also a Conservative Member of Parliament. He was a fussy man who was constantly worried about the danger of attack and kept asking for more troops. Yet he had cause, for on one occasion he complained that in Calgary he had only fifty men, forty rounds of ammunition, no cannon, and no scouts. When the Half-Breed Scrip Commission came to town he was worried that speculators were getting the local Metis drunk and cheating them and this might lead to trouble. Some local men accused him of being a coward but it is likely that Amyot's detractors were Liberals, taking advantage of the fact that the commander was a Member of Parliament. A Calgary war correspondent implied as much when he wrote that "the traditional opponents of the Government sit on convenient nail barrels and invent disasters to Major-General Strange and his command . . . a pastime of those who fly Grit colors." In particular, he singled out Henry Bleecker as the source of the trouble. Bleecker was the town solicitor and pal of

Mayor Murdoch. The war correspondent described him as "ex-secretary of the Grit Association at Belleville, Ont., who has taken an active part in keeping up an agitation in this district…Bleecker poses as a lawyer, politician, agitator, Conservative, and Grit all at once. He is the most remarkable specimen of hypocrisy and humbug that I have met in the western country."[17]

By early May the Metis were defeated and the Indians who had opposed the military were in disarray. After the last vestiges of the rebellion were cleared away during June and July, the troops began to return home. In mid-July, Steele's Scouts marched into Calgary four abreast and under an archway of evergreens decorated with flags and the mottoes, "Welcome home again" and "Calgary welcomes Alberta's heroes."

The men were weather-beaten and their clothes were worn out but they dutifully gathered in front of the Bayne Hotel where they heard speeches of congratulation and cheers from the gathered throngs. In the campaign they had suffered three men wounded and none killed but they had experienced great hardship in the field. Now they were home and would receive a total of $125,000 in back pay which was owing them.

That night, Calgary celebrated so loudly and with so much booze that a dozen hotel operators were arrested for illegally selling liquor. This almost incited a riot as the liquor interests in Calgary—known as the whiskey ring—rallied to the defence of the bootleggers. But then the crowd went home laughing when they learned that the men would appear the following day before the local justice of the peace; he was none other than Mayor Murdoch, one of the supporters of the whiskey ring.

For Calgary, it was back to business as usual.

JERRY TRAVIS AND THE WHISKEY RING

His friends called him Jerry but by the summer of 1886, the press had labelled Jeremiah Travis an Eastern carpetbagger, a crank, and a knave. He was at the centre of one of the most vitriolic controversies that ever engulfed Calgary. It resulted in lawsuits, jail terms, and Calgary having two mayors and councils in office at the same time.

By the time he came to Alberta, Jerry Travis had already experienced a long and colourful career. He was editor of *The Patriot* in St. John which strongly opposed New Brunswick joining Confederation and helped defeat the Conservatives who favoured union with Canada. After graduating from Harvard Law School, Travis went into partnership with Charles Duff and in 1881 he switched to the Conservatives, taking half of St. John's Liberals with him.

As a lawyer, he was neither modest nor restrained about his abilities. He considered himself to be one of Canada's leading authorities on constitutional law and was often at odds with the political establishment. On one occasion he became embroiled in a controversy between federal and provincial authorities relating to temperance laws. As a result he wrote a scathing pamphlet attacking the New Brunswick supreme court and created a sensation both in New Brunswick and in Ottawa.[1]

In the federal election of 1882, Travis campaigned on behalf of Sir Leonard Tilley and was said to have influenced St. John's vote in favour of the Conservatives. As a reward, he was promised a judgeship and moved to Manitoba where he hoped to receive an appointment. Tilley, who was federal Minister of Finance, supported him but the appointment went elsewhere. Disappointed, Travis returned to Ottawa and on July 30, 1885, after considerable lobbying, he was given the newly created posting as stipendiary magistrate for the District Court of Alberta, with judicial offices in Calgary.

By this time, Travis was married with two grown daughters, Elizabeth and Julia. He was a devout Anglican, a teetotaller, and a strong proponent of the temperance movement. He was described by a friend as a person whose temperament was "singularly mercurial." He had "a form that is spare even to gauntness but with such a superfluity of mental and physical energy that nothing seems to tire him."[2]

Without realizing it, Travis was stepping into a maelstrom when he accepted the Calgary appointment. In 1874, when the Mounted Police came west, their main concern was in halting the whiskey traffic which was causing so much chaos among the Indians. To assist in this campaign, the North-West Territories Act was passed in 1875 establishing prohibition in the Territories. This law, and later regulations, permitted the police to search without warrants, confiscate and destroy liquor, and convict a person on flimsy evidence. The only way liquor could be imported for personal consumption was through a permit issued by the lieutenant-governor.

This law achieved its goal and within a short time the illicit whiskey trade to Indians had been virtually abolished. However, in 1882-83 when the CPR was built, newly arriving settlers found that they too were bound by these regulations. Some of the men were from the eastern provinces where drinking laws were liberal and others from the western United States where such laws were virtually non-existent. Often the arrivals were young single men whose main centres of entertainment had been saloons, gambling houses, and brothels.

It did not take long for a criminal element in Calgary to respond to their needs. Pimps and madams provided the girls, illegal gambling was rampant, and importing and selling liquor became a big business. Some men opened hotels or "temperance saloons" to market their wares while others were in the business of transporting liquor in barrels labelled molasses, in valises with false bottoms, and in the personal gear of CPR trainmen.

The Mounted Police had the odious duty of trying to enforce the hated prohibition law. Their attitude was sympathetic but direct; they had no liking for the law but as long as it was on the books, they would enforce it. As Commissioner A.G. Irvine wrote in 1884, "The suppression of this traffic is the most disagreeable duty which the police are called upon to perform." He then urged that a civilian magistrate be appointed because the "odium that has been so freely lavished upon police officers who are justices of the peace is largely due to the want of such an official."[3]

Calgary was still a new town which faced many economic problems; one of them resulted in considerable friction between the Mayor George Murdoch and the Mounted Police. Under the local statutes, the town police could arrest persons only for violating local ordinances; anything related to federal or territorial law went to the Mounties. The problem was that any fines which the Mounted Police collected were sent to Regina or Ottawa, thus removing much-needed cash from the community. Fines for local infractions, on the other hand, went into the town's coffers.

The trouble was that an unruly drunk could be arrested by the town cops for disturbing the peace or by the Mounties for illegal possession of liquor. As a result, there was sometimes a question as to who would make the arrests and at one point Mayor Murdoch became so incensed at the diligence of the Mounted Police that he sent a blistering letter to Ottawa, demanding that they stay out of his town.

The chief of police during these free-and-easy years was John Ingram, a tough two-fisted cop who had been kicked out of the Winnipeg police. Born in St. Thomas, Ontario, he became Winnipeg's first chief of police in 1874 but lasted hardly a year. His problems climaxed during a three-week period when he was charged successively with beating up one of his own policemen, beating up a citizen who had been driving his buggy too fast, and being caught as a found-in in a house of ill-fame. He stayed around Winnipeg after he was fired, presumably as a gambler, and continued to appear before the magistrate on various charges. At last, after a police court appearance for assault in the summer of 1884, he followed the railway west to Medicine Hat where he was promptly arrested for gambling. Finding the town too law-abiding, he continued on to Calgary where, early in 1885, he was hired as the town's first police chief.

Buried among his responsibilities for licensing vendors, maintaining the local pound, and keeping speeders off the streets, Ingram had one overriding duty: to bring money into the town's treasury. This could best be done by controlling, not discouraging, the illicit activities of bootlegging and prostitution. By agreement, madams and saloon keepers were arrested periodically and inevitably given fines instead of jail sentences. In return, the police chief protected them from rowdies and drunks who might have interfered with their business.

As a result, Calgary was a wide-open town. A visitor described how one of the town fathers—perhaps Mayor Murdoch—invited him for a drink. He stated: "We proceeded across the street, mounted a flight of stairs, a mysterious knock was given at an ordinary looking door, we were scrutinized for a second, then invited in to a luxuriously appointed bar, where a dozen other people were already drinking. There are a dozen places like this in town of which everybody knows."[4]

When Jerry Travis arrived in Calgary in the early autumn of 1885, he must have been appalled at the frontier conditions which contrasted so sharply with the communities back East. He was told that the rowdy element was sizeable and that the respectable community was unwilling or unable to do anything about them. Travis learned that when businessman George Marsh tried to get a brothel closed down, the mayor himself had asked him not to press the matter as the prostitutes were a source of revenue for the town. Marsh told Judge Travis about the existence of a whiskey ring and said "it was made up of those who were supposed to be in the

whiskey business and their supporters; he had heard it stated that Bleecker and Murdoch belong to that ring."[5] Henry Bleecker was the town solicitor. Travis also heard that the mayor and another lawyer, E.P. Davis, had been seen in a Calgary brothel, the latter reportedly being too drunk to stand. Not only that, but the mayor and Chief Ingram were allegedly running a protection racket.[6] Just after Travis's arrival, Ingram had gone to the owner of a newly opened saloon "and informed him that in effect, all the saloons keepers had to bribe them to protect them, keep them advised of intended raids on them, etc."[7] This must have been unsettling for Travis, for there would be occasions when he would share the bench with Murdoch, who was a justice of the peace, and both Bleecker and Davis would be appearing before him.

On November 2, the Mounties received a tip that alderman Simon John Clarke and his partner John Beaudoin were selling liquor so two constables in civilian dress were sent to investigate. They had no need for a warrant, as the law gave them the right to enter "any shop, store, hut, tent, wigwam, dwelling or building" where alcohol was suspected of being kept or sold.[8] However, when they began the search, Clarke forcibly tried to stop them. He grabbed one constable by the shoulder and threatened him with a bottle, then held the two men at bay for fully ten minutes before they could make their search. By that time, no liquor could be found.

The Mounted Police charged Clarke with resisting arrest and assault. Four days later he appeared before Travis, with Henry Bleecker and E.P. Davis acting for his defence. Others of the whiskey ring also were there with Mayor Murdoch testifying as to Clarke's good character. Travis heard the evidence but had little patience with the declarations of innocence or Bleecker's plea that the town councillor be let off with a fine. In his summation, Travis made a number of observations, as noted by a reporter from the anti-Murdoch *Calgary Tribune*:

> He censured the [town] police and the town authorities who claimed that the matter belonged to them, that the act was so openly violated and so much drunkenness prevailed in Calgary. He instanced a case where he himself had seen two men drunk on the street on Sunday, one with two stones in his hand, ready to damage life or property on the least provocation, and another instance where a woman had come to him suffering from wounds inflicted by a drunken husband.[9]

Travis then stunned the audience, and the whiskey ring in particular, when he sentenced Clarke to six months at hard labour with no option of a fine. When the news spread through town there were cries of anger and two days later an "indignation meeting" was held at Boynton Hall.

It was a rowdy affair, presumably called by the Calgary town council, for Mayor Murdoch took the chair and Councillor Joseph Millward outlined details of the Clarke arrest. Then the three leading lights of the whiskey ring took over. Lawyer Bleecker made a long and impassioned speech, followed by diatribes from Mayor Murdoch and lawyer Davis. In the end, the noisy crowd agreed to send a deputation to Ottawa to have the Travis decision overturned and to tell the Mounted Police "to

cease any further interference with the corporation of the town of Calgary."[10] A man who had attended the meeting said that the crowd consisted mostly of Calgary's rowdy element. Afterwards, he heard a man say "that a barrel should be filled with dynamite and placed under Judge Travis and blow him to hell."[11] Another warned that if Travis was not removed from Calgary before spring, "he would be carried out a dead man."[12]

Travis, with his mercurial temper, was furious when he heard about the meeting and the fact that the two Calgary lawyers had been in attendance. However, he had other problems to deal with. A short time later when he needed his Clerk of the Court, Hugh S. Cayley, to make up a jury list he found the man out on the street "stupidly drunk." He sent him home with instructions to appear the following day but he did not show up. Travis had already experienced other problems with Cayley besides his drinking. These included his sloppy record keeping and his questionable practice of keeping court funds in his own bank account. Accordingly, Travis fired Cayley and replaced him with a more reliable man.

The only problem was that Hugh Cayley was also the editor of the *Calgary Herald* and had been on the fringes of the whiskey crowd. Now he wholeheartedly joined the dissidents and his newspaper became a strident opponent of Judge Travis.

As for the magistrate, he was angered rather than cowed by the vicious attacks. He saw his role as one who needed to bring law and order to a town where the mayor, council, and some of the leading lawyers were in league with criminals. He did not believe it was his

responsibility to question the suitability of the prohibition law; that was up to the politicians. His task was to see that the existing laws were properly enforced and that the community was protected from the criminal elements. Unfortunately, he was blessed with neither tact nor compassion in carrying out these duties.

The trouble continued with a meeting on December 1 when the town council sat as a Court of Revision to examine the voters' list in preparation for the January 5 election. Mayor Murdoch was in Ottawa on the Clarke affair but before he left, he and councillor I.S. Freeze had given the town clerk a list of 73 names to be added to the voters' list. This was a huge number, considering that previously the list had contained only 212 registered voters, and presumably had been done to assure the re-election of the existing council. G.C. Marsh, a supporter of hotelman James Reilly for mayor, tried to protest but to no avail. He then charged the mayor and council with corruption and the matter was scheduled to come before the courts on December 26.

Meanwhile, Travis was not the kind of man to sit back quietly and take the criticism which was being heaped upon him by the *Calgary Herald*, a newspaper which he referred to as "that dirty, slanderous little sheet."[13] Instead, he charged Cayley with contempt of court, particularly for publishing an anonymous article by "Justitia." In the article, the writer claimed that Cayley had been dismissed because he had published a report of the indignation meeting, that Travis was "arbitrary and tyrannical" and that he had made himself obnoxious "by the unjustness of his decisions."[14]

On December 15, Travis used his regular sitting of court to respond to the various criticisms which had appeared in the *Herald*. He defended his actions in dealing with Clarke and Cayley, then spoke of Mayor Murdoch's collusion with the whiskey merchants. He also startled the audience by revealing that lawyer E.P. Davis was guilty of misrepresentation by referring to himself as a barrister. In fact, he said the man was only a two-year law student who had never passed his bar exams. Accordingly, Davis would no longer be permitted to practise and that even if he became a lawyer, he was barred from Travis's court for two years.

When Cayley appeared before Judge Travis on the contempt charge, he was represented by lawyer Bleecker.

At the outset, Cayley's lawyer claimed that a person could not be cited for contempt if the offence was "committed out of court."[15] Rather, Travis could only lay charges of slander and try to prove them in a court of law. Travis disagreed, then reviewed numerous articles which had appeared in the *Herald*. He focused on the item by "Justitia" and indicated that he might be prepared to drop the charges and direct them against the author of the article if his name was revealed. Travis was convinced that E.P. Davis had written it. However, Cayley refused.

Travis then gave Cayley the option of apologizing to the court and publishing a retraction or being fined $400 or three months in jail. He said he sympathized with Cayley as "he believed the young man had been badly advised by parties who had no real friendship for him but who were interested from a selfish motive."[16] Again Cayley refused to pay the fine and was told to report to the Mounted Police jail on January 4 to begin serving his sentence. On the appointed day, his jailing was turned into a three-ring circus. A large crowd placed him in a wagon which was drawn by hand and "led by the town band, escorted him around the streets with cheers."[17] According to one account, the parade stopped at each saloon along the route "to thaw out the band's instruments" and arrived at the jail in a state of revelry.[18]

On December 26, Travis examined the case against Mayor Murdoch and the town council. Again, the accused were represented by Bleecker who claimed that Travis did not have the right to question the decisions of a Court of

Revision. Again Travis disagreed. He learned that the men proposed for the voters' list had not given sworn testimony as to their qualifications, did not appear in person, and their names had not been checked against a list of taxpayers. Councillors were not familiar with most of the names and in some instances only their surnames were given.

Judge Travis believed that corruption had occurred; he disqualified Mayor Murdoch and councillors Dr. Neville Lindsay, Joseph Millward, and I.S. Freeze, then barred them from holding office for two years. Privately, he said he chose two years because by then "it is hoped law and order will be firmly established here."[19]

By this time, the names of Murdoch, Lindsay, and Freeze were already on the ballots for the civic election on January 5, 1886. Somehow, the nominations officer—who supported the Murdoch faction—failed to remove them, nor did he strike off the 73 friends of Murdoch who had been added to the voters' list. When the votes were counted, Murdoch, Lindsay, and Freeze had been returned by a resounding majority.[20] In addition, James Bannerman and T.W. Soules had been elected to the town council.

The results were immediately protested by James Reilly who petitioned the court to have the election set aside. Travis agreed. He disqualified Murdoch, Lindsay, and Freeze from the new council and replaced them with James Reilly and two of his slate—Archibald Grant and C.N. Davidson. Bannerman and Soules, who had not been involved in the controversy, were retained and supported Reilly.

The response of E.P. Davis—who in addition to being a lawyer was chairman of the local Liberal association—was to seek an opinion from an Ottawa lawyer, F.H. Chrysler, an active Liberal party worker. Chrysler stated that the Travis action had been illegal and on that basis, Murdoch was still the mayor and should refuse to recognize Reilly and his slate. This left Calgary with two mayors, two councils, and two "official" seals. It also gave the town two clerks, for Reilly immediately sacked the incumbent clerk who had remained faithful to Murdoch and replaced him with a man of his own.

Over the next several months, neither side was able to run the town. The Murdoch group had no legal standing in the eyes of the court and the Reilly group could not function because the town books had mysteriously disappeared. One disgruntled taxpayer complained that the streets were not being maintained, there was no fire protection, and taxes weren't being collected. In short, Calgary had become "virtually disincorporated."[21]

Until this time, the dispute had been a power struggle between Murdoch's group and Judge Travis. One side subscribed to a free and easy western lifestyle which was willing to turn a blind eye to the prohibition laws. Its supporters asserted that the "whiskey ring" was a figment of Travis's imagination. The opposing view was represented by the short-tempered judge who believed in following the letter of the law and was appalled by the excessive drinking and the collusion of town council. If left to themselves the two sides might have resolved their differences, either by treating liquor-related problems as municipal infractions or by reducing the incidence of intoxication through more stringent enforcement.

However, E.P. Davis saw the Travis affair as a political matter which could be used to embarrass the Conservative government in Ottawa. In mid-December, a letter was written to Chrysler, the Liberal lawyer, asking him to engineer the removal of Travis. Chrysler suggested that they "commence a newspaper war which must end in removing Travis from his position."[22]

Shortly afterwards, letters were sent to the *Toronto Globe* and the *Manitoba Free Press,* both Liberal newspapers, attacking the magistrate. While Cayley was in jail Davis took over writing for the *Calgary Herald* and had friends writing letters to other Canadian newspapers.

The *Calgary Tribune,* which supported Travis, condemned the campaign:

Bleecker is well known in the east as a Grit of the worst description; he is notorious in that respect wherever he has lived . . . Then Murdoch does not deny his allegiance to the Gritty Party; and what of James Martin and Augustus Carney, and many others—all Grits. Why Davis, the man who was recently made editor of the Herald, is a dyed-in-the-wool Grit. Poor Cayley has been rather hardly used by these people. He has been made to a certain extent, the scape-goat.[23]

Travis was angry about the campaign, complaining

directly to Prime Minister John A. Macdonald about "the manner in which I have been vilified through the Press all over the Dominion by such a drunken, utterly worthless set as the Bleecker-Murdoch-Cayley-Davis quartette."[24]

During this period, there was a strong sentiment in favour of Judge Travis. Methodist and Anglican ministers praised him for his efforts in suppressing the whiskey ring while many private citizens welcomed a diligent and incorrupt-ible judge to combat the town's lawlessness. A petition praising the magistrate for "ably, justly and fearlessly administering the law of our Dominion"[25] was signed by more than 85 per cent of the town's businessmen including James Walker, G.C. King, G.E. Jacques, James Lougheed, Rev. Joshua Dyke, and James Linton. Significantly, James Reilly was the only hotelman or saloon keeper to sign. A similar petition in support of Travis came from the leading merchants of Edmonton where he regularly held court.

However, the cam-paign to discredit Travis and embarrass the government succeeded. When editor Cayley was jailed, the Minister of Justice asked the magis-trate to turn him loose but Travis refused. Three weeks later, acting on pressures from Cayley's father who was a former Tory cabinet minister, the government ordered his release. This was Travis's first setback and the results were immediately evident. According to the Mounted Police, "Cayley's imprisonment had a good effect on the community. Things had quieted down but broke out afresh when Cayley was released."[26]

Further results of the anti-Travis campaign soon fol-lowed as the strident calls of the *Calgary Herald, Manitoba Free Press,* and the *Globe* were heard. Finally, on March 22, Judge Thomas Taylor of Winnipeg was appointed a commissioner to investigate the charges. Meanwhile, Travis was relieved of his duties and was replaced by Stipendiary Magistrate Charles B. Rouleau until the mat-ter was settled.

The hearings were held from June 18 to July 3, 1886, with Bleecker and Davis as complain-ants and Travis acting on his own behalf. There were fifteen charges, ranging from the perse-cution of Mayor Mur-doch, editor Cayley, and the two lawyers, to ille-gally installing James Reilly as mayor of Cal-gary. Dozens of witnesses were heard including William "Jumbo" Fisk, a self-confessed gambler, a couple of ministers, and a number of businessmen.

During the course of the hearings, Travis pre-sented some damning evidence against his accusers. Testimony was given that lawyer Davis had been found drunk and unconscious on his way back from a brothel;[27] Bleecker had once been put to bed because he was too drunk to stand, and on another occasion he suggested that Travis be eliminated "as they would do in towns of the Western States";[28] Hugh Cayley had been convicted of liquor offences, and was shown to have lied under oath when he denied being editor of the *Calgary Herald;* and Mayor Murdoch had appeared at Travis's house "in a state in which no gentleman would show himself before the ladies of another gentleman's house."[29] Travis was accused at the hearings of being dic-

tatorial, overly harsh in his convictions, insulting to lawyers in his courtroom, and acting illegally in convicting Cayley and in disqualifying the Calgary town council.

Taylor's report was submitted to the Department of Justice a month later but the government sat on it for almost a year before releasing it. By this time the Conservatives in Ottawa had already decided that Travis was too much of an embarrassment for them to keep but also he was too outspoken for them to simply fire him. Instead, they introduced a new system of Supreme Courts to the North-West Territory and the positions of stipendiary magistrates were discontinued. Travis's name was not among the appointments to the new courts nor did he ever serve on the bench again. Instead, he was given a $700 annual pension and told to return to private practice.

Similarly, the North-West Council decided not to wait for the Taylor report before resolving Calgary's dual mayoralty problem. Undoubtedly influenced by Travis's revelations, the Council had no wish to let Murdoch and his crowd continue their old ways. In November, 1886, they directed that a new election be held and when the votes were in, George C. King had become the new mayor. And at its first meeting, the new council replaced Henry Bleecker as the town solicitor and Murdoch never again was elected to high office. The clique was broken. Observed a townsman four years later, "Some of the leaders left for pastures new, others sank into oblivion, while the better educated turned over a new leaf and became respectable citizens."[30]

It was perhaps an anticlimax, but Travis was shocked in June of 1887 when Judge Taylor's report was finally submitted to Parliament. The judge disagreed with virtually everything that Travis had done. He concurred with him only on the dismissal of Cayley as his clerk. He said that Davis' disbarment had been arbitrary and unjustified; that prosecuting Cayley for contempt may have been legal but was an extreme act and not in accord with the spirit of the law; and that while Murdoch and his council may have been guilty of corrupt practices, he had no authority to disqualify them and install James Reilly's slate in their place.

"It is beyond all doubt," wrote Taylor, "that there existed among the population of Calgary a lawless ele-

ment, dangerous to the peace, and good order of society. In dealing with this element, Mr. Travis had a difficult task, but he did not pursue a prudent course."[31]

By this time, Travis had already lost his posting and, instead of practising law, he began to invest in Calgary real estate. Both his daughters had married Albertans— Elizabeth to John Barter, manager of the Quorn Ranch, and Julia to J.S. Gibb, a Calgary merchant. By the time of his death in 1911 Travis had become a wealthy man and was described as "one of the most picturesque old timers of Calgary."[32] Yet he never forgot nor forgave the whiskey ring and their friends for the way they had treated him when he tried to bring law and order to the wide-open frontier community.

In retrospect, perhaps one of the most perceptive observations about the whole affair came from the editor of a newspaper in St. John, New Brunswick, which incidentally had been the home town of both Jerry Travis and George Murdoch. During the heat of battle, the editor noted:

> That our late townsman, Jeremiah Travis, is making himself felt in the neighborhood of Calgary is clear. He is pursuing a bold and resolute career, and neither turning to the right or left for fear or favor . . . It may be that the abstract sense of justice which seems to influence Judge Travis has led him astray . . . Perhaps a gradual process of educating the Calgary public up to right ideas of law and order would have been better than the abrupt and emphatic lessons furnished by the stipendiary . . . Judge Travis is laying up for himself a legacy of dislike, but he would not swerve from a right or wrong position though the shattered heavens should fall.[33]

Travis may have been hounded from office by his opponents, yet strangely enough he succeeded in his mission of bringing some modicum of law and order to Calgary. By the time he left office, he had so focused attention on the town's lawlessness that it could no longer be ignored. While Calgary continued to have prostitutes, gambling, and illegal liquor, never again would these activities be seen as the work of an organized "whiskey ring" supported by the mayor, chief of police, and the town council.

FIRE AND SANDSTONE

The Murdoch-Travis dispute may have been exciting at the time but it also had some far-reaching consequences. The most serious was the burning of a major part of Calgary's business section. Newly established towns were expected to experience their baptism of fire but in Calgary's case to have escaped a holocaust would have been a miracle. Rows of wooden buildings, inadequate fire-fighting equipment, and a town council in disarray proved to be a lethal combination.

From the time Calgary was incorporated as a town in November of 1884, there had been an expressed demand for fire protection but the mayor and council had been slow to respond. In February, 1885, just after J.L. Bowen's house had burned to the ground, the *Calgary Nor'Wester* complained of council's laxity. It said the only reason many residents had supported incorporation in the first place had been for fire protection. "Now the town has been incorporated for some months and as yet no move has been made to secure us against fire except the passing of a bylaw for fire prevention, which will never be enforced uniformly."[1] It complained that Calgary had neither a bucket brigade nor a volunteer hook and ladder company to fight fires.

The response of the town council to the Bowen fire was threefold: it authorized the digging of eight wells for fire use; it planned to organize a volunteer brigade; and it investigated the purchase of a chemical engine. By the autumn of 1885, however, none of these schemes had proven very successful.

The eight wells had been dug, but the *Calgary Tribune* complained that they were "worse than useless."[2] Most were said to contain no water and none had pumps installed. A volunteer fire brigade was organized in August with George Constantine as captain but four months later when no ladders, buckets, or other fire-fighting equipment had been purchased, he resigned.

As for the chemical engine, the town had a chance to buy one from a Winnipeg firm for $1,100 plus duty with a year to pay, provided that a sufficient number of responsible businessmen would cosign the note. However, the cosigners could not be found "either because they thought the purchase a poor one, or they had no trust in the body of men who were conducting it."[3] The subject bounced back and forth in council until the end of 1885, at which time the engine was finally bought, the price having risen to $1,600 plus duty. The purchase was made just before Judge Travis disqualified the Murdoch council but when the Reilly council tried to take office at the beginning of 1886, the official records had disappeared. As a result, when the engine was delivered there was no money forthcoming to pay for it so the machine was locked up in a shed near the railway station.

Town business was at a virtual standstill in 1886 as Calgary tried to cope with two mayors and two town councils. Taxes were not collected, council meetings held by either group were in dispute, and little money remained in the town's coffers to carry on normal business.

Meanwhile, Calgary businessmen had to pay excessively high fire insurance rates on their buildings and goods because of the lack of proper fire protection. As a result, most businesses were under-insured while others were uninsured because their owners could not afford the six per cent rate being offered. They were told that this would be reduced by a full twenty-five per cent if the town got the necessary fire-fighting equipment.

During this time, the civic government may have been at a standstill but the town itself was growing rapidly. During the previous year, eighteen business buildings had been erected, as well as four saloons, five livery stables, and thirty-four dwellings. Almost all were wooden frame struc-

A DISASTROUS FIRE IN 1886 DESTROYED MUCH OF ATLANTIC (9TH) AVENUE. THIS PHOTOGRAPH BY ALEXANDER ROSS SHOWS THE EASTERN EDGE OF THE FIRE, WHICH HAD BEEN HALTED BY TEARING DOWN GEORGE MURDOCH'S HARNESS SHOP. (GLENBOW, NA-298-3)

tures although in 1886, a few sandstone and brick structures did begin to appear. For example, George King's post office and Dunne & Lineham's butcher shop were built of sandstone while Trott's drug store was made of brick with sandstone facing—all new in 1886. These, however, were exceptions. As a commercial traveller noted, Stephen Avenue was "a street of hastily constructed frame shells, called buildings."[4] A reporter for the *London Times* saw Calgary as

> the most unfinished town I have yet found in the Canadian Northwest. Building goes on everywhere. The streets are strewn and in some cases almost blockaded with building materials, and large stone buildings are going up, as well as almost countless wooden dwellings. The town has 1,500 people and has grown so rapidly that they have not time either to pave the streets or to construct sidewalks.[5]

These conditions set the stage for Calgary's big fire of November 7, 1886. It started about 5 a.m. behind Parrish & Son's flour and feed store at the north-west corner of 9th (Atlantic) Avenue and Centre (McTavish) Street. Within fifteen minutes, the alarm was sounded by ringing the bell at the Anglican church but by that time the flames had already spread to Lamont's tin shop next door and east across Centre Street to Pullman's Saloon and the Union Hotel. The fire also moved north along Centre Street to the Sherman House where the south wall of the building was engulfed in flames by the time the boarders fled to safety.

Virtually the whole town responded to the Sunday morning calamity. Some helped haul furniture and provisions out of endangered buildings while others tried to fight the fire. Some men remembered the chemical engine and, law or no law, they broke down the door of the storage shed and pressed it into service.

There was a stiff wind blowing from the west but the fire seemed intent on destroying the entire business district along 9th Avenue both upwind and downwind. There was also a fear that it might jump the alley to 8th (Stephen) Avenue and destroy the two blocks of businesses there.

On 9th Avenue, the fire swept relentlessly west towards 1st Street West. It demolished the Massey Manufacturing Company's warehouse, then burned down the Athletic and Mountain View hotels. Behind the Athletic Hotel, the small private home of Charles Sparrow was threatened but E.R. Rogers grabbed a Babcock extinguisher from his hardware store and put out the flames which had ignited one corner of the house. When the conflagration was over, the Sparrow house was fire blackened but safe. And so were the town's financial records which were being kept in the house.

Beyond the two hotels, the fire needed only to get past Straube's gun shop to have a clear run to the west end of the block. However, the building was little more than a shack so a group of men dragged it onto the street and away from the line of fire. Not only was the building saved but the vacant area became an effective barrier to prevent the fire from reaching Sam Shaw's house and other buildings along the block.

Meanwhile, the fire continued to ravage its way east on 9th Avenue. After wiping out the Pullman Saloon and Union Hotel, it struck Ellis' store. By this time, the town was out in full force and willing hands soon cleared the building of its stock of goods. However, it was evident that the blaze would take out the entire block if it wasn't stopped. After a brief discussion with the newly elected mayor, George King, a gang of men descended on Mortimer's Bakery and Murdoch's harness shop which were next in the line of fire. They tried to blow up the two buildings with gunpowder but failed so men with ropes and axes ripped the two buildings to pieces and dragged them out on the street.

The plan worked and the next three buildings along 9th Avenue—I.S. Freeze's general store, John Patterson's shoe store, and the Grand Central Hotel—escaped the blaze.

The fire also roared down Centre Street, striking Dunne & Lineham's old butcher shop on the south-west corner of 8th (Stephen) Avenue; it might have destroyed it had the volunteers not worked so hard. The same applied to the Royal Hotel across the street. Wet blankets were hung over the roof and out the windows to protect the walls and while some of the blankets were scorched, the building was saved.

A little farther along, the warehouse of I.G. Baker was destroyed but the store itself, on the north-east corner of Centre and 8th survived. It was one of the few log buildings in the fire area and successfully withstood the flames. That was as far as the fire got on 8th Avenue. It threatened a few shacks used as private dwellings or storage sheds along the alley but these were pulled down so that the fire could not get to the main buildings on the next street.

There were a number of close calls. When the fire reached I.G. Baker's warehouse, the manager remembered a keg of gunpowder inside. He dashed into the burning building and carried it away just before the entire structure was engulfed in flames. In another warehouse, fire-fighters discovered twenty cases of coal oil and feared that if they exploded they might spread the fire. Instead, they simply burst into flames and sent clouds of black smoke billowing into the morning air. And when crowds had that worry solved, they were hard pressed to tell the difference between the detonation of 2,000 rounds of ammunition and explosions of numerous cans of overheated fruit. None of the bullets caused any damage, but Alex Grant was struck in the head by an exploding tin can.

When it was over, eighteen businesses, warehouses, and dwellings had been destroyed while other firms had suffered the loss or damage of goods and furniture. In addition, A. Carey, of the Union Hotel, had $500 in the pocket of his waistcoat which went up in flames while Tom McLellan left behind a hundred dollars when he fled his hotel room. In all, the total loss of buildings and goods amounted to $103,200, with less than a quarter of this amount covered by insurance.

The cause of the fire was never learned but because it had started near a pile of baled hay, townsmen immediately suspected arson. In case there was a fire bug on the loose, Mayor King threatened him with instant death should he reappear. He told his audience, "If you find any . . . man setting fire to any building, I hand him over to you and you may deal with him as you like."[6] A financial newspaper in Winnipeg, however, placed the blame for the fire in another quarter.

The unfortunate civic broil which occurred at Calgary last winter, and which resulted in the town being left for nearly a year without a legally qualified council board, has been directly responsible for the calamity which has befallen the place. The crying need of some system of protection from fire was apparent to every citizen of the place, but owing to the civic muddle nothing could be done in the matter.[7]

Whatever the cause, Calgary acted quickly to prevent any further such losses. The new council immediately ordered that the town wells be deepened, the volunteer fire brigade be activated, and arrangements be made to buy a steam fire engine and two hose reels. A year later, a proper fire hall was built on the north side of 7th Avenue between Centre and 1st Street East.

ONE OF THE FIRST SAND-STONE BUILDINGS ERECTED IN CALGARY AFTER THE BIG FIRE OF 1886 WAS THE COURT-HOUSE. DESPITE PUBLIC PROTESTS, IT WAS DEMOLISHED IN 1958 TO MAKE WAY FOR A NEW COURT-HOUSE. (GLENBOW, NA-1693-2)

In spite of the disaster, merchants lost none of their optimism and enthusiasm about the future of Calgary. They were utterly convinced that sometime soon—probably very soon—the town would be inundated with immigrants and the prairies would be flooded with farmers and ranchers. There was only one thing to do: rebuild and plan ahead.

But with the bitter experience of the fire behind them, they now looked with renewed interest at the town's only brick factory, run by F.J. Peel, and Joe Butlin's sandstone quarry two miles up the Elbow River. Soon there was a rush of orders from merchants and others who wanted permanence in their new buildings. Before long, additional quarries opened at various points in and around Calgary as sandstone received preference over flammable wood products. At one point, half the tradesmen in Calgary were employed in the sandstone industry.

The first major sandstone building to be constructed after the fire was Knox Presbyterian Church, completed in 1887, while the first major public building was the courthouse, built in 1888. Meanwhile, Stephen Avenue became

THE ALBERTA HOTEL, AT
THE CORNER OF STEPHEN
(8TH) AVENUE AND
SCARTH (1ST STREET
WEST), WAS BUILT IN 1888.
NOTE THE CONSTRUC-
TION MATERIALS IN
THE FOREGROUND.
ALTHOUGH MODIFIED,
THIS BUILDING IS STILL
STANDING. (GLENBOW,
NA-3981-10)

bar, and was said to have been visited on one occasion by Butch Cassidy.

With the United States border less than a 150 miles from Calgary, there was a constant movement of Americans and Canadians back and forth on a regular basis. Some of them had criminal records and found a safe haven across the line if they broke the other country's laws. In 1884, Constable Blake of the Mounted Police tried to arrest a man named Jack Maguire, an American whiskey dealer, while he was saddling his horse in Fitzsimmons' stables. The policeman was unarmed so when the wanted man pulled a pepperpot pistol on him, Blake had to let him go. Less than an hour later, a posse of six armed policemen set out on the fugitive's trail south but he eluded them and fled to Montana.

Also, Calgary's only so-called "gunfight" involved an escape across the line. In 1886, a fiddle dance was held at Ellis' hall, an old restaurant near the original I.G. Baker store. It was mostly a Metis affair and there was a notice-able shortage of women, so each man had to wait his turn and dance about every third dance. However, one of the participants, John Bertrand—known locally as the Black Kid—ignored the social graces and after ten straight dances he was roundly chastised by Hank Forbes, a former detective for the South-West Stock Growers Association. According to the *Calgary Herald*:

It is well understood all over the world, at dances, that when one gentleman insults another by saying that other "ain't no good anyhow," the insult has to be wiped out in blood. The Black Kid proceeded to wipe it out in the customary style, and with such fair aver-age success that Mr. Forbes felt it incumbent to return to town over the midnight plain to fetch his shooting iron and proceed in a more scientific manner.[1]

a veritable showplace for sandstone and brick buildings. Visitors, accustomed to wooden frame buildings which dominated most prairie towns, were impressed by the aura of permanence given to the foothills town.

According to historian Richard Cunniffe, some of the sandstone buildings constructed while Calgary still had town status included: Hutchings & Riley, saddlers, and Linton Block in 1887; I.G. Baker Block and Alberta Hotel in 1888; Bank of Montreal and Calgary Hardware, 1889; Alexander Block, Clarence Block, Lougheed Block, and Lineham Block in 1890; and Alexander Corner in 1891.[8] In addition, a number of churches and private res-idences also made use of sandstone or brick during this period.

The lesson had been a harsh one, but the fire of 1886 left a permanent impact upon the face of downtown Calgary.

GUNFIGHTERS AND KILLERS

In the early years, Calgary had its share of "Wild West" characters who could be compared to gunfighters on the American frontier. For example, in the early 1890s, Calgary was home to the famous outlaw Harry Longbaugh—alias the Sundance Kid—although his only crime while here was to injure a horse while breaking it. He was in partnership at the Grand Central Hotel, tended

When Forbes appeared at the door of the hall with his six shooter in hand, the Black Kid dived to the floor and tried to escape by crawling through the detective's legs. While the Kid was in this exposed position, Forbes fired twice, the first bullet going through his hat and the second striking the floor. The Kid managed to reach the door and was fleeing around a corner when Forbes fired again, the bullet grazing the Kid's side. With a howl, he fell to the ground at which time Forbes walked up to him and fired a fourth shot at close range, which should have killed him. Instead, Forbes was such a lousy shot that the bullet just cut the sleeve of the Kid's coat and grazed his forearm. By this time the crowd was pouring outside so Forbes hurried away into the night. Next morning, the police heard that he was already on his way to his former stamping grounds in Montana.

Between the time that Calgary became a community in 1883 and received city status in 1894 there were only five murders in the immediate vicinity of Calgary. The first was a simple murder-robbery which occurred in 1884 when Jess Williams stabbed and killed a storekeeper during a robbery. He was summarily hanged at the police barracks seven weeks later. His was Calgary's first execution. A little more than two months later, John McManus stabbed and killed Bill Reed, better known as Buckskin Shorty, during a drunken quarrel about four miles south of town. Both men where whiskey smugglers. McManus was sentenced to six months at hard labour in the Calgary police barracks. After the second murder in less than six months, a Montana newspaper commented that "Calgary will soon become the Chicago of the northwest."[2]

Two years passed before the next murder. But this one was a classic mystery and remains so today.

The incident started on August 23, 1886, with the robbery of a stage coach which was on its regular run from Edmonton to Calgary. It had just passed Dickson's stopping house, near the present Airdrie, and was crossing a coulee near the Twin Buttes when two men suddenly jumped from the grass and ordered it to stop. Both wore masks made from fragments of a Union Jack; these covered their entire faces so that only their eyes were showing.

When the robbery was over, the driver and passengers were sent on foot back to the stopping house. The holdup men unhitched the team, rode them to the place where their own horses were cached, abandoned their masks and overalls, and disappeared.

When police enquired at Cochrane, they learned that two strangers had been seen passing through the village two days before the holdup, heading north-east towards Dickson's stopping house. The day after the robbery, these same men had taken breakfast at the railway station before heading west towards the mountains.

The police traced them to Morley but lost their trail beyond that point. Later, two horses which had been stolen near Calgary were found in the mountains at Donald, B.C.

Then, to add to the mystery, the day after the robbery, "Clinker" Scott was found dead in his cabin. His real name was Scott Krueger but he had received his nickname "Clinker" when he misidentified a clinker from a coal stove as a valuable ore specimen. He had tried prospecting but by 1884 he had found it more profitable to become a dealer in illicit whiskey. He had a small shack on the Bow River in the present Bowness district. At that time it was eight miles out of town and close to the iron railroad bridges that spanned the river.

Baptiste Annas and Alex Larondel were haying near the Scott place when they found a hidden camp with a

buckboard and a quantity of flour. Recalling that a buckboard had been stolen from S.A. Ramsay, they rode to Calgary and informed the owner of their discovery. The next day, Ramsay and Larondel rode to the camp but the wagon was gone so they followed its tracks which led directly towards "Clinker" Scott's. When the men arrived there, they found Scott lying dead on his cabin floor, a bullet wound in his chest and his empty money belt on the floor. He obviously had been baking bread when he was attacked for his hands were still covered with flour.

Suspicion for both the stage holdup and the murder pointed to two known criminals, Charles Lafferty and

IN A DRAMATIC SERIES OF EVENTS, THE CALGARY-EDMONTON STAGE COACH, SEEN HERE IN 1888, WAS HELD UP BY ROBBERS, AND THE FOLLOWING DAY, "CLINKER" SCOTT WAS MURDERED. NO ONE WAS EVER CONVICTED OF THE CRIMES. (GLENBOW, NA-1162-3)

Comm: Herchmer — or — N.W.M.Police "The Guardian of the North West." — Calgary 1893 —

John Young. They were members of a gang working in the neighbourhood west of Calgary. "Clinker" Scott was also believed to have been a member of the gang.

Five months earlier, in February 1886, Lafferty and Young had cached eleven kegs of whiskey along the Bow River and were transporting them to Edmonton when they were caught on Nose Creek. The men were found guilty, given jail terms, and their horses, wagon, and harness were sold at public auction. They were released from confinement at the beginning of August and were in desperate need of money.

After the holdup and murder, Lafferty dropped completely out of sight but the police learned that Young was in the vicinity of Canmore where he was believed to be working with a logging crew. Three months later, in December, 1886, Young wrote to the Mounted Police and offered to prove his innocence if they would promise not to prosecute him. The police refused but on December 15 he gave up unconditionally.

At the hearing, a policeman testified seeing Young wearing overalls similar to those used by the bandits but neither one of the passengers nor the stage driver could pick Young out of a lineup. The fact the both robbers had been wearing overalls and had full face masks during the holdup made identification difficult. Another witness who saw the two holdup men hanging around Dickson's stopping house recognized one who was called "Charlie" but could not identify the accused. For his part, Young claimed to have been working steadily at the lumber camps near Canmore all summer. After hearing the testimonies, Judge Rouleau ruled that there was insufficient evidence to proceed with a trial and discharged the prisoner.

It is likely that Lafferty and Young, broke after their aborted whiskey expedition, decided to rob the stage coach. People who knew "Clinker" Scott claimed he "would not likely be a party to anything in the nature of a stage robbery"[3] and believed there was a falling out among the gang. Scott was then murdered either in an argument before the men went on the robbery or afterwards when they were disappointed at their small take and decided to rob their former companion of $425 he had in his possession. If either scenario is correct, they got away with it for no one was ever convicted of the murder or the stage holdup.

Three years passed before Calgary had its next murder and this one created another sensation. Not only was the killing violent and bloody but the murderer, William "Jumbo" Fisk, was a well-known Calgarian.

On February 28, 1886, Fisk returned to Calgary from the town of Anthracite, near Banff, and noticed a number of Indian girls standing on a downtown street corner near Hull's Opera House. He beckoned to one— a Cree named Rosalie New Grass—and she dutifully followed him to the Turf Club, a ramshackle saloon on the west side of Centre Street between 8th and 9th avenues. Fisk had owned it until about a month before. He asked the bartender, George Kelsey, for a key to an upstairs room and indicated he was going to have sex with the girl.

Later, when Kelsey went upstairs there were sounds of groaning coming from the room so Kelsey locked the door so the couple wouldn't be disturbed. Around six o'clock when he heard Fisk knocking he went upstairs to let him out. The first thing he noticed was that the man had blood on his face and clothes. He testified:

> I walked into the room and saw some blood on the wall and on the bed clothes. She was lying with her head towards the foot of the bed. I put my head down close to her mouth and I thought I could hear her breathing.[4]

Even though it was obvious that the girl had been severely injured, neither man tried to help her. Fisk went to another room to wash his hands, then the pair went out for supper at the nearby Windsor Hotel. When they returned a couple of hours later, Rosalie New Grass was dead.

Fisk immediately sought out George Murdoch, former Calgary mayor, who was a justice of the peace. He advised Fisk to give himself up to the police and he was placed under arrest.

The news came as a shock to the Calgary community. Fisk was not a sterling citizen but he had always been known as a quiet inoffensive person. According to the *Tribune,* Fisk "is a good natured citizen who wouldn't hurt a feather."[5]

He was from a good family in Iroquois, Ontario, and had come west in 1882 with his uncle, W.H. Williams, a reporter for the Toronto *Globe.*[6] Although he was a blacksmith by profession, he had first earned his living in Calgary by selling whiskey and then became a gambler. He had been arrested several times for drunkenness and gambling but had remained popular because of his good nature. In 1885 he was a volunteer in the Alberta Field Force and lost a finger while in the service. A year later, he started to train race horses to compete with the gambling crowd and then opened the Turf Club.

The victim, Rosalie New Grass, was a teenager when she was killed. Her father, New Grass or *See-ah-kus-ka,* had been a head man of Little Pine's band near Battleford.[7] There were five in the family—New Grass, his wife, a son Okema, Rosalie, and a sister. During the Riel Rebellion, New Grass moved to Hobbema, north of Red Deer, and became a member of Samson's band but by 1887, the family had migrated to Shaganappi Point on the western outskirts of Calgary. There, together with other Cree Indians, they had eked out a precarious existence by doing odd jobs around town and working for nearby farmers and ranchers. A few of the women, like Rosalie, turned to prostitution. Some measure of the town's attitude towards her—as opposed to its initial sympathy for the killer—was indicated in a headline which stated that the victim was "A Dissolute Young Squaw."[8]

At the trial, the doctor's report showed "such an amount of fiendish brutality in mutilating the victim when in life, that the atrocities of Jack the Ripper seem mild by comparison."[9] The girl suffered great agony, biting through her own lip during a paroxysm of pain. Yet Fisk and the bartender had casually gone to supper while the girl was dying.

The evidence against Fisk was overwhelming. At one point, a Mounted Police detective testified that one of the bloodstains on the wall was that of a hand which was minus a finger. The prisoner was directed to hold up his left hand and the jury saw that his little finger was missing.

After the judge had given his charge to the jury, they were locked in his chambers on Friday afternoon and even Fisk's friends expected a quick decision. However the jury sent out two messages during the evening that they couldn't agree on a verdict. Next morning they shocked everyone in the courtroom by declaring that they had found the accused not guilty. Judge Rouleau refused to accept the verdict and sent the jury back to chambers. An hour later he called them out again and asked if they all agreed with the not guilty verdict. The foreman admitted they didn't, so Rouleau dismissed them and called for a new trial.

At the next sitting of the Supreme Court three months later, the same evidence was reviewed by a new jury. The nine men were told by the judge that if the man was guilty, they had to decide whether he should be convicted of murder or manslaughter. It took them only a couple of hours to come back with the verdict of manslaughter and Fisk was sentenced to fourteen years at hard labour.

The racial overtones of the case were obvious. The *Tribune* said the first verdict had been a disgrace to Calgary. "The idea which seems to possess the minds of some people," said the editor, "that because a crime or offence is committed against an Indian, therefore the crime is lessened, is inhuman in the extreme."[10] Yet that's the way it was at the Fisk trial. As Bob Edwards said in later years, "Fisk got off with 14 years but he should have been hanged."[11]

The fifth and final murder to occur in Calgary before the town received city status was a sad affair involving another victim from the little band of vagabond Crees who were trying to survive on the fringes of Calgary society. In 1893, nineteen-year-old Snake Child was drinking with another man named Sinew when they had a violent quarrel and Snake Child was beaten to death with a tent pole. Sinew pleaded guilty and was sentenced to ten years in the penitentiary but the judge emphasized that the real culprit was the illegal whiskey obtained from a local bootlegger.

Two weeks later, Calgary became a city.

TRYING TO CREATE AN IMAGE OF THE "WILD WEST," THESE ENGLISHMEN AT THE COCHRANE RANCHE, WEST OF CALGARY, TOOK THIS PHOTOGRAPH ABOUT 1886 AND CALLED IT "A FALLEN VICTIM." IT WAS MEANT TO IMPRESS THE FOLKS BACK HOME. (GLENBOW, NA-239-3)

A CITY IS BORN

WAITING FOR THE BOOM

BY THE EARLY 1890S, CALGARY HAD BECOME A PROGRESSIVE TOWN WITH A BRIGHT FUTURE.
IT WAS ON THE MAIN LINE OF THE CPR SERVING A MARKET AREA WHICH EXTENDED SOUTH TO THE
AMERICAN BORDER AND NORTH TO THE ARCTIC CIRCLE. IT ALSO WAS SURROUNDED BY THOUSANDS
OF ACRES OF VACANT LAND WHICH NEEDED ONLY AN INFLUX OF HOMESTEADERS
TO MAKE CALGARY A GREAT CITY.

The local boosters thought the land boom would happen when the transcontinental railway was finished in 1885 but it didn't. They blamed the Riel Rebellion and went on improving the community, positive that their day would come. The town obtained electricity and telephone service in 1887 and waterworks in 1891. It had a population of 3,876 by 1891, a considerable advance over the 1884 figure of 428 when Calgary became a town but a far cry from what the locals had expected.

Yet the town was filled with optimism. Special editions of the *Dominion Illustrated* and *The Globe,* both from Toronto, and the *Western World* from Winnipeg, all extolled the virtues of the prairie town. In 1890, the *Dominion Illustrated* spoke of the community as being as well supplied with "the luxuries of life as any eastern city."[1] It praised the town's electric lights and telephones, a system of waterworks being installed, its parks, public buildings, businesses, and hotel accommodation. With the construction of new railways, it was sure Calgary would be the main centre along the line of the CPR. "Of the future of Calgary," it concluded, "no one need entertain any apprehension."[2]

The Globe was equally optimistic, quoting Sir William Van Horne that Calgary was "a second Denver." Its reporter who visited the town in 1891 was impressed with the appearance of the downtown area. He wrote:

Last year the Alexander block, a handsome stone structure, was completed at a cost of over $60,000; the Lougheed Block was erected at a similar cost; the McLean Block, the Barber Block and the Calgary Hardware Company's blocks were also built at costs ranging from ten to twenty thousand dollars. The CPR have built a substantial dining hall and are also erecting a station of cut stone and pressed brick which will be a decided addition to the large number of fine buildings already in the town.[3]

The construction of the Calgary & Edmonton Railway in 1890-91, and the extension of this line to Macleod a year later, made merchants positive that the town would soon experience an explosion in its growth rate. But it didn't. In the next ten years, Calgary expanded by only a paltry 215 souls to a 1901 population of 4,091.

The reason was simple: Canada, and the West in particular, lapsed into a recession just when settlers should have been pouring in and the cash registers should have been ringing merrily in the downtown stores. As much as Calgary would like to have seen itself as a metropolitan centre it was really a small town that depended upon its market area of farmers and ranchers for its existence. And

the early 1890s were a bad time for the rural people, both homesteaders and cattlemen. The period from 1891 to 1894 had everything they most feared—drouth, disease, bitterly cold winters, prairie fires, depressed prices, and high freight rates.

Beginning in 1891 there was a drouth with poor crops right across the West. This was followed by two more dry years and depressed wheat prices. At the beginning of 1894—on Calgary's birthday as a city—a business newspaper commented that "two years in succession of depressed markets have had a crushing effect upon many

of our farmers."[4] In addition, a new American tariff began to exclude many agricultural products. At the same time, CPR freight rates were unreasonably high, thus discouraging new settlers.

Meanwhile, the ranchers suffered a major setback in their export business when the British government seized a boatload of Canadian cattle in 1891, claiming the animals had a highly communicable form of pleuro-pneumonia. The cattle were destroyed and an embargo placed on any further imports from Canada. Hard on the heels of this disaster came late spring snowstorms in 1893 which killed many calves and weak cows. A year later, a depression swept the United States and affected virtually all imports from Canada—grain, cattle, and manufactured goods. By the end of 1894, a three-year-old cow in top condition was worth only twenty-five dollars and wheat dropped to forty-two cents a bushel.

BECAUSE OF ITS SANDSTONE BUILDINGS, CALGARY IN 1889 LOOKED MORE PERMANENT AND SUBSTANTIAL THAN MANY PRAIRIE TOWNS. THIS IS A VIEW OF STEPHEN (8TH) AVENUE LOOKING EAST FROM SCARTH (1ST STREET WEST). IN THE BACKGROUND IS AN ARCH TO HONOUR LORD STANLEY, GOVERNOR GENERAL OF CANADA, WHO WAS VISITING THE TOWN. (GLENBOW, NA-2864-13233)

THE LOUGHEED BLOCK WAS BUILT BY JAMES LOUGHEED ON THE NORTH SIDE OF STEPHEN (8TH) AVENUE BETWEEN MCTAVISH (CENTRE) AND SCARTH (1ST STREET WEST) AT THE SITE OF THE PRESENT TD BANK. IN THIS 1891 VIEW, ED HODDER IS ON HORSEBACK AT CENTRE WHILE FRANK STONE, OF THE COLONIZATION COMPANY, LEANS OUT OF THE UPSTAIRS WINDOW AT RIGHT. NEXT DOOR IS MARIAGGI'S RESTAURANT, THE UPSTAIRS SERVING AS THE FIRST ROOMS OF THE RANCHMEN'S CLUB. (GLENBOW, NA-3795-1)

"A time of retrenchment has set in all over the West," stated a Winnipeg paper, "and a limiting of purchases, with a radical curtailment of credit has been adopted by all, farmer and trader."[5]

In spite of the fact that Calgary decided to achieve city status in 1894, it was hit hard by the depressed economy. After the building of the C&E railway, the town failed to grow and many firms were forced to reduce staff while others changed hands at a rapid rate. For

example, between 1892 and 1893, the number of Calgary businesses and professions dropped to 196 during which time twenty-seven businesses closed down or were replaced. Many were small firms such as barbers, tailors, and liverymen.[6] In one year, a local benevolent club issued transfer cards to no less than fifty members who were moving elsewhere. A few months after Calgary became a city, a local newspaper made the following wry comment about the tight money situation:

> The Tribune has been accused of springing a huge joke upon the public by the publication of the advertisement announcing that a five dollar bill had been dropped on Stephen Avenue yesterday. There is no such thing—the party states—as a five-dollar bill in the city.[7]

The second half of the decade was far better than the first although the economy was still languishing in a moribund state. The drouth ended but the period was notable in Calgary for a lack of growth and no significant new construction. In 1896, however, Laurier's new Liberal government in Ottawa started to do something about the immigration problem. Under the direction of Clifford Sifton, plans were made to finally fill the vacant prairies with the long awaited settlers. Calgary, which had been waiting for more than a decade, might at last see the boom it had long been seeking.

LEFT COLUMN: ONE DID NOT NEED TO TRAVEL FAR FROM DOWNTOWN CALGARY TO REACH THE RURAL AREAS. WILLIAM BRUCE'S FARM, SEEN HERE IN 1894, WAS LOCATED AT THE PRESENT SITE OF THE BRENTWOOD SHOPPING CENTRE. ON THE RAKE IS DAVE BRUCE, ON THE MOWER IS BRUCE HUNTER, AND ON HORSEBACK IN THE FOREGROUND IS WILLIAM BRUCE. (GLENBOW, NA-1097-1)

TOP: THE SPARSELY FURNISHED CABIN OF OSBORNE BROWN WAS PHOTOGRAPHED ON THE ELBOW RIVER NEAR CALGARY IN 1890. NOTE THE COTTON LINING IN THE CEILING; THE ROOF IS PROBABLY SOD AND LOOSE SOIL HAS FILTERED DOWN TO CREATE SAGGING POCKETS OF DIRT. BROWN WAS AN ENGLISHMAN AND MEMBER OF THE CALGARY POLO CLUB. (GLENBOW, NA-3913-1)

CENTRE: ONE OF THE MOST IMPRESSIVE HOUSES IN CALGARY IN THE 1890S WAS BOW BEND SHACK, OWNED BY WILLIAM PEARCE. THIS WAS LOCATED AT THE PRESENT INGLEWOOD BIRD SANCTUARY. (GLENBOW, NA-3898-1)

BOTTOM: THE BANK OF MONTREAL WAS LOCATED ON THE NORTHEAST CORNER OF STEPHEN (8TH) AVENUE AND SCARTH (1ST STREET WEST). (GLENBOW, NA-1009-2)

CALGARY WAS SURE IT WOULD EXPERIENCE A BOOM WHEN THE CALGARY & EDMONTON RAILWAY WAS BUILT IN 1890-91. HERE, THE HON. EDGAR DEWDNEY, MINISTER OF THE INTERIOR, TURNS THE FIRST SOD FOR THE RAILWAY ON JULY 21, 1890. THE BOOM, HOWEVER, DIDN'T HAPPEN. INSTEAD, CALGARY SLIPPED INTO A RECESSION. (GLENBOW, NA-3320-8)

WHEN CALGARY BECAME A CITY

The idea of Calgary becoming the first city in the North-West Territory came in the heady days after the building of the Calgary & Edmonton Railway when the town revelled in unbridled optimism. New buildings were going up as fast as the stone could be quarried, wholesale houses were being established, and merchants hoped the long-awaited prosperity was just over the horizon.

By early 1892, a local newspaper was already referring to the town fathers as "The City Council" and there were frequent references to the community's imminent population explosion. It was prophesied that "Alberta will double its population within the next two years" and that Calgary would be the main beneficiary of the increased trade.[1] In an editorial, the *Tribune* commented:

> Strangers coming in cannot but be struck by the number of new buildings—nearly all of them substantial stone buildings, too—which have been recently put up, or which are now in course of erection. The impression created is that Calgary people have the utmost confidence in the future of their town, and as confidence begets confidence, it is easily understood why Calgary has the reputation of being the best and most solid town between Winnipeg and Vancouver.[2]

But the onset of a national recession cooled some of the civic ardour and city status was no longer a priority item for the town council or the public. In neither of the civic elections of 1892 nor 1893 was the subject even raised. When Alexander Lucas was elected mayor in 1892 his campaign centred upon a more pressing matter—the financial affairs of the town. By 1893, he was being accused of excessive spending and his detractors said he had turned the town's $8,000 surplus into an $18,000 deficit in a single year. They showed that $10,000 had been borrowed from the Bank of Montreal and the mayor had to admit it had not been repaid.

One of the problems seemed to be that the council was trying to pay for capital projects out of annual operating funds. This had been possible when such works were limited to sidewalks and road grading, but now that the town was installing a sewer system the costs were exorbitant.

The voters obviously believed Mayor Lucas was doing a good job for he was returned to office in 1893 with double the votes of his only rival, Dr. Neville Lindsay. But the problem of funding capital works continued. One solution was to obtain city status and have a provision within its charter to borrow money for capital projects through debentures and extend the repayment over a long period of years.

On May 17, 1893, four months after the new council had been installed, a notice appeared that the Town of Calgary would apply to the Legislative Assembly of the North-West Territories "for an Ordinance changing the name of the said Corporation to 'The City of Calgary.'"[3] Arthur L. Sifton, the town's solicitor, was given the task of writing a proposed charter which could be discussed at public meetings before being submitted to the Legislative Assembly in Regina in August.

However, as the date for the Legislative Assembly meetings drew near, a number of Calgarians became concerned about a lack of consultation. An editorial complained, "The town council has not given the citizens of Calgary any reasons for taking the proposed step; nor has it placed before them any of the details of those enlarged municipal powers for which it is applying to the Legislature."[4]

The drafting of the charter—a 120-page document—was more demanding than Sifton had estimated and it wasn't completed until the beginning of August. With the Legislative Assembly meeting only weeks away, the Calgary mayor and council shipped the document off to Regina with no consultation with the Calgary public. Once it was printed, the town fathers planned to have a number of copies available for distribution "about the time the bill is introduced into the Assembly."[5]

Naturally, rumours abounded about the charter and its impact on Calgary. Some feared it would raise taxes while others were sure it would give the mayor and council dictatorial powers. There were questions about the qualification of candidates, who could vote, and what actions of council required a plebiscite. Frustrated by a

ALEXANDER LUCAS WAS THE LAST MAYOR TO SERVE WHILE CALGARY WAS STILL A TOWN. HE DECIDED NOT TO RUN FOR MAYOR OF THE CITY BUT WAS ELECTED TO THE FIRST CITY COUNCIL. (GLENBOW, LVA.65.11.7)

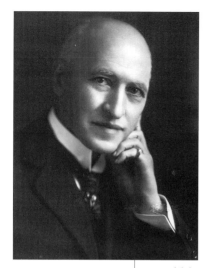

lack of information, a number of ratepayers circulated a petition asking that the request for city status be withdrawn.

This unrest finally crystallized the town council into action and late in August a meeting was called at Hull's Opera House—about a week before the charter was scheduled to be given first reading.

The meeting was packed as Sifton explained the proposed charter. Considering the rumours which had been floating around, the meeting was quiet and orderly. The solicitor reviewed the only copy of the document in town and tried to explain its pertinent points. He said that Calgary's boundaries would be increased to take in the Eau Claire property north of town and the Rouleauville community near the Catholic mission on the Elbow River, that the city would be divided into wards, and outlined the rules governing elections and the passing of by-laws.

Those in attendance appreciated the work of the solicitor and council but insisted that they must have time to study draft and recommend changes. A committee led by James Lougheed was formed and included such leading citizens as James Reilly, W.R. Hull, W.H. Cushing, Peter Prince, G.C. King, James Bannerman, and Father Lestanc. Their first action was to wire Regina with a demand that if the Legislative Assembly approved the charter it should come into effect only after a vote in which two-thirds of the Calgary ratepayers approved it. This was an unusual step and in order to accomplish it, the demand had to become part of the charter itself. Clause 176 stated:

This Ordinance shall come into effect upon the first day of January next after a majority of two-thirds of the resident ratepayers has been recorded in favor of its adoption . . . [6]

On August 29, the Legislative Assembly gave assent to receive the charter for consideration. It became known as Bill 33, An Ordinance to Incorporate "The City of Calgary." It was given first reading on September 8 and second reading four days later. At this time a number of amendments were made, some coming from the Calgary

committee and others from legal advisers to the Assembly.

The plan to include the Eau Claire properties and Rouleauville within the boundaries of the city was abandoned. The approved boundaries were 14th Street on the west, 17th Avenue on the south, and 15th Street on the east. The north boundary followed the Bow River except for the Eau Claire land north of 1st Avenue SW.

Some of the other amendments included: removing the requirement that electors be British subjects; reducing the penalty for wilful malfeasance of office at elections from $100 to $10; making it illegal for candidates to hire vehicles to take voters to polling stations; reducing the amount of real property required to be eligible to vote from $500 to $400; reducing the interest to be charged on back taxes from 10% to 6%; and limiting the type of industries which could be owned by the city.

The Bill was given third and final reading on September 13 and was accorded royal assent three days later. The date for the Calgary plebiscite was set for

October 16 and during the campaigning, local reaction was mixed. The *Calgary Herald,* in particular, was opposed to some of the individual clauses while its rival, the *Tribune* believed that "the adoption of the charter in even so crude a form will be a step in advance of the present mode of municipal existence. Weak points can be strengthened as required afterwards."[7] The ratepayers obviously agreed, for when the votes were counted, there were 326 in favour and only nine against. It was the largest turnout of ratepayers in Calgary's young history. Commented a journalist:

On the first day of January next, Calgary will put on her new garb and dignity. She will then occupy the proud position of being the premier city—and the only one for some time to come—in the North-West Territories. Yesterday's voting was a surprise to the most sanguine supporter of the City Charter . . . The vote showed that the people were interested sufficiently to consider the time opportune to take a step onward in municipal affairs. Every man who was in town possessing qualifications entitling him to vote, except some seventy, recorded his opinion that the Charter was what he wanted.[8]

In preparation for Calgary's new status, Councillors Wesley Orr and J.S. Feehan were given the task of making a city seal but Calgarians had to wait until 1902 before a city crest was designed and adopted.[9] To celebrate Calgary's forthcoming city status, the mayor invited the newly appointed Lieutenant-Governor, Charles H. Mackintosh, to make a special visit. He agreed to come for two days on December 20 and 21 as his first official function since his appointment. The festivities included speeches, a reception, and a ball in aid of the hospital fund. A tour of the town took the official party to Mounted Police barracks, the brewery, CPR offices, the Catholic convent school, and the Holy Cross Hospital. At a special ceremony, Mackintosh presented the mayor with an original letter of 1876 in which Colonel Irvine had recommended the name for Calgary.

Under the new charter, Mayor Lucas and his council remained in office until an election was held. This was set for January 15, 1894. The city charter provided for a mayor, nine aldermen, and two members of the school board. There were three new wards, each to have three aldermen. Ward One was east and Ward Two was west of Centre Street, both north of the CPR line, and Ward Three was south of the CPR line.

After the New Year's Day celebrations, the campaigning began on a serious and often vitriolic note. Lucas decided not to run for mayor but became an aldermanic candidate in Ward One. As for the rest of the town council, Wesley Orr was running for mayor against W.H. Cushing; E. Watson was a candidate in Ward One, R.J. Hutchings and J.H. Millward in Ward Two, and J.S. Feehan in Ward Three. Only Councillor Wendell Maclean was not a candidate for the city council.

Ex-Mayor Lucas and some members of his council received stinging criticisms for the way they had handled the town's finances. During 1893, the Fire, Light & Water Committee had overspent its budget by $1,000; the Police & Relief Committee by $700; the Public Works Committee by $120; and the schools by more than $2,000. By the time the various figures were tallied up, the council had overspent by some $13,000. When added to the $10,000 loan still outstanding with the Bank of Montreal from the previous year and other expenses, the City of Calgary was starting off with a $27,000 deficit—not a very auspicious beginning.

James Reilly, who had been mayor of the town immediately prior to Lucas, and James Bannerman, a former member of the council, both attacked Lucas' record. This was not surprising, for both were running against him in Ward One. Reilly had some choice words for the

THESE CALGARIANS WERE AMONG THE LEADERS WHO ARRANGED FOR CALGARY'S CITY STATUS. SEEN HERE IN FRONT OF THE TOWN HALL IN 1890 ARE, FRONT ROW: WESLEY F. ORR, MAYOR J.D. LAFFERTY, AND TOWN SOLICITOR ARTHUR L. SIFTON; BACK ROW: PATRICK J. NOLAN, CHIEF TOM ENGLISH, CST. JAMES FRASER, CST. THOMAS LIPPINGTON, AND SENATOR JAMES LOUGHEED. (GLENBOW, NA-21-3)

way Mayor Lucas had left the town with a large debt, referring to his tenure as "a monstrosity of maladministration."[10] But the real invective was unleashed by insurance agent R.A. Janes who was not a candidate for office. According to a reporter:

The speech he made was full of venom in its attack on the mayor, the members of the council, the press . . . and the auditors. He attacked the system of borrowing money without asking permission from the people, the irrigation projects of the town and the electric light companies. No opportunity was lost to say something against the ex-mayor, and the language used descended to abusive and ill-advised personalities.[11]

The underlying themes of the campaign, however, were of retrenchment and reform. One candidate after another promised to correct the excesses of the Lucas administration by laying off staff, cutting expenses, and calling public meetings before making any unexpected major expenditures. Most candidates attacked Lucas' plans to build a new town hall, considering it to be an unaffordable expense.

On voting day, the turnout showed that Calgary's first civic election was a huge success. A total of 461 persons voted and "there were not more than ten ratepayers within reasonable distance of the city who did not exercise their franchise."[12] The turnout was even greater than the October ballot to decide on the city charter.

The race for the mayoralty was a close one, with Wesley Orr winning by just 21 votes over his opponent, W.H. Cushing. The vote was 241 to 220. In the three wards, the bitterest fight was in Ward One where a strong effort was made to defeat ex-Mayor Lucas. However, he managed to be one of the three winners. A.J. Cameron received 155 votes, Joseph Bannerman 146, and Lucas 137. In Ward Two, the winners were J.E. Jacques 138, J.A. Nolan 111, and R.J. Hutchings 86. In Ward Three: J.S. Feehan 100, A. McBride 98, and Thomas Underwood 59.

That evening, brooms were soaked with coal oil and set afire for a torchlight parade down the snow-covered streets of the city. Leading the parade was the fire brigade band while Mayor-elect Orr was carried on the shoulders of several stalwart men. When the procession reached the Queen's Hotel, Orr was carried to a sulky sleigh and after a considerable delay for speeches and refreshments, he was pulled down the street by a joyful gang of supporters. When they got to the Alberta Hotel, there were more delays and speeches, and they were off again, this time to the Royal Hotel where the celebrations ended with the playing of the national anthem.

Calgary had, indeed, become a city in grand style.

WESLEY F. ORR WAS THE FIRST MAYOR OF THE CITY OF CALGARY, SERVING IN 1894-95 AND IN 1897. HE WAS AN ENTREPRENEUR, BUSINESSMAN, AND CIVIC BOOSTER. (GLENBOW, LVA.65.11.8)

THE RANCHMEN'S CLUB

When the elite Ranchmen's Club was formed about 1891, it combined the best features of private British clubs and the free and easy ways of western ranchers. It was ostentatious and conservative, yet very convivial. It brought the British class system to Calgary but related it to cowmen and pastoral life.

The relationship of an elite social organization to the ranching industry was not unexpected. More than any other pursuit in the West, ranching was associated with the landed gentry of England. Among the ranch owners during the 1880s were such notables as Sir Alexander Staveley Hill, Sir John Walrond-Walrond, Sir Francis De Winton, and members of the Quorn Hunt Club. Owners also included a number of wealthy investors from Ontario and Quebec.

Ranching had been intimately associated with Calgary from the beginning. Cowboys trailed Cochrane Ranch cattle past the palisaded walls of Fort Calgary on their way to the range in 1880 and by the time the railway arrived three years later, the industry was already well established. The first thing many visitors saw on their arrival were cowboys wearing chaps and spurs driving horses or cattle through the centre of the village. Much of the talk was about the British market, roundups, and the price of cattle.

Typical of the ranchers of that era was A.C. Fraser, an Englishman from Wallingford. When family business called him back to the Old Country, he sold his ranche (with an "e," you know) to the Hon. Sydney Trench, "who also acquires the horses, polo ponies and one of the best equipped ranche houses and buildings in the West."[1]

By 1890, big ranches like the Cochrane, Bar U, Walrond, and Oxley were dominating the industry, while many smaller ranches were successfully competing for the open range. Calgary was a major shipping point for cattle and a number of ranchers maintained rooms at the leading hotels and were frequent visitors to the town.

According to one of the club's traditions, six ranchers, a lawyer, a real estate dealer, and a banker met in a converted boxcar in 1890 to form a group called "The Wolves' Den." These men included A.E. Cross of the A7 Ranch; Herbert Samson and Ben Harford of the Bar XY; Duncan Macpherson of the High River Horse Ranch;

H.B. Alexander of the Two Dot; D.H. Andrews of the 76 Ranch; lawyer J.P.J. Jephson, realtor T.S.C. Lee (who also dabbled in ranching), and banker A.D. Braithwaite.

According to Cross' biographer, "They would play a little poker and plan the future industrial West . . . One night the thoroughly squiffed friends left the boxcar and caroused through the streets of Calgary howling like a pack of wolves."[2] They were arrested but, needless to say, they were released next morning.

The actual relationship between The Wolves' Den and the Ranchmen's Club is murky. It seems that The Wolves' Den was set up to circumvent the stringent liquor laws and to give a number of affluent citizens a place to drink and play cards. However, the liquor laws were changed in 1891, just about the time that some of the Wolves called a meeting to form the Ranchmen's Club.

Twenty-seven ranchers and businessmen assembled in rented quarters, each paying $50 to become charter members. Realtor Lee was elected the first president and

A. E. Cross

"Jolly Jolly Brewer"

Calgary 1893

he set to work with A.E. Cross, Duncan Macpherson, and Fred Stimson (of the Bar U) to have the club legally constituted through an ordinance of the North-West Territorial Government. This was accomplished early in 1892.

The rules of the club were based upon those of St. James Club in Montreal—the oldest British-style club in Canada. It restricted membership to men over the age of twenty-one, prohibited the discussion of politics and religion, excluded dogs (but not horses) from the club rooms, and prohibited smoking in the dining area. The 1913 rule book probably reflects the earlier period when it prohibits conversation in the library, dice playing, card games on Sundays, bringing one's own liquor onto the premises, and bringing into the club as a guest anyone who had been blackballed or expelled from membership. And it was clear that this was a men's club, not only in its membership requirements but in its regulations that members could invite only "gentlemen who do not reside within a thirty-three mile radius of the Club house."[3]

Temporarily, the club had its headquarters in rooms over Mariaggi's Restaurant on Stephen Avenue. Meals were brought up through a dumb waiter and a whole line of drinks were available from the bar. However, an early rule stated that drinks had to be mixed in the presence of the club member, presumably to prevent any substitution of inferior brands. Clearly, drinking and eating were uppermost in the minds of the early members.

In 1892, the club built new quarters on McIntyre (now 7th) Avenue at the site of the present Bay Parkade. This two-storey brick building provided a bar, library, billiard room, lodgings, and other facilities. And as if to reinforce its British ties, seven of the first ten subscriptions for the library were to English magazines, mostly sporting journals.

A reporter observed that in front of the Ranchmen's Club could be found "the steeds of men who have contributed beyond measure to the history of southern Alberta. Business and professional men of the little pioneer town, ranchers of English and American origin . . . were wont to gather of an evening for comradeship within its old brick walls."[4]

According to its official history, one of the club's first and most pressing problems was to gain a liquor permit. Alfred Cross used all his influence as a brewer and member of the Territorial legislature and, after paying $400 in

ONE OF THE ORGANIZERS AND SUPPORTERS OF THE RANCHMEN'S CLUB WAS RANCHER AND ENTREPRENEUR ALFRED E. CROSS. HE WAS PHOTOGRAPHED IN 1893 BY R. RANDOLPH BRUCE IN THE "WOLF'S DEN," MEETING PLACE FOR AN INFORMAL GROUP KNOWN AS THE "PACK OF WESTERN WOLVES." (GLENBOW, NA-2307-21)

fees, he was ultimately successful. The licences were "really pretty substantial for those days," states the club history. "Two year old whiskey in that year (1892) was $1.25 a gallon and 'old' whiskey $2.00 a gallon."[5] The most popular drink was Glen Grant Scotch whiskey which was shipped direct from Edinburgh in 40-gallon barrels.

No sooner was the clubhouse built than Calgary slipped into a recession and the group became hard pressed to pay for it. By 1896 they were in such dire straits that the members seriously considered closing down and disbanding the club. Only when a dozen members advanced funds to cover the debts was a disaster averted and the future of the club assured.

During the real estate boom, the club sold its properties in 1912 and built an imposing new structure on the corner of 13th Street and 6th Avenue SW. When it was opened in 1914, it was a lavish structure, which ultimately featured oak panelling, a carved staircase, stained glass windows, and a western motif on the exterior with terra cotta figures of bucking horses.

With the onset of prohibition in 1916, the club was in real danger of losing its life's blood. Initially, a small room was designated on the third floor as a place where members could cache their own bottles and carry on the age-old traditions of the club. Later, when the provincial government decreed that liquor could be consumed only in rooms with beds (i.e. hotel rooms), members obligingly moved a bed into the room and designated the space as "Mr. Smith's bedroom."

In 1919, another tradition was added to the Ranchmen's Club when Edward, the Prince of Wales, was an honoured guest. He had just received an honorary chieftainship from the Stoney tribe and somehow during the evening, the inebriated club members thought it would be a fine idea to hold an Indian pow-wow. Accordingly, a bonfire was lit on the hardwood floor in the entrance hall and members had a lively time prancing around it. The scars were still evident years later when the area was renovated.

Also during the evening, members decided to pay special attention to Bob Newbolt, an oldtime British rancher who had come to the banquet in full evening dress—a rare occurrence for him. To commemorate the event, the revellers began to autograph the front of his shirt. R.B. Bennett, A.E. Cross, lawyers M.S. McCarthy and M.C. Bernard, and a host of others—including the Prince of Wales—all scrawled their signatures on the stiff front. This item is now a treasured possession of the Glenbow Museum.

Over the years, the membership of the club has been impressive; besides the oldtime ranchers, there have been a prime minister, two premiers, seven chief justices, two presidents of the Canadian Bar Association, one federal cabinet minister, three holders of the Victoria Cross, and numerous senior executives.

Throughout the years, the Ranchmen's Club was a male bastion, as were the private clubs of England. The first chink in its armour of male domination came in the 1920s, when a sports annex was added to the club for squash and badminton courts. Women were invited to participate and out of this eventually grew a new category of "Lady Associate Members." However, they had to enter via the side door of the club, as did any female guests of members. They also ate in a segregated dining room and were never, never allowed to walk through the front doors.

After World War Two, the West's booming economy saw the rise of other private clubs in Calgary but the Ranchmen's remained the elder statesman—conservative, sedate, and unchanging in times of change. The philosophies of its members were, according to a reporter, "about as far right as you can get in Canada and still remain respectable."[6] There was usually a waiting list for membership, and the social prestige and business advantages of being a member were immeasurable.

In 1980, the club began to build a new structure adjoining the clubhouse on the west. Included were new dining rooms and club rooms, and a tall condominium tower. As part of the overall plan, the old building also was completely renovated.

By this time, the Ranchmen's Club was beginning to be criticized for its policy against admitting women as full members. During renovations, the club confirmed that:

the east entrance and main floor will still be restricted to "men only" because as [club president] Bob Phibbs says: "It's tradition, the way it has always been." Although criticized by so-called "libbers" for its policies regarding women, Phibbs maintains the charge is unfair. "We allow women on the second and third floors and they have their own dining rooms (open to both sexes). They can also enter with men through the (new) main door. The only thing we ask is that they let the guys have the first floor."[7]

But the changing times buffeted the Ranchmen's Club during the rest of the decade. The Calgary Professional Club and the Commerce Club had never restricted women members, and in 1989 the Calgary Petroleum Club and Calgary 400 Club crumbled in the face of persistent opposition and permitted women to join.

In 1992, a faction within the Ranchmen's Club forced a vote on the admission of women. "It's time to decide what kind of club the Ranchmen's wants to be," said a lawyer member, "a gentleman's social club or a business-oriented support club."[8] When the ballots were counted, there were 126 in favour of admitting women and 82 opposed—less than the two-thirds majority required for it to pass.

Angrily, the publisher of the *Calgary Herald* announced he was resigning and others soon threatened to join him. When the club faced a possible 40 per cent loss of membership because of the vote, the opposition reluctantly acquiesed. A new ballot early in 1993 approved the admission of women members, 147 to 24. Then, in a strange reversal of events, one room was designated for the exclusive use of men. From once having had the freedom to range through the entire club without ever seeing a woman, a century later the traditionalists were relegated to a single room if they wanted the type of privacy which once had been the hallmark of the English clubs.

"If the pro-fems carry the day," added a reporter, "the Ranchmen's will be no more. The first thing to go will have to be the name. It's too sexist for today's politically sensitive society."[9]

But more than a hundred years of history are not easily swept aside. As the oldest organization in Calgary, the Ranchmen's Club still reflects a proud heritage of ranchers, statesmen, good food, and plenty to drink—especially the latter.

THE TERRIBLE FLOODS

Calgary experienced its first major flood in 1884 but because the town was so small, all it did was wash away the bridges across the Elbow. But that wasn't the case in 1897 or in 1902 when the swollen waters of the Bow and Elbow struck the town in a chaos of floating logs, mud, and debris.

By 1897, with a population of almost 4,000, the city had expanded to the low areas along both rivers. The section around the Langevin Bridge in particular was heavily populated with low and middle income families. Many of them raised chickens and geese while a few had their own milk cows and perhaps a few hogs and teams of horses. Their outbuildings included at least one shed and a barn. There were some beautiful flower gardens and many of the homes were enclosed by attractive picket fences. Wooden sidewalks provided protection for pedestrians from mud after the normal spring rains.

But 1897 wasn't a normal year. There had been heavy snows in the mountains during the winter and in early June the rain had pelted down steadily for ten days. In Calgary almost five inches fell in a single week.

People knew the rivers were running high but no one expected the volume of water which struck the city on the night of June 17. Around seven o'clock, as the seething waters were getting dangerously close to the top of the banks, the fire brigade and Mounted Police went from house to house in the low-lying areas, warning the residents to leave. Some loaded their possessions on wagons provided by the rescue workers and amid the pouring rain they were able to save their most precious furniture and clothing. By ten o'clock, some of the teams were wading through flood waters a foot deep as the river swirled down the streets and carried away the sidewalks.

Some people chose to ignore the warnings; one woman declared she'd rather be dead if her house and furniture were washed away. A man, a former sailor, claimed he was not afraid of water and refused to go. An hour later, he with his wife and children were standing on chairs and tables screaming for help as the water cascaded through the house. They stood helplessly as the furniture floated away, along with chickens, turkeys, and ducks. At last, the firemen heard their call and carried them out on their backs. The ex-sailor wanted the men to go back for the few belongings still in the house but by then the water had become a raging torrent.

When the Bow River crested at ten o'clock, it was 17.52 feet above normal and was discharging 99,000 cubic feet of water per second. That's more than three times higher than the worst floods of the 1930s and 1940s. The muddy waters were filled with logs from the mills upstream, trees uprooted by the storms, and the

scattered remains of houses, sheds, and barns. As the water rose, the debris smashed first against the Bow Marsh Bridge at 10th Street West and then the Langevin Bridge at 4th Street East. At five o'clock on the morning of the 18th, a section of the Bow Marsh Bridge finally collapsed and was carried away by the flood. "It went down the river with a tremendous rush," said a reporter, "and the spectators feared for the safety of the Langevin Bridge when the enormous mass of heavy timbers struck it. The piers however withstood the shock of the great battering ram which shortly afterwards broke up and went on toward the Saskatchewan in pieces."[1]

Meanwhile, the crest of the Elbow River was only six hours behind that of the Bow. During the night, "Irish" Mellon, owner of the Blue Rock Hotel near the Catholic mission, checked the level of the stream and was shocked at the speed at which it was rising. Soon the river was rushing over the Mission Bridge and within a half an hour it had risen more than four feet. It finally crested about four o'clock, having risen six feet during the night.

As soon as he saw what was happening, Mellon sent a messenger to warn the people downstream. At the racetrack (presently Stampede Park) the stables and dwellings were in two feet of water. According to a reporter:

The men were all sleeping soundly, and after they were awakened, it was no inviting task to get to the horses and get them out, but it had to be done, and the 11 horses preparing for the Jubilee races were soon safely landed.[2]

Also along the Elbow, William Pearce's flume for his irrigation works was washed away, the stone piers for a new bridge were destroyed, the brickworks taken over by the flood, and a number of homes had to be abandoned.

At daybreak, the sight was awesome. E.R. Rogers, who lived on the north side of the Bow, noted that from his vantage point "the two rivers and the numerous lakes formed by the overflow during the night look like an archipelago."[3] At least forty-six families had fled their homes near the Langevin Bridge. Dozens of buildings had been swept away while others were inundated with water to their eaves. Besides the loss of buildings and furniture—estimated at more than a quarter of a million dollars—there were scores of chickens, hogs, cattle, and other animals carried away by the flood waters.

In the present Bowness district, the CPR Bridge held but a mile of tracks leading up to it were washed away. Similarly, the tracks to the CPR Bridge on the Edmonton line were destroyed, while the railway bridge across the Elbow was intact but unsafe to cross. This meant that the transcontinental line was cut both east and west of the city, as was the northern line to Edmonton.

Along the Bow, the Alberta Irrigation Company's headgates were washed away while James Walker's house and buildings were destroyed when flood waters cut into the bank for more than fifty feet.

There were numerous examples of heroism and pathos during the night. Harry Turner rescued a chicken that was floating by on a piece of board and decided to keep it as a pet. And two men, Godin and Richard, risked their lives in a canoe to rescue a dog which was chained to a building floating away in the flood.

The firemen and police who worked all night were the real heroes of the flood. Through their efforts, not a single life was lost. The refugees were taken to any available place out of the rain—churches, hotels, even the town jail. Next morning, citizens from all parts of the city pitched in to help. As soon as the water receded, CPR crews were out working on the bridges and their approaches. More than 400 men were put to work in the Bowness area alone to restore train service as quickly as possible.

A few people became unpopular during the flood. One was an unnamed alderman who rushed up to a fireman and shouted, "Who the hell ordered all those drays and who's going to pay for them?"[4] The men had been working all night while the alderman had been sleeping. The old hands just laughed and ignored him; they had heard such stupid outbursts from aldermen before. It may have been this same alderman who was said to have refused to allow money to be spent for hot coffee and food for the rescuers. However, the *Herald* discounted the story, saying that, "No man who has lived in the west for a few years could have his bowels of compassion bound up so hard and fast."[5]

The *Calgary Herald* summarized the tragedy of the flood by saying that "Only a philosopher could see the destruction around him and bear up with equanimity." As an example, it pointed to a man who had probably the best garden in town and a house that had been surrounded by flowers, shrubs, and trees. "The house is now canted over in the river, not a vestige of a tree, plant or bed remains, and his loss cannot be far short of a thousand dollars."[6]

The flood had been a "once in a century" occurrence, according to the experts. They said that conditions which would cause both the Bow and Elbow rivers to crest at almost the same time were so rare that it wouldn't occur more than once in a hundred years. Then five years later the Bow River went on the rampage again, this time by itself, but the results were almost as bad.

In spite of the damage done by the flood of '97, some people insisted on moving back to the area near the Langevin Bridge, although not as many as before. In the spring of 1902 the rains returned, almost nine inches falling in May and another ten inches in June. On July 3, a deluge of nearly two inches of rain was dumped on the city and the Bow rose six inches before noon. With the memory of the '97 flood still fresh in their minds, the fireman under Chief "Cappy" Smart sent out the orders to evacuate. The water did not reach the flood stage as quickly as the last time but by the morning of July 4 a number of houses close to the Langevin Bridge were surrounded by water.

Some of the occupants had ignored the orders to leave and now they were stranded. Chief Smart commandeered a boat and was lowered downstream by means of a long rope. When he got to the first house he rescued a woman and child and then went back for a second woman. He floated down to another house where a man was sitting on the top rail of his fence, fending off logs and debris with a long pole. After bringing him to safety Smart went to a third house where two men were still sleeping, even though the water was cascading around the building.

By mid-morning, the flood waters extended in a long arch from the present Centre Street Bridge to the corner of 6th Avenue and 4th Street SE and east to the edge of the Mounted Police barracks. Upstream, the present districts of Sunnyside, Hillhurst, and Riverdale were all under water. The southern approaches to the Bow Marsh and Langevin bridges were flooded but the structures themselves remained firm. At its peak, the river was 16.7 feet above normal—a foot less than the 1897 flood but still high enough for a couple of dozen families to be rendered homeless. In addition, the power house was flooded and the city was without electricity.

Because the north side of the river was cut off from the south, an enterprising citizen named Birney bought a small rowboat from the Mounted Police and went into business as a ferryman, taking people across the raging torrent at twenty-five cents a head. Some praised him for his ambition but others thought he was taking advantage of other people's misfortunes. Finally, the city provided its own free rowboat service and Birney was out of business.

Meanwhile, the railway bridges at Bowness and east of the city were badly damaged. A student at the nearby Indian school, Herbert Bull Calf, wrote home, "The Big Bow River bridge about one mile from the School has been nearly washed away, just bent badly in the middle, the trains cannot go across the bridge. The middle stone pier is cut into two parts & it may fall to pieces any minute."[7] With the transcontinental line out of commission, trains were halted east and west of the city. At Gleichen, two Number One westbound trains and the Imperial Limited were stalled while the eastbound Number Two and a second Imperial Limited were stopped at Banff. In addition, another three trains were stranded in Calgary. In all, some 2,000 railway travellers were held up until the tracks could be repaired.

One of those left at Gleichen was the poet and author, E. Pauline Johnson. She had a delightful time picking mushrooms, watching Indian horse races, and visiting a nearby Blackfoot camp. Finally, the train ventured on to Calgary, stopping on the east side of the Bow River. There, she noted:

The taut steel bridge was shattered, crooked and disjointed; no train could pass across it for days to come. We detrained, almost six hundred strong, our luggage, the express goods and the meals were wheeled across by a perfect army of employees. The Divisional Superintendent from Calgary, Mr. J. Niblock, met us and personally handed us one by one in Indian file across the cobwebby structure that was temporarily erected above the ties for transferring purposes. We boarded another train, and in a half hour we swelled the dense crowd at the station platform in Calgary.[8]

Johnson went to Bowness to look at the damage to the twin bridges there. One of them had collapsed and she saw eastbound passengers crossing the river on planks which had been fastened to the ties of the other bridge. Baggage, mail and express goods lined the track for 200 yards, ready to be carried across. But even as she watched, a piledriver arrived and workers began to repair the damaged trestle.

Unlike the flood of '97, this one was not without tragedy. At Bowness, railway repairman Gregory Crechita was working on the cribbing when he slipped and fell into the river. His comrades tried to catch him but he was carried away by the wild torrent. And just north of the city, Thomas Campbell tried to cross Nose Creek but his horse was swept off its feet and the man drowned.

But the most poignant tragedy occurred while the flood waters were receding. A number of children went down to the river near 1st Street East to watch the debris floating by. When a log drifted close to the shore, six-year-old Clifford McClellan tried to grab it but fell into the water. The current quickly carried him downstream while his thirteen-year-old sister, Florence, ran along the bank, looking for a way to rescue him. When she came to a little promontory she stretched out her hands to seize him but he was too far away. In a last desperate attempt, she plunged into the water and grabbed him but the current was too swift for her to get back to shore. The last time anyone saw them alive they were locked in each other's arms.

In the next thirty years, Calgary experienced only three more spring floods—in 1915, 1929, and 1932—but none of them came close to the high water marks of 1897 and 1902. And if the hundred-year predictions are correct, the next one shouldn't happen until 1997.

ARTIST GERALD TAILFEATHERS PORTRAYS A BLACKFOOT CAMP MOVING ACROSS THE PRAIRIES IN THE BUFFALO DAYS. THIS TEMPERA PAINTING WAS SPECIALLY COMMISSIONED BY GLENBOW IN 1960. (GLENBOW, FG.60.45.11)

THE STAMPEDE IS THE TITLE OF THIS OIL PAINTING BY CANADIAN ARTIST FREDERICK VERNER. (GLENBOW, VF.55.28)

FORT CALGARY IN WINTER, PAINTED BY MOUNTED POLICE SURGEON RICHARD NEVITT IN 1876. AT LEFT, DEVIL'S HEAD MOUNTAIN STANDS OUT ON THE WESTERN HORIZON. (GLENBOW, 74.7.53)

A MONTANA TRADER, ANDY MCGOWAN, PAINTED THIS VIEW OF CALGARY IN THE 1870S. IN THE FOREGROUND ARE THE BUILDINGS OF I.G. BAKER & CO., WHILE AT RIGHT IS THE HUDSON'S BAY CO. STORE, WITH FORT CALGARY AT CENTRE BACK. THE WATERCOLOUR, PART OF A SERIES SHOWING EVENTS AT THE FORT, WAS LATER ACQUIRED BY INSP. WILLIAM WINDER. (GLENBOW, NA-98-1)

THIS STRIKING VIEW OF
KAN-TE-WAS-TE-WIN, OR
GOOD BROAD WOMAN,
WAS PAINTED AT
CALGARY BY EDWARD
ROPER IN THE 1880S.
(NATIONAL ARCHIVES OF
CANADA, 1989/446)

AGNES GARDNER
ENTITLED THIS WATER-
COLOUR PAINTING,
**INDIAN ENCAMPMENT
AND COMMENCEMENT
OF THE ROCKY
MOUNTAINS FROM
THE RAILWAY NEAR
CALGARY.** (NATIONAL
ARCHIVES OF CANADA,
1990/312)

THREE HUNDRED TROOPS OF THE 65TH MOUNT ROYAL REGIMENT ARRIVED IN CALGARY IN APRIL 1885, ALLAYING FEARS THAT THE TOWN MIGHT BE ATTACKED BY REBELS. THIS IS THE UNIFORM OF THE MONTREAL REGIMENT. PRINTED ON SILK, IT WAS PART OF A SERIES OF PRIZES ENCLOSED WITH CIGARETTES AT THE TURN OF THE CENTURY. (GLENBOW CULTURAL HISTORY DEPARTMENT)

WALTER CHESTERTON PAINTED THIS WATERCOLOUR VIEW OF INDIANS FORDING THE BOW RIVER AT CALGARY IN THE 1880S. (NATIONAL ARCHIVES OF CANADA, 1967/31)

THESE TWO WELLS, DINGMAN NOS. 1 AND 2, SET OFF A FRENZY OF OIL SPECULATION AND DEVELOPMENT IN 1914. ALTHOUGH MUCH OF THE EARLY PROMOTION WAS FRAUDULENT, TURNER VALLEY DID BECOME ONE OF CANADA'S LEADING OIL PRODUCERS. THIS PAINTING IS BY ROLAND GISSING. (GLENBOW, 57.35)

LABOURERS AT WORK IN CALGARY WERE CAPTURED IN THIS 1939 WATER-COLOUR BY MARGARET SHELTON. (GLENBOW, 983.97.3)

A VIEW OF DOWNTOWN CALGARY WAS PAINTED BY MYRTLE JACKSON ABOUT 1932. IN THE BACKGROUND, THE FEDERAL PUBLIC BUILDING DOMINATES THE SKYLINE. THE WORK COMBINES THE MEDIA OF WATER-COLOUR WITH PEN AND INK. (GLENBOW, 57.40)

ARTIST E.J. HUGHES PRODUCED THIS WATER-COLOUR OF CALGARY ABOUT 1955. HE OFFERS A PASTORAL URBAN/RURAL SCENE WITH TREES ON THE NORTH HILL DOMINATING THE FOREGROUND WHILE THE FOOTHILLS AND ROCKIES ON THE SKYLINE ENCLOSE A LANDSCAPE OF BUILDINGS INTERSPERSED WITH TREES. (GLENBOW, HEJ.57.21)

ONE OF THE UNIQUE FEATURES OF THE CALGARY STAMPEDE IS THE CHUCKWAGON RACE, INTRODUCED BY GUY WEADICK IN 1923. BRITISH ARTIST JOHN GILROY PROVIDES HIS OWN INTERPRETATION OF THE EVENT IN THIS 1962 OIL PAINTING. (GLENBOW, 64.27.3)

THE VITALITY OF CALGARY IS CAPTURED IN THIS NIGHT VIEW OF DOWNTOWN CALGARY IN THE 1960S. ARTIST DOUG STEPHENS SHOWS BUSY SHOPPERS ALONG 1ST STREET WEST, WITH THE BAY ON THE RIGHT AND THE PALLISER HOTEL IN THE BACK-GROUND. (GLENBOW, S.69.68)

A NEW CENTURY

OPTIMISM

THE BEGINNING OF THE TWENTIETH CENTURY PROMISED GREAT THINGS FOR CALGARY—
AND FOR THE WEST IN GENERAL. THE LONG RECESSION OF THE 1890S SEEMED TO BE OVER AND THE
LIBERAL GOVERNMENT IN OTTAWA HAD LAUNCHED AN AGGRESSIVE CAMPAIGN TO ATTRACT NEW SETTLERS
FROM EUROPE AND THE UNITED STATES. WITHIN A SHORT TIME, IMMIGRANTS WERE FLOWING IN FROM
GERMANY, THE UKRAINE, AND SCANDINAVIA, HEADING NORTH FOR THE FERTILE LANDS AROUND
EDMONTON. IN SOUTHERN ALBERTA, THE AMERICANS FROM MINNESOTA AND THE MIDWEST
WERE ATTRACTED TO THE OPEN PLAINS.

Yet Calgary was still a small town; the 1901 Dominion census recorded only 4,091 people, barely a ripple above the 1891 figures. The main downtown area was along Atlantic (9th) and Stephen (8th) avenues from Scarth (1st Street West) to Drinkwater (2nd Street East). It consisted of sandstone buildings, wooden livery stables, stores, hotels, and private dwellings. Within the townsite there were more open spaces than there were buildings, with church steeples and the fire hall dominating the horizon.

Most homes had barns in the back yards for horses and milk cows. According to Jack McHugh, "Early in the morning after being milked, the cows would be gathered up by a herdsman and grazed out all day on the open prairie grass. In the evening they would be returned to their respective owners' homes. All that was necessary for the herdsman to do was to turn the cow down the back lane and it would find its own way home alone."[1]

South of the tracks, a number of CPR employees lived along Van Horne (12th) Avenue and beyond them was open prairie south-east to the General Hospital and racetrack, and south to the Catholic mission. Following a prairie trail towards the Elbow River, one came to the Blue Rock Hotel, run by "Irish" Mellon. This marked the beginning of Rouleauville, a small community clustered near the mission and the Elbow River Bridge. There was a sign near the hotel reading "One Mile to Calgary."

Rouleauville had started as a Metis settlement and was distinctively Catholic in its makeup. Indians usually camped in the willows along the river and regularly attended mass at the mission. Sometimes the Sarcees came in a group from their reserve and put on a dance near the base of the present Mount Royal district. "There was a slough there," recalled McHugh, "and they would camp beside it and hold their dances. A gang of us kids used to come out from Calgary and try to play games with the Indian kids but for the most part they were shy and would stick close to their tepees."

In 1901, McIntyre (7th) Avenue West consisted mostly of residences and vacant lots. East of McTavish (Centre) Street were the Presbyterian and Anglican churches, Hull's Opera House, police station, town office, fire hall, and a few small shops. Near the fire hall was a Chinese laundry where the owner also raised vegetables for sale. "I remember," said McHugh, "in the fall of the year, this old man could be seen on the street with a pole over his shoulder and a basket of vegetables hanging from each end. He would go along the street in a little dog trot with his baskets jumping up and down all in rhythm to his pace." On the north-east corner of Scarth (1st Street West) was the Baptist Church while on the north-west corner was Dr. J.D. Lafferty's house; beyond that was open prairie to Bow Marsh Bridge near the present Louise Bridge. Sitting out of the prairie all by itself was the court house while north of town across an open prairie was the Eau Claire mill and employees' houses.

The east end of Calgary was dominated by the Mounted Police barracks while farther out was the brewery, packing plant, and the stockyards. On the north side of the river, there were small settlements near the Bow Marsh and Langevin bridges and the red light district along Nose Creek.

Calgary was still a cowboy and ranching town. In 1901, for example, Ed Taylor was riding downtown along Scarth Street when his horse began to buck. He stayed with her until the animal's legs struck the wooden sidewalk and she plunged to the ground. With one leg pinned, Taylor had to fend the beast off as she tried to bite him, but with the help of a few bystanders he got the

animal to her feet again. "Then," said an onlooker, "straps and cinches were tightened and another fight took place in which the man came out victorious. In a very short time, the horse was utterly cowed and Taylor was enabled to ride it quietly up and down the street."[2]

A visitor in 1900 saw Calgary as "a thriving little hamlet" with sandstone buildings, high taxes, and an inadequate fire department.[3] While walking along Stephen Avenue he was impressed by the variety and informality of dress. He saw a Scotsman in kilts, a dandy dressed in the style of Hyde Park, a Doukhobor in a sheepskin coat, a Ukrainian in traditional calico shirt and wide trousers, and a cowboy with sombrero and chaps, "while everywhere may be seen the ubiquitous native in moccasins and flowing toga." Another visitor writing for a British newspaper found Calgary to be an English town. "It is," he said, "English in the substantial stone buildings; it is English in sentiment; it is English in its social life; it is English in its Ranchman's Club and English in many other respects."[4] But, he added, it was English with a distinctive western flavour.

In the early years of the twentieth century, Calgary saw itself as the predominant city on the prairies west of

IN 1905, STEPHEN (8TH) AVENUE WAS A BUSY THOROUGHFARE. THIS VIEW LOOKS WEST FROM A FEW DOORS WEST OF 1ST STREET EAST. (GLENBOW, NA-468-6)

CALGARY POST OFFICE, LOCATED ON STEPHEN (8TH) AVENUE AND OSLER (1ST STREET EAST), WAS BUILT IN 1894. (GLENBOW, NA-468-24)

THIS 1902 ILLUSTRATION BY C.W. JEFFERYS SHOWS ACTIVITY ON STEPHEN (8TH) AVENUE. IT INCLUDES PEOPLE FROM ALL WALKS OF LIFE IN CALGARY AT THE TURN OF THE CENTURY. (NATIONAL ARCHIVES OF CANADA, C124705)

THE BAR WAS A POPULAR RESORT FOR MEN IN CALGARY UNTIL THE ONSET OF PROHIBITION. THIS IS A VIEW OF THE PALACE HOTEL BAR IN 1903. STANDING IN THE FOREGROUND IS ITS PRO- PRIETOR, CARL WIETING. (GLENBOW, NA-4413-5)

CALGARY CHURCHES AND HOSPITALS.
JUST AFTER TURN OF CENTURY

Winnipeg. It had the advantage of being on the main line of the CPR and even when the Canadian Northern line went through Edmonton in 1905, Calgary did not surrender its role as a wholesale distribution centre. And as homesteading lands opened up along the Calgary & Edmonton Railway and east onto the open prairies, the city's role as a marketing centre expanded. A huge irrigation project developed by the CPR became a major attraction for prairie farmers. One of the highlights for visitors to Calgary was to be taken across the Langevin Bridge and along a trail past the red light district to see the CPR irrigation headgates where water from the Bow River began its long journey to the irrigated fields. Farther east, at Strathmore, demonstration farms exhibited apples and other crops grown with the aid of irrigation.

In 1904, the city fathers decided to abandon the system of street names such as Stephen and Atlantic avenues, replacing them with numbers. Many of the CPR-inspired titles remained permanently embedded in the concrete sidewalks but disappeared from signposts and city maps.[5] Meanwhile, the civic government took over a privately owned waterworks and built its own power plant as it rushed to provide basic amenities to its growing population. Between 1900 and 1914, the city expanded its boundaries three times, spreading north across the Bow River and south past the Elbow River until it encompassed the whole of township twenty-four.

The effects of Calgary's growth between 1900 and 1914 were staggering. There was an increase in every-thing—in the size of the city, the amenities, the shops and businesses, the cash flow, the amount of crime, and the number of real estate salesmen. It was a time for dreamers and schemers, and Calgary had plenty of both. When it was done, the city was overbuilt, oversized, and overspent, but never again would it be a sleepy prairie town.

A CAPITAL IDEA

The suggestion that the West should be divided into provinces was not new, but there needed to be a sizeable population and stable economy before such a goal could become a reality. This was provided after 1900 when thousands of homesteaders flocked to the region as part of a massive immigration scheme.

As early as 1890, Calgary hotelman James Reilly had indicated that the West needed more autonomy and by 1895 he was actively beating the drum in favour of provincial status for Alberta. He was supported by Arthur L. Sifton, another Calgarian, but they were opposed by Fort Macleod lawyer Frederick Haultain, the premier of the North-West Territories, and by Frank Oliver, the crusty editor of the *Edmonton Bulletin*. All were members of the North-West Legislative Assembly, an elected body which met in Regina but was firmly under the thumb of Ottawa.

During the last years of the nineteenth century, Calgary was the centre of agitation for provincial status while Edmonton was generally cool to the idea. The West's first official action was taken in 1896, when Dr. R.G. Brett, the member from Banff, recommended to the Legislative Assembly that the Districts of Alberta and Athabasca become a new province of Alberta. The move was blocked by Premier Haultain who favoured one large province for the vast area between Manitoba and British Columbia. However, the agitation was so strong, particularly from Calgary, that in 1900 the Legislative Assembly asked Ottawa to undertake an enquiry regarding the feasibility of provincial status. Two years later, a draft constitution was written in Regina but it followed Haultain's proposal of one big province.

Either way, Ottawa wasn't interested—at least not until after the general elections of 1904. One of the questions to be resolved for any new province was the rights of Catholic schools, a matter which almost tore Manitoba apart in 1896. Ottawa did not want to raise the ire of Catholic Quebec or Protestant Ontario just before an election.

At this time, the federal government was firmly in the hands of the Liberals so when no action was forthcoming, the Conservatives took up the cause of western autonomy. Members of the Territorial legislature were ostensibly non-partisan but Dr. Brett and Frederick Haultain were known to be Conservatives while Frank Oliver was an avowed Liberal. With the federal Conservatives stepping into the fray, the question of provincial autonomy became split along party lines. However, Prime Minister Wilfrid Laurier promised during the campaign that if the Liberals were re-elected, he would institute provincehood in the West.

The Liberals won the federal election of 1904 but they were reluctant to proceed with the formation of one big province as expounded by Conservative Haultain. There was a fear that such a large province might exert too much political influence, especially if Haultain were elected premier. Frank Oliver was cool to the whole idea. "It is but fair at the outset to say that the people of the Territories are by no means unanimously in favour of the immediate granting of provincial autonomy," he wrote in the *Edmonton Bulletin.*

Yet Laurier's promise could not be ignored, so early in 1905 legislation was introduced to the House of Commons. Instead of one large province, however, it provided for two—Alberta and Saskatchewan. Calgarians were pleased. As the *Herald* stated, "This can be regarded as excellent news for Calgary . . . With such an arrangement, Calgary will be the natural geographical centre and very likely to be selected as the capital."[1]

The legislation also made special provisions for Catholic or "separate" schools; this caused Sir Clifford Sifton, Minister of the Interior, to resign in anger. He was replaced by Frank Oliver, the Edmonton Liberal who was now empowered to implement the terms of the new Alberta Act. The *Calgary Herald* applauded the move for it believed that Oliver would work for the best interests of Alberta as a whole, not just for Edmonton. But to their shock, Calgarians learned that the new Act would name Edmonton, not Calgary, as the provisional capital of the province.

A meeting of the Calgary Board of Trade was held and a delegation dispatched to Ottawa to convince Laurier to change his mind. The group included some of Calgary's most important citizens: Mayor John Emerson, saddlemaker R.J. Hutchings, James Walker, Dr. E.H. Rouleau, W.M. Davidson, Charles A. Stewart, and W.H. Cushing. It was an all-party delegation, with the latter three being Liberals. When Oliver heard about the group, he immediately went to Ottawa himself to head them off. "Your government," he told the prime minister, "is still in honour bound to give the preference to where your friends are in the large majority, as compared with the place where your opponents are in the majority."[2] Laurier listened to Oliver, not the Calgary delegation, and Edmonton was named the provisional capital.

The choice was supposed to be temporary and would remain in effect only until a new provincial government could choose the permanent capital. However, there was a fear that the precedent caused by the selection would greatly affect the final outcome. "Under the cloak of political expediency," complained the *Herald*, "every rule of fair play and representative government has been violated . . . The Calgary representatives have been met openly with the suggestion at Ottawa: 'Had Calgary sent a Liberal to Parliament, things might have been different.' This is atrocious. Following to its legitimate conclusion, it makes support of the government a virtue, and support of the Opposition a crime."[3]

Furthermore, when the time came to draw the electoral boundaries for the new province, Oliver ignored the practice of appointing a bipartisan committee and sat down with fellow Liberal Peter Talbot to do it themselves. When they were finished, the twin cities of Edmonton and Strathcona had six seats in the new legislature and Calgary only one. It was the most flagrant piece of gerrymandering ever perpetrated on a new province, yet Oliver got away with it, even when the House of Commons was told that southern Alberta had a population of 120,834 and the north only 69,021.

Although there were probably more card-carrying Conservatives than Liberals in the new province, the influence of the federal Liberals on the provincial scene

RICHARD B. BENNETT WAS A SUCCESSFUL CALGARY LAWYER AND MEMBER OF THE TERRITORIAL LEGISLATURE WHEN ALBERTA BECAME A PROVINCE IN 1905. HE LATER BECAME PRIME MINISTER OF CANADA. (GLENBOW, NA-861-1)

was pervasive. Armed with the authority to lay the groundwork for the new province, they also set out to assure the future of their party. Given the influence of Oliver, no one was surprised when Liberals were named to the top positions in Alberta. George H. V. Bulyea, of Regina, was appointed Alberta's first lieutenant-governor and he selected Alexander Rutherford, a Liberal stalwart from Strathcona, to be the interim premier. Rutherford, in turn, named a five-man Liberal cabinet.

During the campaign for Alberta's first election late in 1905, the influence of the Liberals was immediately evident, even in the south. Accusations were made of patronage and bribery, both on the part of the federal Liberals and their provincial counterparts. Near the latter stages of the campaign, electors in northern Alberta were

told that a vote for the Conservatives was a vote for having the capital moved to Calgary. On election day, the Liberals swept the province, taking twenty-three of the twenty-five seats. Even the lone Calgary seat went to a Liberal, W.H. Cushing defeating R.B. Bennett.

After that, the selection of a permanent capital was almost a formality. According to historian Lewis G. Thomas:

The choice . . . aroused more public interest than any other act of the session. There were numerous contenders for the honour, but the real struggle was between Edmonton and Calgary. The issue transcended politics. The most enthusiastic supporter of Calgary's claims was her member, the Honourable

ALBERTA'S FIRST CABINET IN 1905 INCLUDED W.H.CUSHING, LOWER LEFT, A LUMBERMAN FROM CALGARY. OTHERS, LEFT TO RIGHT, ARE: W.T. FINDLAY, MEDICINE HAT; A.C. RUTHERFORD, STRATHCONA; LIEUT.-GOV. G.H.V. BULYEA; TOP: CHARLES C. CROSS, EDMONTON; AND DR. L.G. DEVEBER, LETHBRIDGE. (PROVINCIAL ARCHIVES OF ALBERTA, R117)

80

W.H. Cushing, and he was a cabinet minister. Cushing argued that Calgary was the business centre of the province, that the agitation for provincial status had been initiated in Calgary, that the cost of building would be less in Calgary . . . and that Calgary offered a free site.[4]

Edmontonians argued just as persuasively but in the end the vote was along geographical lines and the south simply didn't have enough votes. Six southern Albertans from Calgary, Lethbridge, Macleod, High River, Red Deer, Gleichen, Cardston, and Rosebud, all voted in favour of Calgary, but sixteen other members supported Edmonton.

Calgary had been soundly defeated but there was still another matter which needed to be settled. Later in the session, Premier Rutherford introduced legislation to establish a university for the province. In Saskatchewan, Regina had beat out Saskatoon for the provincial capital but in compensation, the northern city became the site of the university. Calgarians expected the same action to be followed by Alberta so they were visibly disappointed when the University Act failed to specify a location.

Rutherford had a strong personal interest in higher education and when the federal government refused to provide funds for a university site, he quietly purchased land in his own constituency of Strathcona, right across the river from Edmonton. Then, after the end of the second session in 1907, he announced that this would be the site of the University of Alberta. Judging from the press, the attitude of Calgarians was one of resignation. As the *Herald* commented: "The people of the south have tolerated the injustice of the location of the capital being fixed at the instigation of a clique of extreme party men interested in Edmonton. At that time the feeling of injustice was somewhat assuaged by assurances that the university would be placed at Calgary or some other point not in the north. Now that selfish and hoggish element has again turned down the south."[5] To make matters worse, five years later, Edmonton and Strathcona were amalgamated as a single city, giving it both the provincial capital and the university.

And then, as if that wasn't bad enough, when Calgary tried to establish its own university in 1912, the Edmonton-based provincial government blocked its attempt to achieve degree-granting status, claiming the province wasn't big enough to support two universities. Unable to give degrees or to affiliate with an eastern university, the Calgary institution withered and finally died in 1915.

These events caused considerable bitterness and resulted in a rivalry between Calgary and Edmonton which has become legendary. Such modern questions as airline routes, the location of convention centres and new industrial branch plants bring forth scathing attacks from each city's newspapers and civic development officers. Similarly, in the field of sports, matches between the hockey Oilers and Flames, and the football Eskimos and Stampeders, make winning a matter of civic pride.

When British poet Rupert Brooke visited Alberta in 1913, he noted, "It is imperative to praise Edmonton in Edmonton, but it is sudden death to praise it in Calgary. The partisans of each city proclaim its superiority to all the others in swiftness of growth, future population, size of buildings, price of land—by all recognized standards of excellence."[6]

THE HUNDRED THOUSAND CLUB

Calgary's great real estate boom started quietly and perhaps a little hesitantly in 1906. The city was still smarting over its loss of the provincial capital to its sister city to the north but was beginning to feel the effects of Clifford Sifton's immigration policies and the improvement in the world economy. The price of wheat had gone up, cattle were in demand, freight rates had been lowered, and there was a general feeling of optimism in the air.

The immigrants coming to the West weren't all farmers and homesteaders; professional people, tradesmen, and investors gravitated to Calgary, adding to the work force or bringing new businesses with them. This growth in turn fuelled the need for more houses and business buildings.

In 1906, the real estate market finally started to expand following gradual growth in the previous three years. As new manufacturing businesses were announced for East Calgary, property values there began to rise.

Similarly, the wholesale district on 9th and 10th avenues experienced a spurt of growth. In the downtown area, residential lots were in demand, mostly to meet the needs of incoming settlers but also because they were being purchased by speculators. By the summer of 1906, the *Calgary Herald* observed that "prices in the centre of the city are almost prohibitary to the working man who contemplates building a home. Within a half mile of the post office the man who is earning $50 to $60 a month would find it difficult to build at current prices. Within this radius there are practically no lots at less than $400."[1]

During the spring and summer, speculators were among the new arrivals, many of them hailing from the United States. They began to deal in suburban property, sometimes doubling the prices in six months. In Hillhurst, lots which had been selling for $75 in January were fetching $150 by July. In the Mission district, a lot on the corner of 17th Avenue and 4th Street SW jumped from $400 to $1,140 while at the Mills Estate above Scotchman's Hill, prices rose from $150 to $200.

The president of the Board of Trade, C.W. Rowley, said during the summer that "I do not know of any place in Canada where the growth is so rapid as it is in this city."[2] Among the new enterprises he noted were a mill by Calgary Milling Company, a factory for Alberta Biscuit Company, and warehouses for Winnipeg Paint & Glass, W.H. Brock & Company, G.F. Stephens & Company, and Ames Holden Company while in the planning stage was a warehouse for J.I. Case, the implement manufacturers.

"The surrounding country is developing quite as rapidly," he said. "Everywhere the American farmer is driving the ranchers back to the foot of the Rockies and in a few short years ranching in Alberta will be a thing of the past."[3]

The state of Calgary's economy—which had remained stagnant until late in 1902—was reflected in the property assessment figures which jumped to $7.7 million in 1906 and then skyrocketed to reach $132 million by 1913. Much of it, of course, was based on speculation.

But in the euphoria of rising property values and industrial growth, boosters believed that Calgary's potential was unlimited. When a Seattle magazine quoted a railway official's prediction that the city would have a population of 100,000 in fifteen years, they couldn't help but agree.

The question of population was always a sensitive matter for it was perceived to be the unequivocal indicator of prosperity and success. Thus when the Dominion census set Calgary's population at 14,203 for 1906, local boosters were sure the figure was low; even Henderson's directory, published in Winnipeg, gave an estimate of 20,000.

During the discussion of population figures, Fred Lynne, local manager of Bradstreets, a firm of financial advisers, decided to make the growth of the city his personal goal. He announced to the press that he was forming the Fifty Thousand Club, an organization which

would be dedicated to increasing Calgary's population to 50,000 by the year 1916. The Calgary Board of Trade, City Council, the daily newspapers, and probably every real estate salesman in town endorsed the idea. Lynne pointed out that Dallas had a Hundred and Fifty Thousand Club, Vancouver a Hundred Thousand Club, and that both cities had found this to be an effective means of promoting their centres.

An inaugural meeting was called for November 8, 1906, and an appeal was sent out for everyone to attend—men, women, children, and babies. According to an enthusiastic booster:

Men are wanted because they can reach men. Women are wanted because they can reach women, and sometimes have a slight influence over men. Children are wanted because they will become inoculated with the idea and also have an influence on uncles, aunts, and cousins not in Sunny Alberta. Babies are wanted because they will help increase the

CHARLES W. ROWLEY, PRESIDENT OF THE BOARD OF TRADE, GAVE HIS FULL SUPPORT IN 1906 TO A CAMPAIGN WHICH WOULD SEE 100,000 PEOPLE IN CALGARY IN TEN YEARS. (GLENBOW, NA-813-3)

LUKE DRAPER'S GROCERY STORE WAS DOING A THRIVING BUSINESS WHEN THIS PHOTOGRAPH WAS TAKEN AT THE BEGINNING OF CALGARY'S EXPANSION IN 1906. THE STORE WAS LOCATED ON 17TH AVENUE NEAR 2ND STREET SW. LEFT TO RIGHT ARE DELIVERYMAN SIDNEY BLIGHT, DICK TENNANT, AN UNIDENTIFIED CUSTOMER, AND OWNER LUKE DRAPER. (GLENBOW, NA-2959-9)

population, that is, they will grow up and can continue the good work.[4]

The initial meeting of the Fifty Thousand Club was a grand affair. It started off with a parade, led by the Calgary Citizens' Band and featuring boys with flaming torchlights as well as numerous "snorting, buzzing automobiles, filled with ladies and fur-clad gentlemen."[5] They made their way down Stephen Avenue to 1st Street West amid an explosion of fireworks and then congregated in the hall at Alexander Corner.

The meeting was officially opened by Mayor John Emerson and conducted by Senator James Lougheed, a man who was heavily involved in real estate. Lougheed praised the work of the organizers and said there was "no limit set to what can be done by enthusiasm and co-operation."[6] In turn, each of the organizers spoke, using such grand phrases as, "Calgary at present stands before America as an example of what can be done," and "Calgary should always lead in the western provinces."

But then R.J. Hutchings, the pioneer saddlemaker,

arose to announce that he was opposed to the formation of a Fifty Thousand Club. There was a hushed disbelief in the audience, for Hutchings was known to be one of Calgary's strongest boosters. "No," he said, "I am not in favor of a 50,000 club—but a 100,000 one!" His comments were greeted with wild enthusiasm. After all, a Seattle magazine had predicted a hundred thousand people for Calgary in fifteen years, so why stop at fifty thousand? In the euphoria of the meeting anything was possible.

Furniture dealer F.F. Higgs heartily endorsed the idea, claiming Calgary already had reached a point "where the next fifty or sixty thousand would be easier obtained than the first fifteen thousand. If we could make an increase of fifteen thousand in ten years past, we ought to make the hundred thousand in the next ten."

Riding on the crest of these optimistic outpourings, saddlemaker Hutchings was elected president of the Hundred Thousand Club, J.S. Scott of the *Calgary Herald* was named secretary, and Higgs was chosen treasurer. Among its officers were such Calgary luminaries as the Hon. W.H. Cushing, M.S. McCarthy, Fred C. Lowes, and R.A. Brocklebank. The club's objective was "to make Calgary the foremost city in the West, both commercially

and industrially, to induce manufacturers and capitalists to locate here and thus increase the population to 100,000."[7] Membership fees were set at a dollar a year, with women and children free. Calgary businesses would be expected to make donations to carry on the work of the non-profit club.

At this initial meeting, reality had given way to unbridled optimism. No one was prepared to accept the official census figures of 14,000 and even Henderson's estimate of 20,000 seemed low to some of the boosters. Given the pace of settlement, the active real estate market, and the explosion of new construction, a goal of 100,000 people in ten years was thought to be quite reasonable.

As soon as the club was formed, the Great West Land Company donated seventy-five dollars in gold for the best essay on the advantages of Calgary. The winner was E.L. Richardson, general manager of the Calgary Exhibition. The Hundred Thousand Club was so excited about his entry that the information was immediately published in an illustrated booklet, *Calgary Alberta: Commercial Metropolis of Western Canada,* and circulated all across the nation. Over the next several months, it became the primary tool for the promotion of the city.

Not surprisingly, it was an exercise in superlatives. It extolled the climate of Sunny Alberta, its impressive crop yields, the potential of irrigation, and the success of ranching. It emphasized the natural resources available for industrial use—water and electric power, natural gas, and vast coal fields—then went on to list the city's public and private schools and colleges. Richardson concluded by reviewing Calgary's growth, describing the city as "the commercial and industrial capital of Alberta."[8]

Calgarians tried to outdo each other in predicting a rosy future for the city as a result of the Hundred Thousand Club. Perhaps the most imaginative effort was a word picture of Calgary in 1916, ten years hence, after the fabled 100,000 mark had been met and exceeded. Arriving at a magnificent railway depot, a traveller in 1916 would be taken to an 800-room hotel, travelling along streets with eight-storey buildings and passing trolley cars and noiseless motor buses. On the hills overlooking the city would be great mansions. In this imaginary scenario, Sarah Bernhardt was appearing at the 3,000-seat Lyric Theatre[9] while at the other end of town 40,000 people were expected to be on hand to see Chicago and Calgary playing the third game in the World Series.

"Guess you do not realize how big this little town is?" said a Calgarian. "Since the 100,000 club started to work about ten years ago, the growth of the city has been phenomenal; and we are now a city of about a hundred and fifty thousand people, connected with every town within a radius of forty miles by suburban electric lines."[10] Needless to say, the imaginary Calgary of 1916 won the World Series.

Reality—at least over the next couple of years—proved to be quite different. During the winter of 1906-07, "a slight depression"[11] descended upon Calgary and remained for two years. In 1907, boosters continued to estimate the city's population at "more than 20,000" which was the same as they had done in 1906. During this time, the Hundred Thousand Club faithfully carried out its mandate, mailing literature, encouraging Calgarians to invite friends, relatives, and business acquaintances to move to the prairie city, and organizing excursions. It had a tent at the Dominion Exhibition and gave prizes for the best "Made in Calgary" window displays. The club moved into the Board of Trade offices and Charles H. Webster became the permanent secretary-treasurer. When he wasn't busy with the club, he worked for the Board of Trade.

Late in 1908, the nation's economy took an upswing and Calgary's faltering boom was revived. Its building permits increased fourfold in a single year and by 1909 its

PART OF THE PROMO-TIONAL ACTIVITIES OF THE HUNDRED THOUSAND CLUB INCLUDED AUTOMOBILE EXCURSIONS, AS INDICATED IN THIS 1912 POSTCARD. (GLENBOW, NA-1314-10)

population was estimated by Henderson's directory at 31,000. This was an impressive figure, if true, but still a far cry from 100,000. There can be little doubt, however, that the numbers were inflated. Even by 1910, when the population was said by promoters to be 44,360, people were talking more about Calgary's future than its present. The issuing of three permits in one day for a hotel, a business block, and a school was front page news. Much of the traffic through the city consisted of farmers buying land or homesteaders looking for a place to settle rather than tycoons establishing new factories.

By 1911, the boom had really swung into high gear. Boosters were estimating the city's population at 60,000 and were appalled and indignant when the official Dominion census put the number at 43,704. Why, they cried, that's where we were a year earlier, and everyone knew Calgary had grown phenomenally since then! The building permits for May alone, worth $3.6 million, were the fourth highest in Canada, surpassing even Toronto and Vancouver. No, Calgary would use its own estimate of 60,000 and not the federal figures.

By the summer of 1911, real estate dealers were experiencing their best year in history. Lots in Mount Royal were going for $2,000, in Mount Pleasant and Rideau Park for $550, and Elbow Park for $300. Even some of the new subdivisions of Pasadena, Eastborough, and Springwell were finding buyers. At that time, Bob Edwards warned his readers that "To the east of Calgary there are nearly 300,000 lots on the market at the present moment. To the north, where the gophers and badgers

gambol on the baldheaded, far from human ken, there are Additions and Parks till you can't rest . . . There is a wholesale bunco game in progress right here in Calgary."[12]

The Hundred Thousand Club was not forgotten now that the boom had really arrived. One of Calgary's most successful promoters, Fred C. Lowes, toured Toronto, Montreal, and New York, during the winter of 1911-12, telling the financiers, "I am firmly convinced that by 1915 the population of this city will have reached 100,000. I base this on what we have done in the past; on the development of the country around us; on industries assured and in prospect like, for instance, the Canadian Pacific shops, work on which, I am assured, will be commenced immediately. This one industry should increase our population ultimately by 20,000."[13]

The year 1912 seemed to confirm even the most optimistic predictions. New subdivisions were put on the market as fast as they could be surveyed. Roxboro Place in the south and Tuxedo on the North Hill became the showplaces of the real estate market and new homes were sold as soon as they were built. During the year, housing was provided for an additional 20,000 people in single family dwellings or apartment houses.

But the most impressive indication of Calgary's success was in the construction of new businesses. During 1912, work started on twenty-two warehouses, six garages, twelve stores, eight office buildings, and a num-

ber of factories, hotels, and government buildings. Among them were the Palliser Hotel, Hudson's Bay Company store, Tregillis's brick factory, CPR shops, Mountain Spring Brewery, a new court house, and a federal customs house. In all, more than $20 million in building permits were issued during the year—a figure that would not be surpassed in Calgary until 1949, forty-seven years later.

During the boom, roads were paved, subways built, streetcar lines laid out, dial telephones and natural gas introduced, bridges, schools, hospitals, churches, and a Carnegie library built, a University of Calgary established, a natural history museum opened, a city beautification plan commissioned from Thomas Mawson, and the first Calgary Stampede held. Even the most conservative booster believed that the city's population had passed 65,000 and reaching the 100,000-mark by 1915 was a certainty. To prove the point, city officials directed the police to make a census to include everyone, even those living in tents in Hillhurst, East Calgary, and along the north side of the Centre Street Bridge. When they were finished, the police had a tally of 61,340 people—not as much as the boosters predicted but far above the Dominion census figures. Instead of accepting this figure, however, promoters preferred a city directory's estimate of 73,000. Either way, the increase was impressive.

Even the Hundred Thousand Club was caught up in the fervour of 1912. The secretary-treasurer, Charles Webster, concluded he could be more profitably engaged investing in the Calgary boom rather than talking about it. Accordingly, he resigned his position and became a real

THE REV. JOHN MCDOUGALL, METHODIST MISSIONARY, DISAGREED WITH AUTHORITIES WHO WANTED TO SUPPRESS NATIVE CULTURE IN AN EFFORT TO TRANSFORM INDIANS INTO RANCHERS AND FARMERS. ONE EXAMPLE OF HIS VIEW-POINT OCCURRED IN 1912 WHEN HE ARRANGED FOR DOZENS OF INDIANS TO PARTICIPATE IN THE FIRST CALGARY STAMPEDE. THIS WAS DONE IN SPITE OF GOVERNMENT POLICIES PROHIBITING SUCH ACTIVITIES. MCDOUGALL IS SEEN HERE, PREPARING TO LEAD THE INDIAN CONTINGENT IN THE PARADE. (GLENBOW, NC-16-167)

BY 1912, DOWNTOWN CALGARY WAS REFLECTING THE RESULTS OF ITS REAL ESTATE BOOM. THIS IS A VIEW OF 8TH AVENUE, LOOKING EAST TOWARDS CENTRE STREET. MANY OF THE BUILDINGS IN THIS PICTURE ARE STILL STANDING. (GLENBOW, NA-644-9)

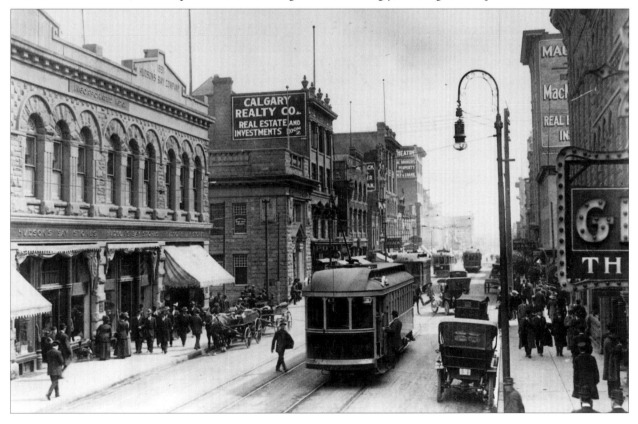

estate broker. By the end of the year, people were predicting that the magic 100,000 figure would be reached by 1913—two years early—so the organization was reconstituted as the Quarter Million Club.[14]

Of course, the buoyant times were not restricted to Calgary; throughout the West, immigrants flooded onto homestead lands, small towns flourished, and cities experienced a rapid growth in population. But the boom could not be sustained. High prices for housing and food, low wages, a limit to the West's agricultural and industrial productivity, and an overheated real estate market all combined in 1913 to bring the whole deck of cards crashing down. Funds from the London and New York money

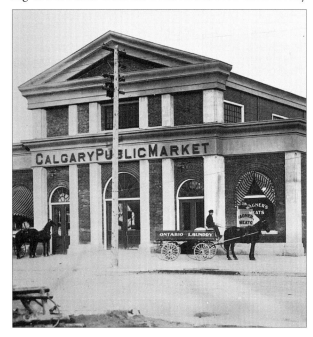

markets dried up and the cash flow for investment came to a sudden halt. During the summer of 1913, a Winnipeg official noted that "the present financial stringency is being felt very acutely throughout the whole Western Country and businessmen are inclined to take a gloomy view of the outlook."[15]

Calgary was luckier than some western cities in that its recession was delayed because of oil discoveries at Turner Valley. A number of entrepreneurs had been searching for oil since the discovery of natural gas in East Calgary in 1905 and on May 14, 1914, this paid off when the Calgary Petroleum Products' well, Dingman No.1, blew in. Overnight, the city became a madhouse as speculators and salesmen switched from real estate to oil. Dozens of companies were formed, stock certificates printed, and offices opened along the city's main thoroughfares. Most of the boom was pure speculation and few wells were ever drilled, causing Bob Edwards to comment, "The oil men are still as busy as bees, thus accounting for so many of us getting stung."[16] Among the companies which actually erected derricks and put drill bits into the earth in 1914 were Calgary Petroleum Products, Black Diamond, Fidelity Oil & Gas, Illinois Alberta, and Stokes-Stevens. The oil was there but more money could be made selling stocks than in actually drilling for oil.

The onset of World War One late in 1914 put an end to all the real estate and oil speculation. For the next four years, Calgary, and the rest of Canada, were preoccupied with the carnage in Europe.

As for the Hundred Thousand Club, it never reached its goal. At the next Dominion census, held in 1916, Calgary's official population was set at 56,514. Perhaps some people had left when the boom went bust and others were fighting in the trenches of Europe but there can be little doubt that Calgary never really came close to achieving its optimistic objective. In fact, Calgary's population did not pass 100,000 until 1946 during the city's second boom—the one that followed the Second World War.

If the promoters had stayed with the original Fifty Thousand Club they would have met their objective but that wasn't the idea. It was characteristic of Calgarians to set impossible goals with the firm belief that somehow they'd be achieved. Calgary tried hard, but didn't make it.

THE PRIVATELY OWNED CENTRE STREET BRIDGE

During the heady days of Calgary's real estate boom, speculators rushed to subdivide new properties and place them on the market as quickly as possible. Those adjacent to the city centre were easy to sell but lots farther afield needed accessibility and, if possible, a view.

The land across the Bow River on the North Hill offered good prospects but access was limited to the Louise Bridge, which led into the village of Hillhurst on the western outskirts of town, and to the Langevin Bridge, which was uncomfortably close to the brothels on Nose Creek. The area immediately north of downtown Calgary was desirable property but it was too hard to reach.

In 1906, entrepreneur A.J. McArthur decided that the prospects were too good to miss, so he acquired a piece of farm land at the top of the hill, subdivided it into lots, and registered it as Crescent Heights. He then formed the

Centre Street Bridge Company Limited and sold shares to other speculators and landholders on the North Hill. As plans progressed, lots were sold on the guarantee of a connecting bridge to the downtown area.

At this time, the area north of the river was not within the city limits so no permission was sought from the local authorities to erect a bridge. Instead, the company simply obtained rights to the properties on each side of the river and proceeded to build a steel and wooden structure.

It was a small narrow bridge consisting of three spans. It made no attempt to follow the north-south configuration of the streets but crossed at right angles to the river in the shortest possible distance. It started about 300 feet west of the present Centre Street Bridge and terminated just east of it.

The promotion was highly successful and by the time the city extended its borders in 1908 to take in Crescent Heights, a small village was already in place. The bridge company built a steep road from the bridge to the top of the hill and the city obligingly constructed wooden stairs for pedestrians. Crescent Heights became a comfortable middle class district with many of its residents regularly walking to and from work, thanks to the private bridge. Meanwhile, other districts such as Mount Pleasant and Rosedale were added to the North Hill and its occupants also became users of the span.

There was no doubt that the bridge was constructed in order to sell lots, just as John Hextall had built the Shouldice Bridge in order to sell lots in the new commu-

nity of Bowness. The only difference was that Hextall was able to make a deal whereby the city took over the bridge and Bowness Park in exchange for a streetcar line. The Crescent Heights promoters weren't so lucky. They offered the $17,000 bridge to the city for the construction costs but found no interest, even when they lowered the price to $10,000.

As soon as the bridge was opened, the city fathers found it provided an excellent short cut to haul gravel from the North Hill for building their downtown cement sidewalks. "So great was the traffic and the havoc to the planking," said company shareholder J.B. Paterson, "that in a short while holes were worn through, and repair was immediately necessary. Because the city had derived a direct benefit, had saved money by a shortened haul for their gravel . . . it was felt by all concerned that the city ought to have kept the bridge in repair."[1] The 1908 City Council agreed but no major improvements were made.

Then, when Calgary's construction boom began to heat up in 1910, contractors found that the base of the North Hill was an excellent place to dump the clay from their excavations. Soon, dozens of heavy wagons were rumbling back and forth over the bridge, further damaging the flooring. The company appealed to the city but all they got was a grudging agreement to make spot repairs and to grade the approaches. It wasn't their bridge, said the city engineer, so they had no responsibility for it. They also said it wasn't worth more than $7,000 but they made no move to buy it, even at that lower price.

By the spring of 1911, the Bow River Bridge

Company had had enough. Early in April, Arthur Bennett, secretary of the company, erected a toll gate and announced plans to charge both vehicles and pedestrians for the right to cross. When the first teamster was turned away he rushed to city hall to complain to the mayor.

Mayor John Mitchell seemed surprised and indignant, claiming that the city had spent large sums of money laying sidewalks and grading roads in Crescent Heights as well as making $3,000 in repairs to the bridge. Not so, replied Bennett. Repairs had been limited to patching a few holes in the floor caused by the heavy loads. As for the improvements in Crescent Heights, this was an ongoing part of the city's responsibility. The heavy wagon traffic had virtually destroyed the flooring in the bridge and if the city wouldn't pay for it, the money would have to come from toll fees.

Calgary contractors were the first to descend upon city hall. The site for the new Hudson's Bay Company store was being excavated and hundreds of loads of clay needed to be dumped on the North Hill site. If the wagons had to use Louise Bridge, the added costs of the circuitous trip would be exorbitant. On the other hand, they were not prepared to pay a fee for every load of clay taken across the bridge.

The second group to complain were the residents of Crescent Heights, especially when they learned that they too would have to pay the toll fee. Their anger was directed at the bridge company. One local resident was particularly irate. "The bridge was built by the property owners north of the Bow River to enhance the value of their land," he said, "and raise the value of the lots they were selling. They advertised the fact to all. A bridge would be built so that people would be within a short distance of the centre of the city, instead of about two miles off, which would have been the case if they had been obliged to go round by the Riverside Bridge or Morley Trail. Do they think people would have bought at those prices, or any price, if they had advertised that it was to be a private bridge and toll gates erected?"[2]

The bridge company, realizing that the backlash from Crescent Heights' residents would undermine its campaign, decided to abandon the toll fee and to close the bridge entirely for all heavy traffic. At the same time, pedestrians, horsemen, light rigs, and automobiles could cross free of charge. While this action wouldn't pay for repairs, at least it would prevent further damage. The company hoped it would also keep the pressure on city hall if the contractors and their heavy wagons were banned. Mayor Mitchell's only response was to declare war on the company by cancelling a $600 item in the civic budget which had been earmarked for minor repairs to the bridge.

A few days later, the directors of the bridge company met with officials at city hall. An officer of the company pointed out that a survey a year earlier had indicated that 1,200 people and more than 100 vehicles used the bridge daily. Estimates for the current year were 2,000 pedestrians and 200 vehicles. Obviously the bridge was now providing a public service and should be purchased by the city for $7,000. However, the meeting turned into a bitter and acrimonious confrontation.

"I am perfectly certain in saying that the council will not entertain your offer, gentlemen," said the mayor. "The bridge is not worth that amount of money."

"In that case," said one of the delegates, "it will be practically up to us to close the bridge. We cannot be responsible for damage suits that may result from persons using it in its present condition and we cannot pay for its maintenance."[3]

When the matter went before City Council, Alderman Adoniram Samis came to the defence of the bridge company. He pointed out that the city had given permission for the telephone company to string its lines across the bridge and that the city itself had wires across it for its electric street lighting. He made a motion that the city offer $6,000 for the structure. Alderman Hornby agreed but lowered the price to $5,000. He did not want to see the bridge closed, saying it "is being used by the public as much as any bridge the city owns. Why should people be forced to walk a considerable distance out of their way owing to the action of the city?"

The mayor and other aldermen were opposed but then another member of council came up with the novel idea of waiting to see if the bridge survived the spring floods. As a result, Mayor Mitchell obligingly made a motion "to have the question shelved until the big rush of water from the mountains."[4] One of the aldermen hoped the bridge would float away and their problem would be solved.

True to its threat, the Bow River Bridge Company closed down the bridge three days after the City Council meeting. Heavy wooden bars were erected at each end and some of the floor boards torn up to make the structure impassable. When he learned of this, city employee William Gardiner sent an urgent message to the commissioners, telling them of the closure. Commented a reporter:

There was a big laugh in the commissioners' office when this little epistle was read. It seemed so funny to the trio . . . However, it may be said that there was no laughter emitted by pedestrians and teamsters who were held up at the approaches of the structure which has caused so much squabbling."[5]

The mayor and aldermen weren't laughing. All the stranded North Hill residents were voters and clearly they were unhappy. As a compromise the mayor offered to raise the matter again at the May council meeting if only the bridge was reopened. However, before the matter could be considered, an irate citizen paid a nocturnal visit to the bridge and used an axe to cut away the barriers. They were immediately replaced and a guard placed at the site until after the council meeting.

The closure had placed the city in the position of making a decision: either build a new Centre Street Bridge immediately or maintain the old one. However, when the mayor put the question to the city commissioners, they admitted that they had no idea how much a new

bridge would cost. The city engineer said that a price of $7,000 for the steel in the old bridge was reasonable and that it would cost more than that to have a new supply delivered to the site; however, he was not prepared to recommend its purchase until he knew the cost of a new structure. At the direction of City Council, the commissioners were told to draw up plans for a new Centre Street Bridge and prepare a by-law for its construction and the purchase of the old bridge.

The Bow River Bridge Company then agreed to open the span for pedestrians; all other traffic would have to use the Louise or Langevin Bridge. Meanwhile, the city commissioners decided to neutralize the influence of both the Bow River Bridge Company and the bridge itself by extending streetcar service into the heart of the North Hill. Until this time, the line went just across the Louise Bridge to serve the residents of Hillhurst and Sunnyside but by July the engineers had pushed it all the way through to Crescent Heights.

"Only within this last six months has [Crescent Heights] formed a part of this great and enterprising city," said an ebullient reporter, "and yet what a change. The village [is now] supplied with car service, bringing the people within a few minutes distance of the centre of the city."[6] Travelling to Crescent Heights was definitely a rural experience. As noted, "It is a treat to get away from the baking streets of the city, and travel across the high lands with the cool breeze playing about you. The wide spreading green of the prairies, dotted with pleasant cottages, whilst out to the west is seen the splendid panorama of the Rocky Mountains. One gets as bright and healthy a trip for a nickel as one could desire."[7]

There can be little doubt that the new line was installed to mollify the Crescent Heights' residents and to defuse a politically sensitive situation. However, it still left the teamsters without their much-needed shortcut so they were obliged to take the roundabout route to reach the base of the North Hill.

In July, arrangements were completed to lease the bridge and open it fully to the public until the ratepayers had a chance to vote on its purchase for $7,000. This item was on the ballot in August but was roundly defeated. The lease was extended and a second vote was taken in March, 1912, this time for $5,000, but the ratepayers again turned it down.

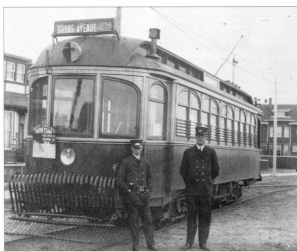

IN ORDER TO PROVIDE A LINK BETWEEN CRESCENT HEIGHTS AND DOWN-TOWN CALGARY, A STREETCAR LINE WAS EXTENDED NORTHWARD FROM SUNNYSIDE IN 1911. CONDUCTORS R.G. HOLLOWAY, LEFT, AND HENRY HOWARD POSE IN FRONT OF THE CRESCENT HEIGHTS CAR IN 1912. (GLENBOW, NA-1299-1)

The commissioners and the bridge company were now at an impasse, for the city had no money or plans for a new Centre Street Bridge but the electorate obviously were not prepared to dole out money for the old one. Another meeting was held and the commissioners offered to buy the bridge for a paltry $1,300, the money to come out of the city's operating budget and thus avoid another humiliating by-law. John Steinbrecker and Arthur Bennett, representatives of the bridge company, didn't like it but there wasn't much they could do. The voters of Calgary had spoken. So on June 15, 1912, they accepted the offer and the Centre Street Bridge officially became the property of the City of Calgary.

It continued to be used during the land boom of 1912 when dozens of new subdivisions were opened on the North Hill. Tuxedo Park became a showpiece while lots were sold in Regal Terrace and Balmoral, bringing thousands more people across the narrow span. Earlier, City Council had appointed a committee to develop a comprehensive plan for the future development of the downtown area, including the Centre Street Bridge, and British planner Thomas Mawson was engaged to make the survey. In the meantime, all development plans were put on hold. When Mawson considered a new Centre Street Bridge, there were two alternatives. One was a grandiose structure which would rise from the south bank to almost the top of the North Hill. The other was a low level bridge with elevators at the north end to raise vehicles to the top of the bank.

When Mawson's final plan was submitted in 1914, the real estate boom had already collapsed and the city had no money to pay for his flamboyant vision of marble buildings, statues, and pretentious towers. A plan for an imposing $469,000 bridge was unanimously rejected by voters late in 1913 but a more modest proposal was approved a year later. Meanwhile, the Centre Street Bridge kept getting older and more decrepit. Then, in June of 1915, when basic construction had already started on the new span, the river finally resolved the problem of the old one. The structure had become dangerously weakened by the rising flood waters and when City Engineer G.W. Craig and Commissioner James H. Garden went to inspect it, the whole north span collapsed and floated away. The two officials were dumped into the water but a fireman with a row boat succeeded

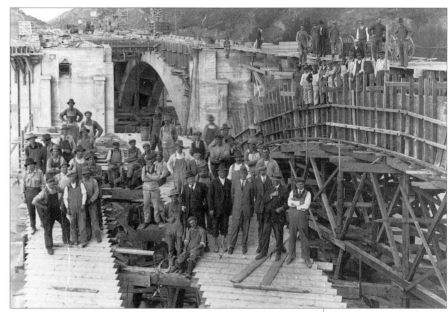

in rescuing them near the Langevin Bridge. A pedestrian crossing the bridge at the same time wasn't so lucky; he was carried out into the main stream and drowned.

The concrete work on the new bridge commenced that year and the new $375,000 Centre Street Bridge, complete with reposing lions and concrete turrets, was opened the following year. As for the old structure built by the Bow River Bridge Company, what was left of it was sold for scrap to the provincial Department of Highways in 1917 for $1,500—for a profit of $200.

THE BIRTH OF CHINATOWN

The Chinese have been a part of Calgary since the first railway construction workers were laid off in British Columbia in the 1880s and came across the mountains looking for work. Some became cooks at ranches, coal mines, and lumber camps while others congregated in places like Calgary where they opened laundries and restaurants or obtained work as domestics. The population was almost entirely male, for the government levied a head tax of fifty dollars and imposed other restrictions on every Chinese entering Canada.

At first the tiny population was scattered throughout the town, the men sometimes living at their places of business. They were quiet and law abiding but often subjected to overt discrimination because of their race and language. They were accused of being habitual gamblers, of sending all their earnings out of the country, and of being unsanitary and spreading disease. In 1892, this discrimination took an ominous turn when a Chinese, newly arrived from Canton, was found to have the dreaded smallpox.

In the weeks that followed, a quarantine camp was established on Nose Creek but in spite of precautions there were several smallpox deaths in the white community. The anger of the townspeople erupted one evening after a drunken crowd left a cricket match and descended on the Chinese merchants, destroying property and beating up several men. The local police and mayor made no effort to intervene and only the quick action of the Mounted Police prevented further trouble.

By 1900 there were about eighty Chinese living in Calgary—all men—and the nucleus of a Chinatown existed on 9th Avenue and on Centre Street by the CPR station. Less than half the town's Chinese population lived there, the rest residing behind their laundries and grocery stores. The focal point of Chinatown was the Kwong Man Yuen Restaurant on Centre Street. In back was a small room where the men could meet and visit.[1]

However, the area could never become a true Chinatown, for it was hemmed in by other downtown establishments. At its peak, it never exceeded a laundry, two grocery stores, two restaurants, and a boarding house. A year later, when a Chinese Christian mission was opened on 10th Avenue, businesses shifted to locations nearby and along 1st Street SW. The first mission building was provided by Thomas Underwood in response to an appeal from the Presbyterian Church. When it proved to be too small, Underwood built a new mission on his own property at 215 - 10th Avenue SW. It was a two-storey frame building with accommodation for thirty-five residents and rooms for English language instruction and religious services.

THOMAS UNDERWOOD, MAYOR OF CALGARY IN 1902-03, WAS A STRONG SUPPORTER OF THE CHINESE COMMUNITY AND ITS CHRISTIAN MISSION. WHEN THE PRESENT CHINATOWN WAS ESTABLISHED, HE HELPED BUILD A NEW MISSION ON 2ND AVENUE SW IN 1911. (GLENBOW, NA-2639-1)

Before long, some twelve Chinese businesses were spread out around the mission. They were described by Jack McHugh as "a few small frame buildings close to Tenth Avenue on the east side, including one or two Chinese restaurants, one or two laundries and some small dwellings. Also I think there was a Chinese merchant selling goods imported from China."[2] A reporter who visited one of the rooming houses in 1909 stated: "Almost every room in the building held Chinese men, talking, gambling, smoking and sleeping. The building is partitioned off in narrow sections, and these sections are again partitioned off in infinitesimal rooms."[3]

Another man went to a Chinese restaurant after midnight when his usual cafe was closed. "Through an uninviting store," he said, "typical of the usual Chinese establishment, we wended our way to an upper room, where three or four tables covered with oil cloth, surrounded with a few chairs, were the only furniture in a room which was otherwise bare and comfortless."[4] The group ordered Chinese noodles—which they were unable to eat with chopsticks—and completed their fare with a pot of tea and "pork and chicken, chopped into small pieces which, dipped in piquant sauce, helped to satisfy our appetites."[5]

Bareness was not necessarily a feature of Chinese establishments. When local Chinese gathered at Wing Kee's hall in 1906 to organize the Chinese Empire Reform Association, the room was decorated with flags, bunting, photographs, literature and mottoes. At one end of the hall was "a many-colored picture of a Chinese God before which was placed oranges, nuts, cake, sweets, etc . . . Over the picture was a canopy of red satin handsomely embroidered with gold and silver lace."[6] Spearheading the new association were Wing Kee, Lam Kee, Louie Bell, Louie Kwong, Charlie Hing, Kwong Man Yuen, Wah Kee, Joe George, Chong Kee, and Sun Hong Lee.

As the population of Calgary expanded during the first decade, so did the Chinese community. About a third of the people lived in the 10th Avenue Chinatown while the rest were across from the CPR station or scattered throughout the city. Of all the locations, the 10th Avenue one seemed to offer the best chance for expansion because of the number of vacant lots in the area.

However, the situation changed suddenly in 1910 when the Canadian Northern Railway laid a branch line into Calgary. Its plans called for the line to reach the downtown area by following a route a hundred feet east of 1st Street SW to 10th Avenue, and there to build sidings, freight sheds, and offices. This would not only wipe out part of the existing Chinatown but it meant a rapid escalation in property values. As most Chinese rented their shops and rooms, they were required to move when much of the land was sold to speculators.

As it turned out, the City of Calgary and Canadian Northern could not agree on terms so the line to the downtown area was never built. By this time, however, the Chinese had already made arrangements to move. Eight merchants led by W.R. Wing purchased property on the corner of Centre Street and 2nd Avenue, just south of the old wooden Centre Street Bridge. Their plans called for a two-storey brick building which would house eight stores with apartments on the second floor. This was the beginning of Chinatown.

When local residents heard about the purchase, they immediately protested to city council and demanded that the sale be disallowed. They wanted Chinese to be moved out of the downtown area and segregated from the rest of the Calgary community. Spokesman for the group, lawyer James Short, said the Chinese "ought to be treated much the same as an infectious disease . . . They live like rabbits in a warren and 30 of them crowd into where five white people would ordinarily reside."[7] He then presented the following petition:

We undersigned ratepayers living nearest to lots 1, 2 and 3 in block 7, plan c, Calgary, hereby petition your honorable body to prevent Chinese from occupying said lots, on the ground that the residence of Chinese in the neighborhood deteriorates the value of the surrounding property, and makes it objectionable as a residential district, contrary to provisions of bylaw 1090.[8]

Among those signing the petition were W.R. Hull, F.H. Brown, S.H. Might, James Short, Thomas Pain, G.B. Cook, and Nat Lynn.

The reaction of the mayor was one of sympathy and helplessness. "They have a permit now and I don't see how we can legally stop them," he told the petitioners. But the feeling was running high among the crowd that jammed the commissioner's office, and the mayor promised to take the matter to city council to see if anything could be done.

An investigation revealed that all the proper specifications and contracts had been filed with the building inspector several weeks earlier. The proposal had been advertised in the newspapers as required by law but no one seemed to have noticed it. Not only that, but when certain parties suggested that the transactions all be handled by architects McDougall & Forester so that no one would know that Chinese were involved, the merchants refused. Commented J.B. Henderson, "With commendable faith in British law and fair play, these Chinese merchants themselves decided on the more straightforward course and let the contract direct, having satisfied themselves that every requirement of the law had been fulfilled."[9] When the building inspector did not receive any protests about the $20,000 building, he issued a building permit. Now, if the city made any attempt to rescind, it would be open to legal action.

The *Calgary Herald* came out strongly against the proposed Chinatown. It claimed that "There is no use trying to argue the thing out by contending that the Chinese must be treated before the law on an equality with our people."[10] It saw Chinatown as "a menace to a white city" and if the Chinese insisted on living in Calgary they should be controlled so as "not to injure the property or endanger the happiness and comfort of the whites."[11]

Some Calgary residents came up with the idea of forcing the Chinese to settle on land near Mewata Park or at Birney's market near the Langevin Bridge. The *Calgary News-Telegram* favoured the latter site as the Chinese would "least interfere or come in contact with the white residents . . . The China men would be practically isolated."[12]

In response to the uproar, the mayor struck a committee made up of twelve ratepayers and twelve chosen by the Chinese community. However, even before it held its first meeting, the *Herald* insisted that the white representatives should not compromise "by giving away in the slightest degree to the present proposals of the Chinese residents."[13]

The committee was an impressive one. On the ratepayers side were James Short, John Emmerson, J.G. and Sheriff Van Wart, A.L. Cameron, Henry Haskins, William Georgeson, W. Livingstone, H.E. Lambert, E.A. Dagg, and J. MacKenzie. For the Chinese were Louie Kwong, Chong Kee, Charlie Yee, Yuen Sun, and Kwong Wing Kee, representing shopkeepers; Ho Lem representing restaurants; Wong Yuen Jan representing travellers; Joe Giough representing laundries; and Wong Chui representing cooks. In addition, the Chinese delegation selected Thomas Underwood, Rev. R.H. Standerwick, W. Porterfield, and T. Humphries to be part of the committee.

By the time the committee held its first public meeting, tempers had cooled and more moderate voices began to be heard. Acting Mayor Brocklebank, parks superintendent J. Buchanan, and commissioner A.G. Graves all favoured leaving the Chinese alone. Dr. Thomas Dawson, the medical health officer, came out strongly in favour of the new Chinatown and refuted statements that the Chinese were unsanitary. "Personally," he said, "a Chinaman is more cleanly than many whites, such as Galicians or a certain class of Italians."[14] Police chief Mackie also came to the defence of the Chinese, stating that they were "a harmless people, and they have not given the police much trouble . . . They have proven themselves to be law-abiding."[15]

When the committee met with the mayor and council, there were a few surprises. For example, both sides objected to the Birney market site, although for different reasons. And Henry Haskins, who was supposed to be part of the ratepayers group, came out strongly in favour of the Chinese. After listening to an argument between an alderman and one of the ratepayers, Haskins observed wryly that "he knew Chinamen who were better than white men present."[16]

Speaking for the Chinese delegation, Ho Lem said he had lived in Calgary for nine years and had no trouble with his neighbours near the CPR station. He didn't think the residents at the new location "were so superior to his white neighbors that they could raise any serious objections."[17] As one person after another rose to speak, it was obvious that the dissidents were receiving little or no support. They seemed to agree with ratepayer William Georgeson who concluded, "We had better let them be."[18]

One positive suggestion which came from the meeting was that overcrowding could contribute to the spread of disease, but that this was true of any people or of any enclave in the city. As a result, the meeting ended by unanimously passing a resolution that "this committee recommend to the council that the bylaws of the city be revised to regulate the number of persons who reside or sleep in a given floor space." No mention was made of the Chinese.

The fight seemed to be over but the dissidents had not given up. Instead, they appeared at the next meeting of city council with a petition recommending that the block of land from 4th Avenue south to the Bow River be rezoned for residential use. Under their proposed regulations, the only way a store could be established in the area would be through a petition of local property owners. Privately, the dissidents said they wanted the by-law on the books only long enough to get rid of the Chinese, then have it revoked so that they could begin promoting their holdings for business use.

The dissidents claimed their petition had been signed by a majority of ratepayers in the proposed area but an investigation showed that there were 418 property owners and only 32 had signed. On that basis, civic authorities refused to act on the petition.

The agitation finally ended there. Over the next few years, more property was purchased in the district and a

HO LEM WAS ONE OF THE LEADERS OF THE CHINESE COMMUNITY AFTER HIS ARRIVAL IN CALGARY ABOUT 1902. HE REPRESENTED THE RESTAURANT OWNERS AT A MEETING WITH CIVIC AUTHORITIES IN 1910 TO DECIDE ON THE FUTURE OF CHINATOWN. THIS PORTRAIT WAS TAKEN IN 1921 WHILE HE WAS ON THE BOARD OF THE CALGARY CHINESE MISSION. (GLENBOW, NA-5520-1)

BOYS AND MISSION STAFF AT THE CHINESE YMCA IN THE TEENS. THE MISSION WAS LOCATED AT 120 SECOND AVENUE SW. (GLENBOW, NA-2193-8)

real Chinatown came into existence. A new Christian mission, partly financed by Thomas Underwood, was built at 120 - 2nd Avenue SW in 1911, followed by the first Chinese YMCA in Canada. Sun Yat Sen visited the community in 1911 and two years later a Chinese National League was formed. By the early 1920s, Calgary's Chinatown had its own school, Freemasons, and family associations or tongs. Many Chinese still preferred to live in other parts of the city, usually near their shops, but Chinatown became the social and cultural centre of Calgary's Chinese community.

WOMEN OF CALGARY

The real estate boom of 1910-12 had a dramatic effect upon the class system in Calgary. The old established families mixed with newly arrived industrialists and paper-rich speculators to such an extent that it was hard to tell the old money from the new. In social gatherings, a jewellery-bedecked woman in a Parisian gown might be the wife of a banker or she could be a secretary or a self-employed real estate agent.

There generally had been four classes of women in Calgary at the turn of the century—the elite, the middle class, the poor, and the "soiled doves." By 1910, the first two categories had become hopelessly muddled, at least in the minds of some people, but all figured prominently in the social life of the community and had their own impact on the development of the city.

Earlier, the elite had been confined to the wives or daughters of well-established successful businessmen, church leaders, or pillars of the community. Men like Justice James F. Macleod, Bishop William C. Pinkham, Pat Burns, James Lougheed, Paddy Nolan, James Walker, and Samuel Shaw had wives and families who reflected the advantages of money and education. The women lived in fine homes with servants, presided at afternoon teas, wore their finest gowns to the theatres and balls, had days set aside for receiving visitors, and usually supported projects which were helpful to the community such as hospitals, churches, and aid to the poor.

However, by 1910 they were being joined by the wives of *nouveau riche* entrepreneurs and Americans

with their own views of an elite society. A local writer, confused by the situation remarked that "one is uncertain just who is in society, with a capital S, and who is outside the pale."[1]

It wasn't always that way. When Mrs. W. Henry Scovil arrived in Calgary in 1902 she was immediately accepted into the social set because of the status of her husband, a manufacturer's agent. Within her first month, she attended a dance given by Calgary bankers in the hall at Alexander Corner; an "at home" and dance by bachelor William Roper Hull at the opera house; and an afternoon tea at the ranch of Col. Lawrence Herchmer. "All the ladies have their afternoon to receive," she said, "but the

EDITH AND CONSTANCE SANDERS, SEEN HERE IN 1901, WERE PART OF CALGARY'S SOCIAL ELITE. THEIR FATHER, GILBERT E. SANDERS, WAS A MOUNTED POLICE OFFICER AND MAGISTRATE. (GLENBOW, NA-919-56)

ONE OF THE SOCIAL CENTRES OF CALGARY AT THE TURN OF THE CENTURY WAS THE PAT BURNS HOME, LOCATED ON 4TH STREET BETWEEN 12TH AND 13TH AVENUES SW. (GLENBOW, NA-1655-1)

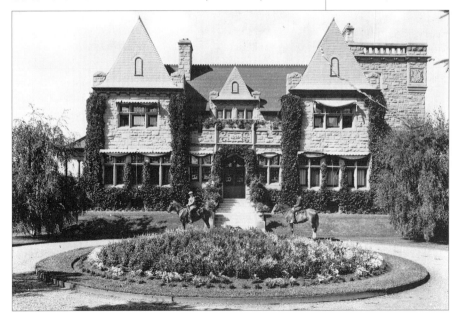

majority receive only once a month, say the second Thursday or perhaps the first Friday."[2]

Two of the *grande dames* of Calgary society during this period were Mrs. Jean Pinkham and Mrs. Isobel Lougheed. Pinkham was the wife of W. Cyprian Pinkham, the Anglican Bishop of Calgary. She had arrived in Calgary in 1889 and from the beginning, her home, Bishop's Court, was a social centre of the town. Jean Pinkham was organizer and first president of the Women's Hospital Aid Society, president of the Anglican Women's Auxiliary, and presided over meetings of the Local Council of Women, Victorian Order of Nurses, and Independent Order Daughters of the Empire. Mrs. Lougheed—later Lady Lougheed—came to Calgary as a girl and later married a lawyer, James Lougheed. When he was appointed to the Senate in 1889, she was already the "first lady" of Calgary. She entertained visiting royalty and was known as a gracious hostess. After the turn of the century, for example, a reporter noted that "Mrs. Lougheed throws open her magnificent home to the many charitable organizations of the city, and her spacious ball room is thronged several times during the season."[3]

By 1910, Calgary's new-found wealth and its booster-ism had drawn a new breed of women into the city, many of them well educated, independent, and decidedly democratic in their views of an elite society. According to one woman, "English dignity, Yankee freedom, and Canadian common sense unite to form an excellent combination, as unique as charming. Society in Calgary is more dignified than in the average American town, more varied than in the average British town, and more sparkling than in the average Canadian town."

A society matron newly arrived from Ontario learned about Calgary's unique social class when she snubbed a Calgary woman who would have been considered a nobody back East, then learned to her horror that she was part of "the Holy of Holies, the innermost shrine of polite society in Calgary." Similarly, an English woman was appalled at the class of women accepted into Calgary society. She commented:

Positively, girls in offices are received everywhere. My husband says it gives him quite a start to meet the girl who took dictation from him that day at a bridge table that same night. And the tradespeople! Fancy meeting your grocer and his wife, as well as your stenographer, at a dinner-dance. Isn't it quite too dreadful?

The genteel women from England and Ontario often considered the Americans to be unsophisticated and gauche. They could not understand how local society could accept a woman like Janet Sparrow, who owned her own insurance and real estate business and drove her own car. Yet she was a respected member of Calgary society, a recognized equestrian, and had won the golf championship at the local country club.

The Americans, on the other hand, had little use for the affectations of British society. One woman who lived in a magnificent home in Mount Royal was appalled at the English, their "haw-haw ways, and their attempts to introduce polo and lawn tennis."

There were a number of clubs and organizations where women played a dominant role. One of these was the Calgary Golf and Country Club. When its new course was officially opened in 1911, the event was reported on the society pages of local newspapers, not in the sports columns. Women like Mrs. Paddy Nolan, Mrs. J.J. Young, and Mrs. Bob Newbolt regularly poured tea at the club on Saturday afternoons and the annual club dance was one of the social events of the year.

In fact, dances were a major part of Calgary's social life. "Never was there a town so devoted to the terpsichorean art," commented a local writer. "Calgarians count that week lost which had not at least one dance, and often there are as many as four dances in one week. The golf club, the hunt club, the tennis club, the cricket club, the Daughters of the Empire, the Girls' Hospital Aid, the old timers, and the Assemblies—these are a few of the regular dances."

Two organizations which were dedicated to education and public service were the Woman's Canadian

Club and the Local Council of Women, both formed in 1911. The former was the largest women's organization in Calgary, with fifty-three charter members and a total membership of 275 within the first month. Its first major project was to work with the Women's Hospital Auxiliary and the Girls' Hospital Auxiliary to combat tuberculosis and to agitate for the construction of a sanatorium for Calgary. They were also involved in public health legislation and city beautification.

The middle class in Calgary included a broad segment of the population. The women included wives of shopkeepers, labourers, and businessmen as well as single girls who often were stenographers, maids, store clerks, teachers, and nurses. A few were Calgary-born but most of them were from elsewhere. Some had come with their families while others had gravitated to the West in a spirit of adventure. Well represented were

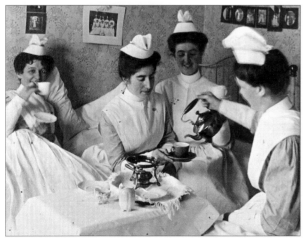

non-English women—German, Italian, Ukrainian, Scandinavian, Black, Oriental—who had been part of the massive immigration from Europe and the United States.

Housing was a problem for many families when they arrived during the boom. If it was summer, they could live in tents until they had a house built or could rent suitable accommodation; otherwise they had to take what they could find. A single woman who came during the summer of 1911 searched for three weeks before she could find suitable furnished accommodation. She started by checking the want ads but by the time she went to the addresses, the places were either already rented or she was "candidly told that the rooms could not be let to ladies, for men are so little bother and are out all day."[4]

Next she tried the real estate offices but the salesmen were interested only in selling her a lot or a finished house. At last she found a salesman who agreed to take her to two furnished places which were for rent. The first was a cosy little bungalow on the North Hill but the rent was a prohibitive $85 a month. The second was a larger old house but it was virtually bare of furnishings for $75 a month. Then, just as she was about ready to give up, "something was presented that really did look and was feasible and we are now happily installed in what might have looked very humble and small three weeks ago but today a truly paradise."[5]

The shortage of housing affected families as well as single women. A man named Will Norman emigrated from Yorkshire and decided to build a home in the Parkhill district. Once he had obtained the property, he sent for his wife and children but they had to live in rented quarters until the house was ready. When they arrived, the family was not impressed. "Dad had cleaned and whitewashed the place and put blue-dotted curtains at the windows," recalled his daughter. "Mom was so happy to be with her man at last that she tried to hold back her disappointment, but later admitted she thought it 'nowt but a cowshed.'"[6]

For much of the boom period, housing always seemed to be inadequate for the burgeoning population. In many instances, all the suites in a new apartment house were rented long before the building was completed. But living in Calgary during the boom period could be an exciting experience, especially for young single women. In 1907, for example, the census showed that

AS OWNERS OF A NEWSPAPER AND A STATIONERY STORE, THE YOUNGS WERE PART OF THE BUSINESS ELITE IN CALGARY. HERE, CORRECTLY ATTIRED FOR A GARDEN PARTY IN 1908 ARE, LEFT TO RIGHT, EFFIE YOUNG, MRS. D.J. YOUNG, LUCILLA YOUNG, MABEL YOUNG, AND MRS. J.J. YOUNG. (GLENBOW, NA-4954-20)

NURSES AT THE CALGARY GENERAL HOSPITAL BREAK FOR TEA IN 1904. NURSING WAS ONE OF THE FEW OCCUPATIONS AVAILABLE TO WOMEN AT THE TURN OF THE CENTURY. (GLENBOW, NA-2600-3)

THIS SECRETARY TAKES DICTATION FROM DANIEL MACLEOD, OF MACLEOD BROTHERS CLOTHIERS, IN THE TEENS. POSITIONS FOR WOMEN AT THAT TIME WERE USUALLY LIMITED TO NURSES, TEACHERS, SECRETARIES, CLERKS, OR HOUSEKEEPERS. (GLENBOW, NA-2640-4)

BY THE TIME OF THE REAL ESTATE BOOM, CALGARY'S LARGELY ENGLISH AND AMERICAN COMMUNITIES HAD BEEN ENRICHED BY IMMIGRANTS FROM GERMANY, THE UKRAINE, ITALY, AND OTHER EUROPEAN AND ASIAN COUNTRIES. THIS IS THE VIOLINI FAMILY, WHO EMIGRATED FROM ITALY TO CANADA. (GLENBOW, NA-5141-1)

there were three men to every woman. "There are so many young men and so few young women," lamented the *Albertan,* "that somebody was bound to get left in the cold."[7]

Upon arriving in the city, a girl was "immediately surrounded by a swarm of masculine butterflies." They invited her to dances, offered to take her on buggy rides, and showered her with theatre tickets. Even girls of no apparent beauty or winning personalities were not immune from the attention of male swains. "I know of one case where a lady was married two months after her arrival in Calgary," said the scribe. "Such instances are very common. This is the happy hunting ground for husbands."

Married women faced less pleasurable times for they often had difficulty in making ends meet. Not only was housing expensive, but the inflated prices extended to retail goods as well. Grocery prices were often double those of Toronto. Not only that, but most storekeepers refused to deal in pennies, rounding prices off to the nearest nickel. Most people grew their own vegetables, otherwise they were purchased from Chinese market gardeners who had large fields in the Pump Hill district. In the fall, local farmers brought loads of potatoes in to the city market.

Entertainment was as varied as the people themselves. A relatively inexpensive family outing consisted of taking the streetcar to Bowness Park for a picnic while in winter there was skating on the Elbow River. Sports of all kinds were common and women often participated. In 1913 a ladies hockey team was formed and played teams in Okotoks, Red Deer, and other places. Women also played softball, curling, tennis, and many other sports available at that time.

With the rapid growth of Calgary and the heavy volume of European immigration, the poor soon became a visible part of the community. They lived in tents and shacks along the Bow River or occupied cheap rooms in East Calgary where they depended upon the largesse of the city, local churches, and philanthropies in order to survive.

Often the woman was the only breadwinner, doing cleaning or housework to bring in a few dollars to support her family, including a sick or drunken husband. In some instances, the families were recent immigrants who should never have passed the government's medical examinations and were ultimately deported. Others had suffered a series of tragedies and reverses and had virtually given up.

In 1912, a reporter visited a tent and shack town near Louise Bridge. "After a trip through one of these settlements," he wrote, "one is forced to confess that the homes of the 'other half' present a pitifully striking contrast to the magnificent abodes of Mount Royal or the palatial dwellings of Calgary's fine residential quarters."[8] He saw a roughly built one-room shack which housed a family of eight. Nearby were an elderly couple who had just run out of food and, "after winding our way through a labyrinth of tents, shacks and other indescribable dwellings," he came to a Scottish family who had spent their last five dollars to rent a miserable hovel for a month. The man was dying of tuberculosis and his pregnant wife was doing her best to hold her family together. There also was a widow whose husband had just died and she was left with three children. She was taking in sewing

and receiving charitable help to buy food and pay the eight-dollar rent for her tiny shack.

Some of the poor were ne'er-do-wells who had drifted to Calgary because of its booming economy. They included gamblers, confidence men, laggards, and other undesirable types. Often they were accompanied by a disillusioned and downtrodden woman who had the task of trying to feed her family and keep a roof over their heads. For example, when a man and his family arrived from

Newcastle, England, they didn't have a cent in their pockets. The family included a husband, pregnant wife, and two children. The man was the son of a prominent English solicitor but he had been a useless loafer in the Old Country and had refused to work. Finally, his father had paid the family's passage to Canada just to get them out the way. In Calgary, the man still wouldn't work so two months later, after the woman had given birth, the whole bunch were sent back to England.

Life could be difficult in other ways. For example, a gruelling experience was recounted by a woman who became ill and was suspected of having smallpox. She was taken to the "pest house," an isolated building on the prairies of North Hill at 16th Avenue NE. She was dumped at the front door and told to find her own way to her quarters. There were eleven patients in the building and no staff; the healthier ones were expected to look after those who were ill and to do the cooking. The only furnishings were beds with no sheets and wooden chairs with hard backs. There were no books, no newspapers, and no blinds on the windows.

"There are no clean towels," the woman reported. "Water is brought up to the hospital every other day and is stored in tubs and old tin cans. The blankets are used time and again. When one patient passes out of the building, the blankets are thrown in a heap to be used by the next person who is sent to the institution."[9]

The woman remained confined until the doctor was convinced that she did not have smallpox. She then had to disinfect her own clothes and check herself out.

When a newspaper reporter asked Dr. Estey, the medical health officer, if the woman's story was true, he admitted that it was. "It isn't a place of which the city can by any means be proud," he said. "It is quite true that the convalescent patients are asked to do work and attend to the needs of the others . . . and, as a matter of fact, it is almost impossible to get anybody to do work in the smallpox hospital."

Besides questionable health services and inadequate housing, the poor also suffered from a lack of employment opportunities, even in the boom times. As a result, teenaged girls were sometimes tempted into prostitution as a way of escaping the misery of daily life. A good example occurred in 1911, when a couple tried to convince sixteen-year-old Bertha Pearson that she should become a prostitute. She had emigrated to Canada from her native Sweden and because of a dispute with her parents she left home to become a servant for a family in East Calgary. While there, she was approached by a woman who invited her to come and live with her. She painted "an attractive picture of living a life of ease and luxury, having lots of money and good clothes, and going to places of entertainment."[10] When the girl showed an interest, she was sent to the red light district but the house had been under surveillance and as soon as Bertha went inside, the place was raided and she was returned to her family.

Prostitution had been a part of Calgary life since the first railway construction crews arrived in 1883. Initially, there had been a small red light district in East Calgary in the shacks which had been abandoned when the town moved to the west side of the Elbow River. Later, the area north of 9th Avenue East and east of 2nd Street East was a haven for prostitutes. Then, when the Langevin Bridge was built, the valley of Nose Creek became a well-established red light district.

In 1906, when reformers demanded a suppression of gambling and prostitution, police chief English stated flatly, "There are no houses of prostitution in Calgary."[11] He also claimed that drunkenness was not conspicuous, there were no illegal saloons, and gambling was almost unknown. Anyone who read his interview in the *Albertan* must have either laughed aloud or snorted in anger. Under Chief English, according to historian James Gray, Calgary was one of the most wide-open towns in the whole Canadian West.[12] There were nine or ten well-known brothels within the city limits, as well as others at Nose Creek and South Coulee outside of town. The latter was just off the Macleod Trail near the Mountain Springs Brewery.

Immediately prior to the civic elections of 1906, there was agitation for a crackdown on the brothels. During this time, a reporter from the *Albertan* visited the houses in a red light district and described what he saw.

These places with two exceptions are all close together on a street which everyone knows—except the chief of police. They are small wooden cottages with

ONE OF CALGARY'S MADAMS DURING THE TEENS WAS IRENE WALKER, WHO WENT UNDER SEVERAL ALIASES INCLUDING PAULINE FAIR. SHE CAME TO CALGARY FROM THE UNITED STATES. (GLENBOW, NA-625-16)

discreet, shuttered fronts. Access is ordinarily obtained from the rear. Within, the bare little boarded rooms do not offer much in the way of gilded luxury; there are none of the rich stuffs, the enervating perfume, the shaded lights usually associated in the imagination with such abodes. A cheap little kerosene lamp supplies the illumination and a decidedly unornamental little round stove the warmth.[13]

In spite of periodic crackdowns, the traffic in girls continued unabated in Calgary during the next three or four years. By 1909, it was apparent that Chief English was not prepared to suppress prostitution and gambling so he was fired and replaced by his deputy, Thomas Mackie. The new chief's philosophy may have been different from those of his predecessor but the results were virtually the same. He could arrest the madams and girls but either they got off with small fines or the charges were dismissed for lack of evidence. Sometimes the women were run out of town, but when this happened they were soon replaced.

When Chief Mackie failed, he was replaced in 1912 by Alfred Cuddy, a professional policeman from Toronto. Cuddy quickly put the bigger houses out of business but he was never able to clean out the downtown area. In the end, the First World War did more to change the prostitution scene in Calgary than any moral reform league or police raids. Nose Creek was too far away from the Sarcee military camp, so the houses were gradually abandoned and the area east of Centre Street resumed its role as Calgary's main red light district. The onset of prohibition in 1916 further reduced the number of brothels, for liquor had been a necessary supplement to the trade.

Prostitution was never completely eradicated from Calgary, but the days of wide-open red light districts,

complicity of the police chief, and general acceptance by the public ended with the demise of Nose Creek.

Not only that, but by the end of the decade the role of many women on the frontier had changed drastically. No longer were they restricted to housework, teaching, and nursing. Women were in business, both as staff and as management; they were involved in social work, the arts, and community activities. They had the vote, served in labour organizations, and were entrepreneurs. At the same time, the social set remained sacrosanct, the old families now mingling comfortably with the newcomers at teas, sporting events, and social gatherings. By the end of World War One, the women of Calgary had evolved from the primitive conditions of the Victorian age and were active participants in a burgeoning city.

WAR AND ITS AFTERMATH

PRELUDE TO BATTLE

CALGARIANS WERE NOT WARLIKE BY INCLINATION BUT THERE WERE ENOUGH EX-IMPERIAL
SOLDIERS AND MOUNTED POLICEMEN AROUND THAT THE IDEA OF HAVING A MILITIA ARMY APPEALED
TO THEM. SOME HAD SERVED IN THE ALBERTA FIELD FORCE OF 1885 WHILE A NUMBER OF OTHERS WERE BOER
WAR VETERANS. BESIDES, COWBOYS AND RANCHERS WERE NATURALLY DRAWN TO CAVALRY UNITS.

Calgary's first experience with a permanent militia force occurred in 1901 when the federal government authorized the formation of three squadrons of militia cavalry for Alberta. One of these, "G" Squadron, was located in Calgary and by 1903 it was conducting a summer camp under canvas on James Walker's property, now the Inglewood Bird Sanctuary. Walker was, of course, an ex-Mountie.

In 1904, the summer soldiers moved to Victoria Park where they trained in horsemanship, musketry, and marching drill. A year later, this group was reorganized as the 15th Light Horse under the benevolent eye of Colonel Walker, their commanding officer. Now that he was in charge, the training camp moved back to his estate.

In 1911, the first major training camp for southern Alberta was held at Reservoir Park, at the present Currie Barracks. There were more than 2,000 militia in attendance from Edmonton, Lethbridge, Medicine Hat, and other centres. By this time, Calgary had several militia units, including the Canadian Army Service Corps, 103rd Regiment (Calgary Rifles), and the 17th Cavalry Field Ambulance. None of them had their own armouries for winter training but rented space wherever they could find it and paraded at local school grounds.

In July, 1914, when Archduke Ferdinand was assassinated in Sarajevo, the *Calgary Herald* stated: "All hope of averting the war catastrophe has been abandoned. All Europe will soon be involved in the greatest conflict the world has ever seen."[1] And when the announcement finally came, newsboys dashed through the streets of Calgary yelling the news and selling "Extras" of the *Albertan, Herald*, and *News-Telegram*. Crowds milled downtown and anxiously watched for bulletins flashed on the *Herald's* notice boards.

"Not even in the height of the real estate or oil excitement was there such an outburst of pent up feelings," commented the *Herald*. "Each fresh bulletin was greeted with enthusiastic cheering and the streets were soon thronged for blocks with people eager for more particulars."[2]

A brass band assembled and crowds joined in singing patriotic songs. There were feelings of exultation and confidence that the British would put a quick end to the military aggressions of the Kaiser.

Perhaps some of the mothers feared for their enthusiastic young sons and their fathers remembered the devastation of the Boer War but they were silent. One comment was that "It is going to be a terrible war, but it will clear up a lot of things." Just how terrible it would be, no one could envision.

One superstitious soul looked toward the western sky and saw that the moon was blood red, an ominous sign. It was just the smoke from the forest fires, someone said, don't worry about it. Calgary was going to war.

At the Reservoir Park, summer training was already underway, so hundreds of weekend soldiers were already in uniform and in training. As soon as recuiting started, they would be the first to go.

CALGARY GOES TO WAR

When war erupted in Europe on August 4, 1914, Calgarians knew that Canada would become involved in the conflict. They were part of the British Empire so any war which involved England was also their war. As the Canadian government began to mobilize militia units for active service, young men flocked to the recruiting offices, anxious to get overseas before the fight was over. Young Britishers enlisted in the Canadian army or booked passage back to the Old Country while Boer War veterans were among the first to offer their services.

E.D. "Buck" Harrison was appointed Calgary's recruiting officer and was given quarters in the basement of a building on 6th Avenue owned by a man offering a sure cure for rheumatism. One of the first to be signed up was an old Imperial sergeant who was sent out onto the streets to let everyone know the office was open. As the men flocked in, they were examined by a medical doctor or, when there were too many applicants, the veterinary captain was pressed into service. As he said, "I have been examining horses all day; surely I can pass a few men."[1]

Three weeks later, the first contingent of 240 soldiers left for Valcartier, Quebec, to be followed by 1,300 officers and men in another three weeks. These soldiers, part

of the First Canadian Division, were training in England before the end of the year.

As soon as they had been dispatched, recruitment started on the Second Canadian Division. Two main infantry battalions were raised in Calgary and district. The 31st Battalion under Lt. Col. A. H. Bell became known as "Bell's Bulldogs" or the "Fighting 31st" while the 50th Battalion under Lt. Col. E.G. Mason was referred to as the "Mason's Man-Eaters" or the "Suicide Battalion." Many Calgarians also joined the "Fighting 10th" Battalion, enlisted in the navy, or were attached to support units of the Canadian Expeditionary Force.

There was a tremendous enthusiasm among the entire population, almost as though the Allies were engaged in a holy war. The *Calgary Herald* at the onset of the conflict said that "success will crown our banners no Britisher doubts, for God is with the right."[2] Patriotic organizations and churches encouraged enlistment, then set to work to provide support for the boys overseas. During war, thousands of socks, ditty bags, and food packages were shipped to England and France. The Salvation Army, Red Cross, Belgian Relief Fund,

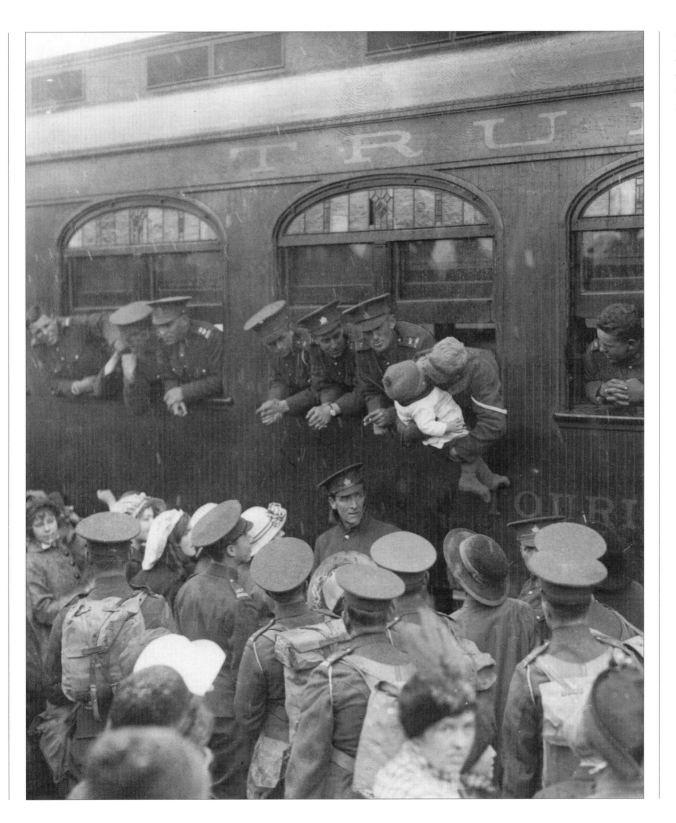

SOLDIERS OF THE 82ND INFANTRY SAY GOODBYE TO THEIR LOVED ONES AT THE CALGARY STATION IN 1916. (GLENBOW, NA-3965-5)

MEMBERS OF THE 50TH
BATTALION, TO BECOME
KNOWN AS THE "SUICIDE
BATTALION," PARADE
THROUGH CALGARY
BEFORE LEAVING FOR
EUROPE. (GLENBOW,
NA-3419-3)

TO HELP IN THE WAR
EFFORT, A CALGARY
NEWSPAPER ORGANIZED
A DRIVE TO COLLECT
KNITTED SOCKS FOR THE
SOLDIERS OVERSEAS.
HERE, A WAGON LOAD IS
READIED FOR SHIPMENT
IN 1916. (GLENBOW,
NA-1567-4)

brother Bill enlisted in the 82nd Battalion (Lieut. Col. W.A. Lowry). A month later, my father, who was past 50, dyed his hair, lied about his age and also enlisted in the 82nd. Then 17 year old Albert, who had just started to work as an apprentice baker, joined the Army Service Corps. At 15, I found myself at the head of the family.[3]

The war provided a much-needed economic boost for the city. The camp at Reservoir Park, which had served as a summer bivouac for the militia, was not adequate for the army's needs so after considerable negotiation, a long-term lease was arranged between the Sarcees and the military authorities for the site of Sarcee Camp, which became the headquarters for Military District 13. It opened in May of 1915 as a tent city with only a few wooden buildings. Within days, it was occupied by the 50th, 51st and 56th Infantry Battalions, the 20th Field Battery, and the 12th and 13th Canadian Mounted Rifles. Also at the camp were the Canadian Army Medical Corps, Service Corps and Ordnance Corps.

As quickly as the new recruits could be trained, they were shipped off to the East and ultimately to the scene of conflict. By the end of the war, some 40,000 men had passed through the camp. As a result, there were lucrative business opportunities as soldiers spent their pay.

Within a short time, a row of wooden buildings which gloried in the name of Sarcee City sprang up along the outskirts of the base. Here, enterprising merchants had a pool hall, two theatres, shooting gallery, photographic and souvenir shop, a bakery, barber shop, tailor shop, and several cafes to help relieve the soldiers of their money. Also, a number of prostitutes moved into the area and peddled their wares from the nearby hills. "After the war ended," said Fred Kennedy, "some wags would insist that the depressions on the prairies were not really buffalo wallows but were actually the work of countless hundreds of soldiers who had humped their way through the twilight hours at the cost of three days pay."[4]

Meanwhile, the glamour of war began to pale as Canadian soldiers died by the thousands in the trenches of France. The killing reached a peak during 1916 when the British and Commonwealth forces lost 60,000 men on the first day of the offensive at The Somme. In a six-

Canadian Patriotic Fund, and other war relief agencies were well supported, as were the war bond drives.

In Calgary, as in most western cities, the war meant shortages—manpower, foodstuffs, and many manufactured goods. In the latter part of the war, sugar, meat, and other commodities were rationed. The newspapers were filled with war news and there were constant pressures to enlist. Fred Kennedy, later a senior newspaperman and columnist at *The Albertan*, recalled what happened in his home:

In the winter of 1914, the war started to involve my family. My brother Tom was the first to go. He enlisted in the 31st Battalion, a unit . . . which soon earned an enviable reputation as a fighting battalion of the first water. In the spring of 1915, my eldest

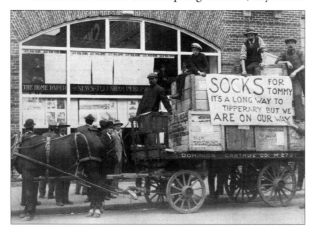

month period, Calgary's 31st Battalion lost more than half its strength, with 130 killed, 495 wounded, and four missing. And in a single battle on September 15, 1916, only 318 of the 722 men of the battalion came through

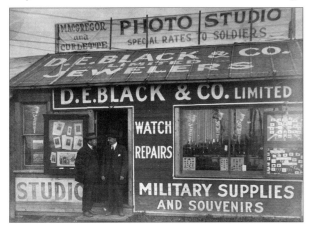

unscathed. The 50th Battalion suffered similar heavy casualties; on November 18 it lost 230 men a fight at the Regina trench. A total of 260 officers and men went "over the top" to attack German lines and only one officer and 30 men came back unwounded. These were mostly Calgary and southern Alberta men.

A disproportionately high number of officers were killed during these attacks. Among them were such notables as Lt. Ernest Pinkham, the son of Bishop Pinkham; Lt. Rex Pryce-Jones, son of department store owner A.W. Pryce-Jones; and Major J. Frank Costigan, son of lawyer John Costigan. Among the many other officers killed in action were Lts. D.J. Campbell, Leonard Hextall, L.R. Swain, Ernest Thom, and E.T. Toole. By the summer of 1916, Calgary's daily newspapers were carrying long lists of the casualties, including photographs of many of the fallen soldiers.

Fred Kennedy was a junior staffer on the *Calgary News-Telegram* at this time. He was paid 25 cents for every officer's photograph he could get from the grieving family, 20 cents for a sergeant or corporal, and 15 cents for a private. "I hated the job right from the start but the financial returns were good," he recalled. "I carried out this assignment for two years, and for years afterwards, I was haunted by the faces of sobbing wives, mothers and children who had not yet recovered from the shock of the 'Sincerely regret to inform you that . . .'" One day, after he had collected eight such photographs, he

returned home to find that his mother had received an official telegram saying that his brother Tom had been wounded in action. "I gave up that job the very next day," he said.

The early war years became prosperous ones for Calgary. Not only were profits to be made from the presence of a large military base, but crops were good and grain prices increased significantly. Although Calgary was a city of 56,000, its fortunes still rose and fell with the agricultural economy.

The war years gave impetus to the reform and social gospel movements to make sweeping changes in the way people lived. One of these occurred when a majority of electors in the province voted in favour of total prohibition. This was implemented on July 1, 1916, and completely altered the social fabric of the province. Bars and liquor stores disappeared and with them went the problems of men spending their entire paycheques on booze, treating their friends, and reeling home perhaps to beat up their wives. But the bars were replaced by the illegal importation of liquor and consequent bootlegging.

A COMMUNITY OF SHOPS AND ENTERTAINMENT MUSHROOMED JUST OUTSIDE OF THE MILITARY CAMP TO SERVE THE NEEDS OF SOLDIERS. KNOWN AS SARCEE CITY, IT INCLUDED THIS SOUVENIR AND WATCH REPAIR SHOP. (GLENBOW, NA-1551-1)

PTE. JOHN PATTISON OF CALGARY WAS AWARDED THE VICTORIA CROSS AT VIMY RIDGE IN 1917. HE WAS WITH THE 50TH BATTALION ATTACKING ENEMY LINES WHEN THEY WERE PINNED DOWN BY A GERMAN MACHINE GUN. PATTISON DASHED FORWARD, HURLED GRENADES AT THE EMPLACEMENT, THEN WIPED OUT THE REMAINING GUNNERS WITH HIS BAYONET. PATTISON WAS KILLED IN ACTION A FEW DAYS LATER. (GLENBOW, NA-4025-1)

Drinking now moved from the men's domain in the bars and entered private homes where it often became a family affair, sometimes with tragic consequences.

Prohibition was distinguished by its failure rather than its success. However, it remained in effect until 1923, when it was replaced by limited beer sales in hotels and strictly controlled government liquor stores.

Another change in society during the war years was extending to women the right to vote. This had long been a goal of the women's movements, encouraged by the suffrage movement in England. The voice of Alberta women was finally heard in 1916 when they were given the provincial vote, and two years later when they got the federal vote. The movement had strong support from the leading women's clubs in Calgary such as the Local Council of Women and Women's Christian Temperance Union, and from leaders like Alice Jamieson, widow of Calgary's former mayor, and Alberta's "Famous Five"— Nellie McClung, Emily Murphy, Louise McKinney, Irene Parlby, and Henrietta Edwards.

In the provincial election in 1917, two women ran for the legislature—Louise McKinney from Claresholm and Roberta McAdams, a nursing sister serving in

England, who ran as one of the two armed services representatives. Both were elected. McAdams served only one term, then married Calgary lawyer Harvey Price. He entered the oil business while she became active in a number of organizations, including the Local Council of Women, Women's Literary Club, Mount Royal Education Club, and the Calgary Council of Home and School.

When the war ended on November 11, 1918, Calgary—and Canada—faced a host of new problems. What to do with the surge of returned veterans? How will

they find jobs? What about the growing dissatisfaction among the labour unions? How can Canada's economy sustain a peacetime economy?

Yet there was the euphoria of parades of returning soldiers, brass bands, waving flags, and decorated archways. In 1919 Calgary organized a huge Victory Stampede—the first since the heady days of 1912—and a few weeks later everyone turned out to welcome Edward, the Prince of Wales. He was a great hero among

returned Canadian soldiers and the general public, not only because he was a son of King George V, but because of the active role he had played in the war. He had spent the latter part of 1918 with the Canadian Corps under General Sir Arthur Currie and was with the Canadians when they entered Lille. To Canadians, he was their own special hero who had been with their boys overseas. As a result, his tour was a triumphant event, with thousands of Calgarians turning out to see the young prince. By the time he left, Calgary was ready to enter the "Roaring Twenties."

ONE BIG UNION

During the prosperity of World War One, labour in the West experienced the most dramatic growth in its history, the unions almost doubling in size. However, wartime restrictions, the high cost of living, poor working conditions, and the intransigence of mine and industrial owners had fostered a large radical element within union ranks. Although the eastern-based Trades and Labour Congress (TLC) tended to be conservative in its approach to union grievances, many of the rank-and-file in the West wanted militant strike action and direct political involvement. The success of the Bolshevik Revolution in Russia was held as an example of what workers could accomplish by unified action.

When the TLC continued to pursue conservative policies at its 1918 annual assembly in Quebec, a group of militant union men organized a Western Labour Conference to be held in Calgary in the spring of 1919. The idea was to unite left-wing supporters and overthrow the conservatives at the next TLC convention.

Calgary was chosen because it was mid-way between the two strongest hotbeds of left-wing militancy—Winnipeg and Vancouver. Also, in an unusual move, the British Columbia Federation of Labour decided to hold its annual meeting in Calgary just before the Western Labour Conference. In this way, the B.C. delegates from the interior would have to travel to only one location.

Calgary in 1919 had some strong left-wing union supporters including A.G. Broatch, a city alderman, and R.J. Tallon, head of the Calgary Trades and Labour Council. The leading organizer of the convention was David Rees, an official of the United Mine Workers of America (UMWA) and vice-president of the TLC. He believed that if the western unions could formulate some progressive policies they would gain the support of eastern unionists and force the TLC to take a more aggressive stand in dealings with management and the government.

The B.C. Federation meetings, held in Calgary's Labour Temple, started to go awry almost from the outset. One of the federation's first resolutions was for a six-hour day and five-day week but when Rees said that such a radical proposal would have to be submitted to their respective international unions in the United States, delegates noisily rejected the idea. Instead, they defiantly

TOP LEFT: LOUISE CRUMMY MCKINNEY WAS A LEADING PROPONENT OF WOMEN'S RIGHTS IN ALBERTA. IN 1917, SHE WAS THE FIRST WOMAN ELECTED TO A LEGISLATURE IN THE BRITISH EMPIRE WHEN SHE BECAME AN ALBERTA MLA. (GLENBOW, NA-1731-3)

TOP RIGHT: ROBERTA MACADAMS WAS A NURSING SISTER IN ENGLAND WHEN SHE BECAME A SUCCESSFUL ARMED SERVICES CANDIDATE FOR THE ALBERTA LEGISLATURE IN 1917. AFTER SERVING ONE TERM SHE BECAME ACTIVE IN A NUMBER OF CALGARY ORGANIZATIONS, INCLUDING THE LOCAL COUNCIL OF WOMEN. (GLENBOW, NA-1476-2)

BOTTOM LEFT: NELLIE MCCLUNG WAS A FAMOUS CANADIAN AUTHOR AND SUPPORTER OF WOMEN'S RIGHTS. HER HOME IS STILL STANDING IN MOUNT ROYAL. (GLENBOW, NA-1514-3)

BOTTOM RIGHT: ALICE JAMIESON, WIFE OF CALGARY'S MAYOR, BECAME THE FIRST WOMAN JUDGE OF A JUVENILE COURT IN THE BRITISH EMPIRE AND CANADA'S SECOND FEMALE MAGISTRATE. (GLENBOW, NA-2315-1)

passed the resolution which called for a general strike if the demand wasn't met.

This direct action came as a surprise to many of the unionists, even the left-wingers, for every delegate there was a member of an international union which had set rules to follow before strike action could take place. But as the meeting continued, delegates became more and more strident in their rejection of the international unions. Thomas Grogan, for example, representing the

A CALGARY NEWSPAPER ARGUED THAT THE BALLOT BOX AND NOT THE VIOLENT DEMONSTRATIONS OF THE OBU WOULD SOLVE THE COUNTRY'S LABOUR PROBLEMS. THIS CARTOON APPEARED IN THE ALBERTA NON PARTISAN ON MAY 22, 1919, JUST BEFORE CALGARY WORKERS WENT OUT ON STRIKE.

The World's Greatest Problem!

THE O.B.U & DIRECT ACTION IS NEEDED TO FREE THE WORKER FROM THE EXPLOITER OF LABOR

HERE IS THE PLACE FOR US TO SETTLE OUR GRIEVANCES PEACEABLY AND PERMANENTLY

THE BALLOT BOX

WHAT IS THE ANSWER?

boilermakers union, "scathingly denounced the international bodies, whom he characterized as tapeworms."[1] By the third day, the radicals had taken control of the meeting and pushed through a resolution, "That this convention recommends to its affiliated memberships that they sever affiliation with their international organizations and that steps be taken to form an industrial organization of all workers."[2]

The Western Labour Conference convened at Paget Hall next to the Anglican cathedral on March 13, 1919, immediately following the stormy British Columbia sessions. There were more than 200 delegates in attendance from the four western provinces and a few from Fort William, Ontario. They represented mine workers, loggers, machinists, fishermen, boilermakers, and a host of other unions. As with the B.C. sessions, David Rees

chaired the opening meeting. He had a detailed agenda to plan a strategy for bringing the TLC more into line with left-wing radicalism.

The sessions started quietly enough. The secretary read a number of predictable resolutions: that the Soviet system of electing representatives from industries was more effective than Canada's present form of government; that sympathy be expressed for the Russian Bolshevik and German Spartacan revolutions; and that jailed union activists be released.

When Rees explained how a united western stand could alter the policies of the TLC, he was quickly rebuffed by one of the delegates who said that the original intention of the conference had changed; there were more important matters to consider. Rees—who was the most respected voice of left-wing moderation at the meeting—tried to reason with the dissidents but without success. To make matters worse, he had to leave the conference after the first day to attend a UMWA meeting in Indianapolis. The chairmanship was then taken by Calgary labour leader R.J. Tallon whose sympathies lay entirely with the radicals. From that point on, a handful of revolutionaries dominated the sessions and convinced the delegates that the aims of labour would be met through radical action.

On March 14, the morning following Rees's departure, the conference agreed to recommend to their unions that they break away from the American Federation of Labor (AFL) and the TLC. In their place they would form a group known as the One Big Union (OBU) which would be based on Marxist philosophies and would bring all workers of Canada into a single union. It was one of the most radical ideas ever proposed in the history of Canadian labour. And to emphasize its left-wing stand, the meeting demanded that Allied troops fighting the Bolsheviks in Russia be immediately withdrawn or the OBU would call a general strike for June 1. It also advocated the use of sympathy strikes if any of its members had clashes with specific industries.

Calgary alderman A.G. Broatch argued against the idea of strikes, remarking that they "had always proved a failure."[3] Instead, he suggested that union members enter the political arena, as he had done, to work from the inside. Joe Knight, an Edmonton delegate, responded that "the waste paper basket is the proper place" for such an idea. But other unionists also favoured political involvement and the matter was argued vociferously before it was finally defeated.

When the conference ended on March 15, Calgary had seen the organization of a Bolshevik-inspired organization which was dedicated to a doctrine of revolutionary unionism. Elected to the central committee were W.A. Pritchard and V.R. Midgley of Vancouver, R.J. Johns of Winnipeg, Joe Knight of Edmonton, and J. Naylor of Cumberland, B.C. They were to develop general policies while the rest of the delegates would take the proposals back to their memberships for ratification by May 1.

Predictably, the *Calgary Herald* immediately attacked the new organization. While admitting "the workers have legitimate cause in certain directions for grievance against capitalism," it urged its readers to guard against "the revolutionary movement which the 'Reds' of the labor organizations in the west would like to force upon us."[4] However, the newspaper believed there was little likelihood that the OBU would ever be accepted by the various unions.

How wrong it was. Although the OBU as an active organization lasted for only three or four years, it left an indelible and violent mark on the history of western labour. Its first test came just two months after the Calgary meeting and before its charter had been ratified by the rank-and-file. When the Winnipeg Trades and Labour Council called for a strike on behalf of the building and metals trade, the organizers of the One Big Union were swift to offer their support. The walkout— the Winnipeg General Strike—was one of the biggest in Canadian history, involving more than 30,000 workers.

When the Winnipeg strike committee appealed to other cities to support them, the Calgary Trades and Labour Council was in complete accord. Led by J.S. Hooley, the labour council was dominated by OBU adherents including R.H. Parkyn, G. Sangster, and R.J. Tallon. However, the strike call sharply divided the union ranks in Calgary, many being opposed either to strike action or to the radicalism of the OBU group.

When the walkout occurred on May 26, the strongest support came from workers at the CPR shops and Riverside Iron Works. These included blacksmiths, sheet metalworkers, pipefitters, and boilermakers, while from other unions came the postal workers, express men, and flour and feed workers. And as the strike wore on, plumbers, steamfitters, telegraphers, and others also walked out. However, some of the unions essential to the success of a general strike—carpenters, bricklayers, electrical workers, painters, printers, and telephone operators— refused to join. At its peak, not more than 2,000 of Calgary's 30,000 union men had taken part in the walkout.

Meanwhile, the federal government and local industries began to take retaliatory action. Businessmen set up a Calgary Citizens Committee to combat the strike and to encourage its members to hire non-union labour during the walkout. The federal government fired the 185 post office employees in Calgary and replaced them with non-union labour, while Dominion Express and Canadian National Railways ordered its striking staff to return to work or face dismissal.

After two weeks of ineffectual strike action, union men began drifting back to work, starting with the express men and followed by the telegraphers and building trades. In Winnipeg, the general strike climaxed on June 21 when the Mounted Police charged into a crowd of strikers, resulting in two people being killed and thirty injured. Four days later, the strikers admitted defeat and returned to work. In Calgary, the last holdouts at the Ogden shops reluctantly went back to their jobs. The Calgary sympathy strike had been a failure.

Within union ranks, the walkout created a violent backlash against the left-wing agitators. A short time later, the Calgary Trades and Labour Council was purged of its OBU supporters and the Mounted Police followed up the action by raiding the homes of known OBU officers. At Alderman Broatch's residence, the police seized the minute books and records of the OBU while in other homes illegal Bolshevik pamphlets and publications were found.

Yet the OBU was not destroyed. While it never again became an influence in Calgary, it drew hundreds of workers to its ranks from other parts of the West and by 1920 it had more than 50,000 members. But the old line labour organizations were not willing to surrender to the radical Marxist upstart. The TLC and AFL united with the Canadian government and major businesses to launch strong counter attacks against the OBU. Then, as divisions occurred within its own body, the union lost rank-and-file support almost as quickly as it had gained it. By 1923 it had been reduced to a minor dissident group and was finally absorbed into the Canadian Labour Congress in 1956.

The formation of the One Big Union had been Calgary's first experience as a centre for dissent but it would not be the last. In 1932, another left-wing group held its organizational meeting in the city. It became the Co-operative Commonwealth Federation (CCF) which later evolved into the New Democratic Party. And three years later, in 1935, Calgary became the site for a meeting of proponents of a new monetary theory for Canada—the Social Credit Party.

BOB EDWARDS AND PROHIBITION

Calgary was up in arms over more than war and labour unions in the teens and twenties. The question of drink became a raging debate which pitched the "wets" against the "drys." And one of the most notable combatants was the redoubtable Robert Chambers "Bob" Edwards. With

BOB EDWARDS, EDITOR OF THE **CALGARY EYE OPENER**. (GLENBOW, NA-450-1)

a skilful blend of humour, news, and comments on social and political events of the day he had developed a faithful following who looked forward to each issue of the *Calgary Eye Opener*, usually published weekly or, as he stated, sometimes "semi-occasionally." As early as 1908 Edwards was printing more than 18,500 copies of his newspaper, with 4,000 being sold in Toronto alone.

From the beginning of his first paper in Wetaskiwin in 1897 to the twenty-year run of the *Eye Opener* from 1902 to 1922, Edwards made no secret of the fact that he had a drinking problem. For example, on January 2, 1903, he wrote:

Yes, yes. This paper will appear henceforth with unfailing regularity. Horace says: 'Mingle a little folly with your wisdom.' We have been following this advice with considerable ardour, but find that it don't pay so we propose trying the converse of the proposition as an experiment.

And on August 3, 1912:

We beg to inform our infuriated subscribers and agonized agents that we have been away at the coast for a holiday and to get the cobwebs blown from our massive brain. Everybody, we feel sure, will be glad to learn that wehadwunhelofatime.

In 1898, when the federal government held a national referendum on prohibition, Edwards was firmly opposed. While admitting that "Alcoholism is a disease which no politician or preacher on earth can handle,"[1] he said that the "unavailing clamor for reform is of no use except for self-glorification, and we have no patience with nonsense of that sort."[2] Later in the campaign he stated, "This talk about eradicating the evil can hardly be taken seriously. One might as well try to sweep back the Atlantic with a broom."[3]

But as the years passed, Edwards witnessed the adverse consequences of the liquor traffic, not only on himself but on the rest of society. He complained how the corner bars were destroying family life, that men with their weekly paycheques often cashed them at the bars and ended up coming home drunk and broke. As for Edwards himself, he was a periodic drinker who would go off on a bat and would finally end up in a Calgary or Banff hospital. He tended to make fun of booze, telling humorous stories, both fictional and real. He delighted readers with such aphorisms as: "Some men are hard drinkers, but others find it absurdly easy," or "Every man has his favorite bird. Ours is the bat," and "The latest stunt is fountain pens filled with whiskey. We have just bought a dozen and expect to do much spirited writing during the coming year."[4]

But drinking had its serious side and Edwards knew it. He had tried to stop on several occasions and once succeeded in staying dry for two years. Each time, however, he succumbed to the temptation and seemed powerless to quit.

When the women's organizations, farmers' groups, and others succeeded in pressuring the Alberta government to call for a vote on prohibition in 1915, Edwards had mixed feelings about it. If he had had a choice, he would have preferred that hard liquor be banned but the sale of wine and beer be permitted. However, the plebiscite called for total prohibition.

Vested interests watched with concern while the newspaperman considered the stand of the *Calgary Eye Opener*. The Licensed Victualers Association, the Bartenders' Union, and the Alberta Federation of Labour all opposed prohibition, while those favouring it included the Temperance and Moral Reform League, Women's Christian Temperance Union, and United Farmers of Alberta. According to Grant MacEwan, the hotel interests tried to convince Edwards to support their cause but made the mistake of offering him a bribe. Later, when he was approached by the temperance forces, they asked for his help but offered him no money.

"That's fine," responded the editor, "because I'm not for sale."[5]

Edwards wasted no time in coming to the support of the temperance peoples. "Whiskey is all right in its place," he said in his July 3, 1915, edition, "but its place is in hell. The liquor traffic hasn't one leg to stand on."

The plebiscite was set for July 21 and Edwards went all out to attack the liquor interests in the issue which would hit the streets four days earlier. But then, according to fellow newspaperman Art Halpen, the hotelmen managed to get him drunk and hoped to keep him that way until after the vote. Edwards did not have his own print shop; rather, he wrote his copy and had the printing work done by the *Albertan*. When the galley proofs were ready, Halpen was sent over to Edwards' office to have them proofread and approved. When Halpen got there, he found Edwards had been drinking but he had not fallen victim to the plot of his opponents. "For two hours," recalled Halpen, "I sat and played the player piano while Bob checked the proofs and gave me the OK to run."[6]

In his hard-hitting columns Edwards said he sympathized with the hotelmen who might be put out of business by prohibition and wondered whether this excited the pity of his readers. Then he continued:

It does ours, but only to a limited extent, for a panorama passes before our eyes of women and little children in humble homes, shy proper food and clothing, lacking warmth in winter and bereft completely of the joy of living, going to sleep in misery and awakening to another day with the dull pain of hopelessness, innocent victims of the damnable traffic of booze; we see a multitude of downcast men, down-and-outers, panhandling for dimes on the street to procure more of that very booze which lost them every job they ever had.[7]

Many people were of the opinion that this eleventh-hour edition of the *Eye Opener* had a definite impact on the vote, which came out strongly in favour of prohibition. It was clear that Edwards was a victim of the liquor traffic and although he may have had some misgivings about the effectiveness of total prohibition, he favoured it over the current situation.

It did not take long, however, for Edwards's cynicism to find root in the effects of prohibition. Rather than totally suppressing the traffic in liquor, the new law merely drove it underground. Soon the bootleggers, moonshiners, and other criminals were becoming rich as drinking moved from the bars to private homes. By 1918, a disillusioned Edwards wrote:

Our views on the subject of prohibition have undergone considerable change since the memorable days when we worked so hard in favor of it. The whole thing has proved a farce. It may be true enough that the elimination of the bar has brought good results by removing temptation from the path of wage-earners with families who had no moral right to divert their money from proper domestic channels, but in other circles, the damage wrought by so-called prohibition has been something fierce.

We have been hammering away at those booze parties in the home for a long time now, with no tangible results outside of an occasional knowing wink and smile from the cognoscenti. Everybody knows of the disgraceful orgies that are pulled off nightly in private homes along our quiet avenues which look so innocent, childlike and bland during the day.[8]

As early as 1920, Edwards was recommending that prohibition be abandoned and replaced with government-owned liquor stores. He believed this would drive the bootleggers out of business and get rid of some of the poisonous booze which was being illegally imported into the province. He pointed out that there was a tremendous traffic in booze across the international border and that the smuggling was "under the control of a lawless, tough, dangerous . . . element who go about with automatics concealed on their persons and carry on just as they please, in defiance of the laws of this country."[9]

Unfortunately, Bob Edwards never lived to see the Alberta government enact the very suggestions he made. Edwards died in 1922 and three years later, prohibition was repealed in favour of government-run liquor stores, just like he wanted.

THE TWENTIES THAT DIDN'T ROAR

They were called the Roaring Twenties but they didn't roar much in Alberta. The decade began with labour unrest, poor crops, depressed grain prices, unemployment, and a problem of what to do with all the returned war veterans. In 1922, for example, Mayor S.H. Adams commented that Calgary was plagued by "unrest and consequent fear for the future"[1] brought about by the readjustment to a peacetime economy. The Board of Trade believed that Calgarians could "no longer look back to the hectic boom days of the war to make comparisons in connection with their balance sheets."

Some disillusioned people migrated to California, Oregon, and Washington, attracted by rumours of a prosperous economy and plenty of work, while others pinned their hopes on a revival of the oil industry. Imperial Oil started to build a refinery at Calgary in 1922 while other companies extended their drilling into Montana and north to Norman Wells. Royalite Oil took over the original discovery wells of Calgary Petroleum Products Limited and revived exploration work at Turner Valley. This paid off in 1924 when the company struck a rich flow of naphtha gas, setting off another flurry of exploration and speculation in the area.

Technological advances, some brought about because of the war, began to impact on Calgary. Silent motion pictures grew from the muddy one-reelers shown in ramshackle buildings to major productions coming out of Hollywood, New York, and London. By 1920, the Allen, Bijou, Dreamland, Empress, Grand, Pantages, and Regent were all in business, to be followed by the Capitol,

BY THE 1920S, SILENT MOVIES HAD BECOME A POPULAR FORM OF ENTERTAINMENT. THIS THEATRE WAS LOCATED ON THE NORTH SIDE OF 8TH AVENUE NEAR 1ST STREET EAST. (GLENBOW, NA-1469-11)

Arcade, and Variety later in the decade. Some offered vaudeville acts during intermissions while an old piano was usually there to provide a musical accompaniment to the flickering pictures. The Palace and Grand theatres also presented live concerts, local theatrical productions, and performances by travelling companies.

During the war, many women had been at last freed from the confines of the home. By the 1920s, a sense of liberation pervaded many United States cities and this attitude was soon carried across the border. According to pioneer Calgarian Margaret Howson, "The twenties were the age of the flapper, this century's first liberated women. These girls cut off their long hair, shortened their skirts to the knee, dieted to achieve as boyish a figure as possible, drank in public, and smoked in public. Enamel nail polish appeared on the scene and the girls

had marcel waves in their hair unless they preferred straight cuts with bangs, and a kiss curl beside each cheek. Fashionable young men in the same period wore white flannels in summer, white shoes and straw boater hats. In winter, coon coats were the thing, with generous pockets for the hip flasks."[2]

The development of radio also had a major impact on the lives and activities of Calgarians. In the spring of 1922, Calgary became one of the first cities on the western prairies to open its own broadcasting station when CHCQ was launched by the *Calgary Herald*. The 10-watt unit was turned on twice a day at 3:30 and 7:45 p.m. and began by playing recorded music. Soon it was besieged by performers who wanted to be part of this wonderful invention. The Palace Theatre orchestra put on live performances while scores of singers, musicians, elocutionists, lecturers, and clergyman began to use the air waves. And to make the new science available to everyone, the *Herald* published detailed information about making crystal sets and technical aspects of radio.

So enthusiastic was the response from Calgarians that the *Herald* decided to upgrade the station and buy more refined equipment. For the technology buffs, the newspaper described its new transmitter as a "large set which is rated as a 2,000 watt machine, [which] consists of four 500-watt oscillators and two 250-watt modulators."[3] The station also had equipment for receiving transmissions, as well as a large studio complete with a grand piano. It was located "directly between the tall steel masts on top of The Herald building."

The station was officially opened on August 29, 1922, with the mayor and president of the Board of Trade doing the honours. Because it had a stronger signal than the old station, it was given the new call num-

bers of CFAC. During that first evening, it filled the air waves with marches, violin, coronet and vocal solos, and music from the Calgary Silver Band.

The radio was a major form of entertainment which was within the reach of almost anyone. For a few pennies, a boy could assemble the copper wire, tin, crystal, and other items needed for a home-made crystal set while for adults, W.W. Grant and other companies sold commercial radios.

If people did not want to sit at home with crystal sets on a warm summer weekend, they could always go to one of Calgary's parks. Riley Park had playgrounds, a cricket pitch, wading pool, and a sandy-bottomed swimming pool that was filled with water from a nearby fire hydrant. In 1922, a reporter noted that "The pool was crowded with youngsters, girls and boys, splashing, swimming, diving and playing in the water."[4] For more great fun, there was a swimming hole at St. George's Island, not far from the Calgary Auto Club's campground. The pool had been made by digging out a natural hollow and allowing it to be fed by the waters of the Bow. Similarly, at Elbow Park a pool was designated by a log boom in the river. "The only dangerous part is marked and there is no need for any accidents to happen here," commented a reporter. There was another swimming hole in a slough at the bottom of the hill just north-east of the Centre Street Bridge, next to the town dump.

THIS LADY OF FASHION IS TYPICAL OF THE "FLAPPER" ERA OF THE 1920S. (GLENBOW, NA-3965-47)

ELSIE CURRIE, HOME SERVICE DIRECTOR FOR CANADIAN WESTERN NATURAL GAS CO. PROVIDED HINTS TO HOUSEWIVES THROUGH HER RADIO BROADCASTS. (GLENBOW, NA-1446-27)

One could play tennis or football at Mewata Park, golf at Shaganappi Park, soccer at Hillhurst Park, or enjoy the beauty of the flower gardens at Central Park. And, of course, there was always the long streetcar ride to the picnic grounds and lagoon at Bowness Park.

By the 1920s, automobiles had become such a fad that you could join an automobile club for a weekend excursion or venture out on your own. The route to Banff was well established and a new road to Windermere was opened in 1922. There was no designated Trans-Canada Highway although the Banff route was being promoted by the Calgary Good Roads Association. Calgary surveyor William Pearce was one of the first to suggest that well-maintained roads could create an entirely new industry for Alberta—tourism. "We have to

the south of us a population of 110,000,000 of which a very considerable percentage of them are very wealthy and liberal in spending it," he said, "and anything that we can obtain from them is that amount of money found. We can assure our neighbours to the south that if they want cool weather in the summer, combined with the most sanitary and agreeable scenic conditions, we can furnish it to them."[5]

In spite of modern facilities such as automobiles, movies, and radios, Calgary was still a cow town in many ways and had never turned its back on its ranching heritage. The Calgary Stampedes of 1912 and 1919 had been isolated events but people never forgot just how popular they were.

The early 1920s were disastrous ones for the Calgary Exhibition so when Guy Weadick suggested that they have another western show, manager E.L. Richardson and other officials decided to take a chance. As the *Herald* commented, "When the Stampede was first mooted the outlook was not promising. Southern Alberta had had three years of insufficient moisture. Low yields and low prices had combined to rob city and country alike of prosperity. It was while conditions were in that state that the more ambitious programme for the exhibition was decided upon."[6]

The 1923 event went under a number of names—the Stampede and Buffalo Barbecue; Calgary Exhibition and Stampede; the Calgary Fair and Stampede; and the Stampede and Exhibition. Like the shows of 1912 and 1919 it was intended to be a one-time extravaganza, complete with rodeo events and Indians as well as an entirely new feature: chuckwagon racing. "In the 'chuck-wagon' race . . . the wagons will be equipped the same as to tent, stove, branding irons, chuck-box, etc. There will be a four horse team, driver and four mounted men who [after the race] will unhitch the team, erect a tent using at least two stakes, set up the stove, and the first smoke through the chimney wins. This race will be a new one and promises to be one of the most thrilling and entertaining on the programme."[7]

The whole week from July 9 to 15 proved to be more exciting and successful than even the promoters had predicted. The Monday parade was three miles long, with five bands and more than 2,000 participants on horseback, floats, or on foot. Calgary's mayor, George

RILEY PARK WAS THE SCENE OF FREQUENT CRICKET MATCHES. THE WOMEN'S MATCH SHOWN HERE TOOK PLACE IN 1921. (GLENBOW, NA-2393-1)

A FAVOURITE WINTER PASTIME FOR CALGARIANS IN THE TEENS AND 1920S WAS SKATING ON FROZEN RIVERS AND PONDS. HERE, PEOPLE ENJOY THEMSELVES ON THE ELBOW RIVER NEAR RIDEAU ROAD. (GLENBOW, NA-479-1)

THE LAGOON AT BOWNESS PARK DREW MANY CALGARIANS TO ITS BANKS DURING THE 1920S AND 1930S. IF A MAN HAD THE PRICE OF A CANOE RENTAL, HE COULD TAKE HIS GIRL FOR A LEISURELY PADDLE AND ADMIRE THE BEAUTY OF THE PARK. (GLENBOW, NA-2019-5)

Webster, led the procession on horseback, and started Calgary's long tradition of "going western" by dressing in a blue silk shirt, pink kerchief, Stetson hat, and leather chaps.

"Residents of Calgary," said the *Herald*, "catching the Stampede spirit, are sporting wide-brimmed cowboy hats and colored shirts and neckerchiefs by the hundreds, adding to the flashing color of the vivid exhibition setting."[8]

Part of the downtown area was closed off for two hours every morning for chuckwagons, street dancing, and entertainment. On the second day, cowboy Ed King rode his horse Tony into the Club Cafe as a publicity stunt. Patrons were told not to worry as the horse was completely "restaurant-broke." Other cowboys amused the crowds by roping passersby—usually good-looking stenographers—as well as demonstrating their riding skills. This was not without danger and during the first day two men and one horse were injured in the parade or during the downtown events. The most serious accident occurred when Pete Knight's horse slipped on the pavement. Knight—later to become one of Canada's most famous rodeo cowboys—was pinned under the horse, suffered a broken ankle, and was out of the competition. Another young cowboy was bucked off his horse and had a minor concussion, and later a runaway team bolted down 8th Avenue plunging through the window of Palace of Eats on the south-west corner of 1st Street West.

In spite of a few rain showers on the first day, the mobs surged to the fair grounds in such numbers that on one occasion the gates had to be closed until those inside were dispersed. They went to the Indian village, wandered down Johnny J. Jones's midway, saw the agricultural exhibits, and took in the rodeo events. And on the final day, patrons feasted on 4,000 pounds of barbecued buffalo meat sandwiches. In the rodeo finals, Dan Riley's outfit from High River won the chuckwagon championship; Pete Vandermeer, the Canadian bucking horse competition; Ken Cooper, bareback riding; Eddie Bowlen, calf roping; C. Patterson, steer riding; and Neil Campbell, the wild horse race. Alberta Kid was declared to be the best bucking horse of the week. The attendance of 138,950 was the largest in the history of Calgary, surpassing even the highly successful 1919

Victory Stampede and far above the 1922 figure of 81,000. Ever since the war, the fair had been losing about $5,000 a year but in 1923 it showed an impressive $20,000 profit.

It wasn't long before people were clamouring for the rodeo to become a permanent part of the annual fair. Mayor Webster led the call, proclaiming that the 1923 event had received publicity all across North America and as soon as better roads were built, he predicted that thousands of tourists would flock to an annual stampede. Perhaps the best comments came from the editorial pages of *The Albertan,* likely from the pen of W.M. Davidson:

The Calgary Stampede with its wonderful success has brought back the old Calgary spirit more than any-

THE PALLISER HOTEL DOMINATED BOTH CALGARY'S SKYLINE AND THE CITY'S HOTEL BUSINESS. THE CPR HOTEL, SEEN HERE IN THE 1920S, WAS CALGARY'S MOST ELEGANT PLACE FOR STAYING OR DINING. A TRAVELLER ONCE COMMENTED THAT "THE PALLISER AND ITS TEN MAGNIFICENT STORIES RISE ABOVE THE SURROUNDING HOVELS AND SHACKS AND HOMELY FRONTIER TOWN LIKE A GRECIAN STATUE ON A CLAM FLAT." (GLENBOW, NA-2399-26)

thing else . . . The Calgary spirit in the past was extreme, perhaps. It inspired people to believe that Calgary and Alberta could achieve more than any other city or province. But the pendulum has been swinging back the other way. We have been losing our confidence. We have been losing our power to assert ourselves. The phenomenal success of the Stampede, which is so essentially a Calgary enterprise, has revived the old spirit of confidence, the old community spirit. We are proud of our city and the achievements of our people.[9]

SOME OF THE LEGENDS OF THE CALGARY STAMPEDE STARTED IN 1923 THROUGH THE HIGH JINKS OF THE COWBOYS. HERE, EDDY KING EMERGES FROM A RIDE THROUGH THE CLUB CAFE. THIS PHOTOGRAPH BECAME A POPULAR POST CARD. (GLENBOW, NA-2768-4)

The enthusiasm of the public and the impressive profits from the 1923 show convinced the Calgary Exhibition Board that the rodeo should indeed become an annual event. After all, where else would one expect to see the Calgary Stampede?

The success of the show did not drive the recession away from Calgary, but two years later—in 1925—the good times returned when the farmers harvested bumper crops. It was a short-lived period of prosperity, however, and came tumbling down four years later with the Wall Street crash.

HUNGRY THIRTIES AND OFF TO WAR AGAIN

DEPRESSION AND WAR

FOR A WHILE IT LOOKED AS THOUGH THE TWENTIES WERE GOING TO END ON A
POSITIVE NOTE. FARMERS WERE HARVESTING BUMPER CROPS, CREDIT WAS EASILY AVAILABLE,
AND PEOPLE WERE SPENDING MONEY WITH CAREFREE ABANDON. IN CALGARY, EATON'S OPENED
A NEW $1 MILLION STORE WHILE ITS COMPETITOR, THE HUDSON'S BAY COMPANY, BEGAN A
MAJOR ADDITION TO ITS DOWNTOWN BUILDING.

But the euphoria of prosperity was dashed in October 1929 with the Wall Street crash when stocks tumbled and the world's overheated money market collapsed. Within a matter of weeks, grain prices fell, creditors began demanding payments that couldn't be made, staff were laid off, and businesses went broke.

Calgary—as well as Canada and the rest of the world—had entered the Great Depression.

At first, businessmen with their usual Calgary optimism were convinced that the downturn in the economy was only temporary and that the city would soon return to its prosperous lifestyle. A start was made on a new Glenmore Reservoir to increase the city's water supply while new schools were built at Rideau Park and Upper Hillhurst. The optimism also extended to the nascent oil industry, with the addition of the Red Coulee field near the Montana border. Production in 1930 of 1.25 million barrels of naphtha and crude oil at Turner Valley set a new record.

Yet offsetting these brave attempts at optimism were the cold facts: bank clearings were down, prices were falling, and more and more people were out of work. By the end of 1930, Mayor Andy Davison admitted that the city was going through one of the most difficult periods he had ever experienced. "The business depression has swelled the army of unemployed," he said, "with the result that large numbers of our citizens are in straitened circumstances."[1] But, like other optimists, he subscribed to the belief that the setback was only temporary and that in 1931, Calgarians would "see the pendulum swing back to normal with the result that prosperity will again reign in the land."

Fat chance. Calgary was just beginning a period of depression which would last for almost a decade. But the first three years were the worst, not only for the depth of the city's malaise and the terrible drouth conditions in the surrounding areas, but because Calgarians needed time to adjust to the depressed conditions.

From the first, a spirit of self-help and co-operation permeated the city. Businesses which had not been badly hit by the downturn began to assist those in need long before the various levels of government were prepared to act. A number of firms led the way by providing money for hot porridge to be served each morning to any unemployed who showed up at a downtown kitchen. Similarly, a few war veteran associations were able to solicit food from various stores and hand it out to their unemployed members. And service organizations, particularly women's clubs, began to collect food, clothing, and money to help the needy.

For example, when the Samaritan Club heard that farmers in the Neville district were suffering through severe conditions in 1930, it collected bales of clothing for them. In reply, the club received the following letter from a grateful drouth-stricken woman:

Can you imagine dust storms so bad that one must drive with lights on at mid-day, or highways blocked with sand so as to make it necessary to detour? This kept up for weeks until the seed was blown from the ground and what early wheat had come up was cut off. Finally, in July, the Russian thistle covered the ground in a sold mass. The result is that hundreds of farmers are facing ruin. The outlook is hopeless—conditions are drastic—for where will the farmer go if he is forced off the land? Living right here and seeing these things pass before my eyes like a vast moving picture is like living in a book—one feels sometimes that one must be dreaming. It is all so unreal![2]

Gradually, the various levels of government accepted the fact that they would have to look after the thousands of unemployed and to help businesses survive until the crisis was over. But the hardship continued throughout the 1930s. The farmers called them the "Dirty Thirties," but perhaps the unemployed groups were more accurate when they referred to this decade as the "Hungry Thirties." And it would take another war to bring the country back to better times.

RIOTS OF THE UNEMPLOYED

Throughout the summer of 1930—the first full year of the Depression—the government had been caught so unprepared for the massive unemployment and drouth conditions that several months were to pass before effective assistance could be provided. In the autumn, the federal government finally offered $20 million to municipalities for make-work projects so that the unemployed could receive relief payments over the winter.

Calgary immediately applied for $750,000 worth of projects, the costs to be shared by the three levels of government. These included lane gravelling, sewer construc-

tion, brush clearing, and laying a new water main. However, the number of unemployed were increasing so rapidly that there was not enough work for even the married men. By October, the city had 900 married men and more than 1,500 single men registered as unemployed.

Meanwhile, arrangements were made for single unemployed men to receive two vouchers daily during the winter—25 cents for food and 25 cents for lodging. "Two or three men can club together," it was noted, "and with their bed tickets obtain a furnished room equipped with electric light, gas stove and cooking utensils. Each man can buy twenty-five cents worth of groceries with his meal ticket. With day-old bread at five cents per loaf, hamburger at three pounds for twenty-five cents, and buttermilk at fifteen cents per gallon, a man who is not working should be able to survive the winter."[1]

One of the first groups to take advantage of the unsettled economic conditions was the Communist Party. Ever since the Bolshevik revolution of 1917 it had compared the capitalist system with the supposed workers' paradise created in Russia. With unemployment now ravaging Canada, it found a ready audience among the unemployed for its message of a workers' revolt.

In December, 1930, the first Communist demonstration took place in Calgary at an open air rally in front of the Labour Bureau. There was a scuffle with the police and five men were arrested for unlawful assembly. By all accounts, it was a tame affair but it served notice that the unemployed and left-wing agitators would be forces to be reckoned with.

Over the winter of 1930-31, the provincial government opened eleven relief camps in the forested areas around Calgary and provided winter employment for a number of single men. Anyone who refused to go to a camp was cut off any assistance. This provided some relief to Calgary but meanwhile the list of unemployed married men continued to grow, reaching 2,127 by mid-winter.

In the following spring, the make-work programs came to an end but the city realized it could not stop its relief assistance. It had already spent far more than it had in its budget, but conditions were so severe that the removal of relief would have meant actual starvation for men and their families. Reluctantly, the city dug deeper into its funds and, with help from the senior governments, made arrangements to operate relief projects during the summer.

The first confrontation between the unemployed and the civic government in 1931 occurred at the May Day parade. Communist marchers, organized under the name of the National Unemployed Workers' Association, waved red flags and sang "The Internationale" as they led more than 2,000 workers towards City Hall. There, city police and Alberta Provincial Police were waiting for them.

"As the banner carriers reached the street," said the *Herald,* "the two details of police converged on them. Emil Jensen and Fred Levenotsky carrying banners in the front rank dropped their poles into a fighting position and the battle was on. Levenotsky went to his knees from a baton blow over the head, while Jensen ducked one baton but caught another over the shoulder."[2]

When a policeman tried to slug Levenotsky again, a woman hit him over the head with a stick, driving his helmet over his eyes. When this happened, the police surged into the crowd, clubbing down anyone within striking distance. "Batons were swung freely," commented the *Herald,* "and after six men had been placed under arrest, the Communists, disheartened by the action of

their leaders in running when the first signs of trouble commenced, dropped their banners and sought safety in the lanes." Marching four abreast, the police cleared the street while another detail of officers smashed the banner poles and tore the banners to ribbons.

When Calgary planned its 1931 summer relief program, it was advised by the Alberta government to restrict it to men who had been registered during the winter and who had not refused to work. However, the city heard pleas from local men who had lost their jobs or left their farms in the early spring and thus wouldn't qualify. As a result the city led with its heart rather than its wallet and decided that any bona fide unemployed person could apply.

Within days, the message had spread to unemployed men all across western Canada, for no other city was offering such a generous program. For working one eight-hour day a week, an unemployed single man would receive daily food and accommodation allowances worth $3.50. "By freight train, blind baggage, and on foot," said a reporter, "wandering transients are flocking into Calgary daily by the score for the purpose of registering under the latest unemployment relief scheme, and by noon Wednesday no less than 1,580 had been registered since the office opened at 9 o'clock Tuesday morning."[3]

UNEMPLOYED WORKERS NUMBERED IN THE HUNDREDS AS THEY MADE AN ORDERLY MARCH THROUGH CALGARY IN THE 1930S. IN SOME INSTANCES, THEIR DEMONSTRATIONS ENDED IN VIOLENCE. (GLENBOW, NA-4532-1)

Shocked by the massive response to its program (which had been intended for local men) the mayor immediately halted further registration. By this time there were 4,719 unemployed single men in the city. When the city commissioners looked at the problem they had created, they realized that the city would be hard pressed to find enough money to pay for the large number who had registered. Accordingly, they decided to stiffen the requirements so that single men would be obliged to work two seven-hour days a week, instead of one eight-hour day. In this way they hoped to discourage some of the malingerers and reduce their numbers.

The results were predictable. The Communist-led National Unemployed Workers' Association organized a strike with several hundred men refusing to work. Mayor Davison's response was to cut off their assistance. This action infuriated more of the workers who joined the strike and that evening, they milled through the downtown streets, congregating along 2nd Street and down 7th Avenue SE, and shouting and yelling around City Hall. At this point, the police ordered the unemployed to go to a nearby vacant lot, known as Red Square, and to stay off the streets. When they arrived, Communist spokesman Phillip Luck stood on an improvised platform and began to harangue the mob so Police Chief David Ritchie immediately sent a sergeant into the crowd to drag him away.

That was the beginning of a brief but violent Red Square riot.

A reporter described the event: "The fight started, and within a few minutes, batons, stones, rocks, clubs were whirling through the air, with police striking and beating those unemployed who resisted, while they, on the other hand, fought back with sticks, stones, and one of them with an iron pipe."[4]

A constable was struck on the head with a brick and knocked unconscious. The attacker was set upon by another policeman who beat him to the ground with his billy club and handcuffed him. As the other police waded into the crowd with their clubs, the strikers broke and fled. A total of six men, most of them bruised and bleeding, were arrested and charged with unlawful assembly.

The actions of the police had the desired effect for on the day following the riot, the unemployed men went back to work and the strike was over. Those who had refused to work the previous day were struck off the relief lists and remained blacklisted.

By the end of 1931, Calgary's employment and economic picture remained grim. When the city held an auction to sell a hundred homes and 2,000 lots which had been seized for non-payment of taxes, they only had three bids. Almost everyone was broke. The city had more than a million dollars in uncollected taxes with only 56 per cent of home owners and businessmen being able to pay. A total of $40,000 had been earmarked for relief to the unemployed during the year but a whopping $216,000 had been spent. There were 6,000 registered unemployed of which fully half were married men with families.

In the following year, teachers' salaries were cut, some schools closed, streetcar service curtailed, and all civic employees' salaries reduced. In addition, a plan was put into place for property owners to work off their back

TWO UNEMPLOYED MEN WAIT FOR A FREIGHT TRAIN TO LEAVE SO THEY CAN GO IN SEARCH OF WORK. LEFT TO RIGHT ARE PAUL GARRECHT AND BILL RUHL. (GLENBOW, NA-5244-8)

taxes. Another way the city saved money was to replace the single men's food vouchers with a soup kitchen. An area under the grandstand at Victoria Park was set aside where more than 2,000 people a day were fed. It was, claimed a reporter, the largest soup kitchen in the British Empire. Each day, the unemployed went through 600 loaves of bread, 170 pounds of butter, a ton of potatoes, 200 pounds of sugar, 140 gallons of milk, and huge quantities of tea, coffee, meat, and porridge. Yet in spite of the quantity, the kitchen cost $250 less per day than the food vouchers.

The political scene remained quiet during 1931 and 1932 but trouble was never very far away. In the spring, the city kept the soup kitchen open for single unemployed men and in the winter continued its support by issuing meal and lodging tickets. By the winter of 1932-33, the massive drain on Calgary's funds had almost sent the city into bankruptcy. Wages were cut for firemen and policemen, three fire halls were closed, and drastic limits placed on spending. But it wasn't enough. In the spring of 1933, the *Herald* reported that "Calgary is as a besieged city with 13,000 persons on relief, another 13,000 making the barest living, and one-third of the population unable to pay taxes."[5] Since the onset of the Depression, salaries in the business sector had dropped by 60 to 65 per cent while the price of wheat—the mainstay of prairie economy—had fallen from $1.15 to 35 cents a bushel.

The only solution for Calgary was to reduce the amount of money spent on the unemployed. This was accomplished by switching to federally funded summer programs in April, a month earlier than usual, and extending them for an additional two months in the fall. It meant that married men would have to work two days a week on civic projects during that time if they expected to get their food and lodging tickets.

The news set off the longest unemployed workers' strike of the entire Depression. When the Workers United Front called a protest meeting, more than 4,000 men and women jammed Victoria Park and agreed to stay off the job. And true to their word, about 500 married men failed to appear for work on the morning of April 3. Mayor Davison responded by giving them two days to report or their relief assistance would be cut by 25 per cent.

On April 24, a mass rally was held at Victoria Park, described as "the largest in the city's history."[6] From the meeting, the thousands of protesters marched four abreast along Macleod Trail to City Hall. They were led by ex-service men wearing their medals and carrying a Union Jack, while a mass of women, including members of the Single Unemployed Girls' Association, brought up the rear.

Fred Nutt and James Newall, supported by left-wing aldermen Harry Humble and R.H. Parkyn, presented the strikers' list of demands to Mayor Davison. These included the re-establishment of winter rates for the single unemployed; restoration of the 25 per cent penalty levied against married strikers; relief increased to $5.00 a week plus a clothing allowance; and that no attempts be made to deport non-resident strikers.

The mayor refused to accede to any of the demands. His only concession was to promise to call a special council meeting if the strikers would go back to work.

The next day, the strike turned violent. A mob of 1,500 strikers gathered at the Victoria Park soup kitchen under the leadership of Fred Nutt of the Central Workers' Council, and James Newall and Eric Poole of the Unemployed Married Men's Association. The crowd was divided into three groups which converged on Mission Hill where some seventy unemployed men were engaged in a make-work project. The strikers called for them to join them but when they refused, they were subjected to boos and catcalls. About fifty police were supposed to protect the workers, but when the strikers suddenly attacked, they were swept aside in the rush. According to a reporter, "Some of the workmen dropped their shovels and ran for cover. A number of others, however, lined up shoulder to shoulder and prepared to defend themselves."[7]

The police regrouped and dashed into the crowd and within moments there was a melee of flying shovels and batons as police, strikers, and workers engaged in a violent fight. Nearby, women screamed at the strikers and urged them into action. One striker hit a policeman over the head with a shovel and barely missed another officer. Two other constables were hurt when struck with shovels and pick handles. When the riot was over, two men were arrested for assault and several ringleaders were taken into custody.

As soon as Mayor Davison heard about the fight, he sent an urgent appeal for help and the Mounted Police immediately dispatched twenty men and horses from Edmonton, another seventeen from Lethbridge, and twenty-five from Regina. Added to the police already in the city, there were now more than sixty federal officers ready for strike battle. Guards were placed on the militia stores at Mewata Armouries and RCMP patrols were visible during the next couple of days. With the May Day parade only a few days off, the police were clearly worried about further violence.[8]

Considering the tension and stringent control existing in Calgary, it was a credit to the strike committee that the May Day parade came off peacefully. More than 3,000 men, women, and children marched from 3rd Street East to Mewata Park, singing such tunes as "The Internationale," "The Red Flag," and "It's a Long way to Tipperary." The mass meeting demanded that the winter relief rates be reinstated, the 25 per cent cut in strikers' payments be paid retroactively, and that all charges be withdrawn against the strikers. The crowd then agreed with a request of local clergymen to suspend the strike for a week so that negotiations could be conducted.

With the help of the Calgary Ministerial Association, a meeting was arranged between the strikers and a special committee of city council. After several hours of discussion, the city agreed to cancel the 25 per cent penalty if the workers would accept the summer rates. The strike leaders in turn modified their demands to seek only the extension of winter food allowances, rather than the whole package of shelter, light, heat, and water. Both sides then recommended these changes to their respective bodies and on May 15—six weeks after the walkout—the strike was officially over

The Depression would not end for another six years but the country gradually shook off its malaise and began seeking solutions. A number of socialists gathered in Calgary in 1932 to form the Co-operative Commonwealth Federation—a left-wing organization

WILLIAM ABERHART, A CALGARY SCHOOL PRINCIPAL, BECAME A PROPONENT OF THE MONETARY THEORIES OF SOCIAL CREDIT AS A WAY OF GETTING RID OF THE DEPRESSION. WHEN THE PROVINCIAL GOVERNMENT REFUSED TO ADOPT THESE PRINCIPLES, ABERHART FORMED THE SOCIAL CREDIT PARTY AND SWEPT THE POLLS IN 1935. HIS MONETARY THEORIES WERE DECLARED ILLEGAL BY THE FEDERAL GOVERNMENT BUT THE PARTY PROVED TO BE A GOOD ONE AND CONTINUED TO HOLD POWER IN ALBERTA UNTIL 1971. (GLENBOW, NA-1250-1)

that ultimately became the New Democratic Party. A year later, a Calgary man told the *Herald* of an Englishman, "Major Douglas by name, who has a system which he claims will help us out of our difficulties."[9] Within a short time, this new monetary theory—Social Credit—caught the imagination of Calgary radio evangelist William Aberhart and was being studied all across the prairies. In 1935, it was translated from theory to political action with the sweeping victory of the Social Credit Party in Alberta's general election.

The first signs of relief from the Depression came late in 1937 when western Canada harvested its first bumper crop since the Wall Street crash. There was a feeling of optimism as Calgary experienced more new construction than it had seen in the decade and Turner Valley had its best oil production year in history. But in the end, it took a war to wipe out the decade-long disaster.

In 1941, a Calgary woman looked back and saw the Thirties as a nightmare experience. She was married in 1931 and she and her husband had eked out a living on a farm before giving up and moving back to Calgary with three children in 1935. Her husband found a temporary job but when he was laid off they were forced to go on relief.

"We received $49 a month from the relief board," she recalled, "and out of this had to pay $15 rent. The only place we could find to live in was a two-roomed suite—it's so hard to find a place when you have children.

"Then, in 1939, the war broke out and my husband enlisted. I got $79 a month allowance, and he got his salary besides, so things began to look up. The first thing we did was move into a house where we wouldn't be so crowded. We have a little back yard and a small garden, so that helps some. We still had to economize though, because we didn't have a bit of furniture and had to buy enough to start us off.

"We're trying to pay off our debts a little at a time. Sometimes it's seemed as if we never would be done, but now that John has steady work, I think we'll be all right. We never have accepted any more aid from the city or anyone that we could possibly help.

"Yes, we've been through the depression but we're beginning to see daylight again. I'm sure that now we'll make it through—alone."[10]

ANOTHER WAR

Everyone knew the Depression was over when Pat Lenihan, one of Calgary's most popular Communist organizers of the unemployed, was arrested in December, 1939, for making inflammatory statements. Not only had the days of unemployed riots passed but the country was now under wartime regulations. Lenihan wasn't convicted but a few weeks later he was sent to an internment camp at Kananaskis, along with enemy aliens and others who were considered national security risks.

When Hitler's armies invaded Poland, Canada began to prepare for war. On September 1, the Department of National Defence issued its first call for troops; those from Alberta were ordered to report to Military District 13 headquarters in Calgary. Authorization was given for recruiting about 4,000 officers and men and by the evening of the first day, more than 300 soldiers had enlisted. Donald McIntyre had the honour of being the first Calgary civilian to volunteer for active service.

The Calgary units mobilized at the outbreak of war included the 1st Battalion, Calgary Highlanders; 23rd and 91st Field Batteries, Royal Canadian Artillery; 13th Field Company, Royal Canadian Engineers; and a number of others.[1] There was no room to house all these troops so barracks were constructed immediately north of Mewata Armouries.

On September 2, a squadron of Hawker Hurricane fighters at the Currie Barracks airport under Squadron Leader Elmer Fullerton was dispatched to Halifax in preparation for war while dozens of young men made enquiries about joining the air force or the navy.

Britain declared war on September 3 and Canada a week later on September 10. By the end of the month, all Calgary units were at full strength and busy training at Sarcee camp, Currie barracks, and Mewata Armouries. Many of the recruits had enlisted for patriotic reasons, particularly those who had strong associations with the Old Country. But others were motivated by the chance of receiving a regular income—the first in their lives. In November, Calgary reported the lowest number of people on its relief rolls since 1930. It was clear that the majority of those on relief were anxious to work but had lacked the opportunity.

During the first few months of the war, prices began to skyrocket and items such as tea and coffee were soon in short supply because of hoarding. But before the profiteers could dominate the market, the Rental Control Board and the Wartime Prices and Trade Board were set up and price controls introduced. This was the beginning of many restrictions which governed the lives of Calgarians for the rest of the war. National registration of all citizens became law and by the summer of 1940 more than 67,000 Calgarians were on the rolls. Each was issued with an identity card which had to be carried at all times.

In 1942, National Selective Service regulations placed stringent restrictions on essential workers and their employers. Many workers could not quit or change jobs without approval and unemployed persons could be forced to take jobs which were assigned to them. Local war industries included an ammonia plant for making explosives, and the conversion of the CPR shops to make naval gun barrels.

Rationing was introduced in 1942, beginning with gasoline. Cars and trucks were classified by their importance to the war effort and an owner received a ration book and a sticker for the windshield. In the beginning, the owner of a car in the "A" category could buy 300 gallons of gas a year while a family car would qualify for 120 gallons. Later in the war, the amounts were reduced or the categories changed so that only the most vital services were assured of an adequate supply of gas. At the same time, the sale of new tires and inner tubes were restricted to essential industries. Even to buy a used tire, one had to produce evidence that the old one was worn out.

Later in 1942, rationing was extended to meat, sugar, coffee, tea, and butter. Each person received a ration book and the merchants tore out the coupons when purchases were made. Alcohol was also rationed, although not very stringently. In 1943, a person could buy one bottle of hard liquor and two bottles of wine a week, as well as a daily ration of beer. Even then, some people were so thirsty that they pressed their teetotalling friends and relatives to apply for permits on their behalf.

During the war, the government regularly posted new regulations and reminders: no cuffs allowed on new trousers; no double breasted suits; extra sugar rations available at canning time; sale of burlap bags limited, etc. In addition, notices appeared in newspapers telling consumers when their coupons were due.

In 1943, cafeterias were required to observe "Meatless Tuesdays." The government suggested that restaurants substitute such delicacies as macaroni and chicken livers, boiled eggs and potato salad, or fricasseed chicken wings. Later in the war, the government added a "Meatless Friday" as well.

Many items became scarce, such as nylon stockings, lipstick, chocolate bars, toothpaste (because of the lead tubes), and antifreeze. A black market existed for some of these items, and anyone who knew an American soldier assigned to the Alaska Highway often had access to the scarce luxury items.

By the spring of 1940, more than 12,000 troops were in training in the Calgary district. The first to leave for Europe were the Highlanders who departed in May of 1940. As the men went overseas, the casualty lists began to appear. Among the first were two Calgary sailors, James Johnson and William Clarke, who were killed when the destroyer *Fraser* was sunk in June, 1940. From that time on, lists appeared regularly giving the names of those killed, wounded, and missing in action. The battles in which they fought in North Africa, Italy, France, and Holland became tragically well known to Calgarians.

Perhaps the most famous—or infamous—engagement involving Canadian troops occurred in 1942 when a raid was made upon the German-held town on Dieppe on the west coast of France. The idea had originated with Lord Mountbatten as a means of gaining experience on amphibious operations. After bombarding the resort with naval and air fire, ground troops protected by tanks and air cover would hit the beaches and invade the town, then make an orderly withdrawal. However, the plan was ill advised and proceeded on the basis of inadequate intelligence reports. Selected for the raid was the 14th Army Tank Regiment (The Calgary Regiment) (Tank), usually called the Calgary Tanks, which was to support British and Canadian commando and infantry units.

From the late arrival of the first landing crafts to the final surrender of the Allied troops, the whole raid was a disaster. A third of the tanks were bogged down on the stony beaches or were immobilized by shell fire, the infantry was pinned down by heavy fire, and ultimately those who could not be rescued were forced to surrender. When it was over, only 2,200 of the 6,000 troops returned to England; the rest were killed or captured. In addition, 106 Allied aircraft were shot down during the assault.

Later, a British officer noted that there was "nothing to be learned from Dieppe, except how not to do it, a little late in the war to learn that lesson."[2]

DURING THE BADLY PLANNED RAID ON DIEPPE IN 1942, THE CALGARY TANK REGIMENT WAS PINNED DOWN ON THE BEACHES. THIS TANK, CHRISTENED "CALGARY," LOST ITS TREAD AND ACTED AS A PILLBOX, FIRING ITS 6-POUNDER CANNON INTO THE TOWN. THE LOADER-OPERATOR, TROOPER DENNIS G. SCOTT, DESCRIBED THE ENGAGEMENT: "WE WERE SITTING WITH NO COVER AND SO HAD A GOOD VIEW OF THE BEACH. LIEUTENANT [BRICE G.] DOUGLAS FOUND ENOUGH TARGETS TO KEEP [TROOPER KEN] SMETHURST BUSY UNTIL WE HAD USED UP ALL OUR AMMUNITION ... MEANWHILE WE WERE ATTRACTING A LOT OF GUN-FIRE. WE TOOK SOME DIRECT HITS ON THE TURRET, HARD ENOUGH THAT THE PAINT WAS MELTING AND RUNNING DOWN ON THE INSIDE. THE HEAT INSIDE, ALONG WITH THE SMELL OF THE SMOKE AND CORDITE, WAS ALMOST UNBEARABLE, SO MUCH SO THAT SERGEANT ALFRED S. WAGSTAFF, WHO WAS DOWN IN THE CO-DRIVER'S SEAT, WAS PUT OUT OF ACTION. WE STAYED IN THE TANK UNTIL WE WERE ORDERED TO SURRENDER." (BUNDESARCHIV, 362/2207/34)

When the British Commonwealth Air Training Plan was initiated, Calgary became a major centre for training Britons, Australians, New Zealanders, and Canadians as pilots, observers, and ground crews. In 1941, the city was selected as the headquarters of Western Command, while flying schools, air observer schools, wireless schools, and other training depots were located in Provincial School of Technology and Art, Currie Barracks, and at other locations in the city.

A number of Calgary men were singled out for honours during the war. The first Canadian soldier to be decorated was a Calgarian, Douglas W. Cunnington, who was awarded the George Medal for conspicuous bravery in 1940. During the midst of a German air raid over London, he dug up a bomb at a busy throughfare and carried it out of harm's way shortly before it exploded. During the Battle of Britain, Flying Officer William L. McKnight destroyed twenty-three German planes for which he received the Distinguished Flying Cross and bar, but was himself shot down over France early in 1941. McKnight Boulevard was later named in his honour.

Another Calgary hero was D.M. "Bitsy" Grant who received the DFC after destroying more than sixty enemy trains and nine aircraft. So successful were his efforts that he starred in a National Film Board documentary, *Train-Busters*. His military career ended when he was shot down in 1943.

During the invasion of France, George E. Nuttall commanded one of the first landing craft to hit the shores of Normandy, while Charles N. Mawer received the DSC while serving on the destroyer *Haida* during the invasion. When his ship encountered five enemy vessels, it destroyed two and damaged the rest. Later, when Canadian troops landed, the Calgary Highlanders were commanded by Donald H. MacLauchlan who was awarded a DSO for the way he led his men during the campaign.

The only Calgarian to be awarded a Victoria Cross in World War Two was Ian W. Bazalgette, a squadron leader in the RAF. In the summer of 1944 he was leading a squadron to mark a target for Allied bombers when his Lancaster was hit by anti-aircraft fire and burst into flames. Despite the danger, and with two crewmen wounded, he succeeded in marking the target, then ordered the uninjured crewmen to leave by parachute.

Bazalgette stayed at the controls, tried to land with the wounded, but the aircraft exploded on impact and all were killed.[3]

While the conflict was taking place in Europe and later in the Pacific, Calgarians supported the war effort in every way possible. War saving certificates were purchased by the thousands; in one drive called "Fifteen Minutes for Calgary," $25,000 worth of war saving stamps were bought in downtown stores. Support was given to the Red Cross, bottle and scrap drives, victory gardens, and other

patriotic efforts. In the annual Victory Loan campaigns, the city consistently exceeded its goal. In 1944, it surpassed its $5 million quota by $400,000 and in 1945 it topped $6.5 million.

This last Victory Loan campaign of the war was a memorable one. During a Victory bond rally, a crowd of 12,000 congregated at Victoria Park on the evening of May 5 for an army show called "Cavalcade of Victory." However, people were no sooner seated when a gigantic storm struck the grounds.

According to the *Herald*, "The sun-lit park was transformed into a roaring tumult of dust and darkness as a raging storm, fanned by an 80 miles an hour wind, roared out of the northwest. Preceded by huge funnel-shaped clouds as black as night . . . the storm drove clouds of dust ahead of it at lightning speed and the crowded grandstand took the full force of the storm."[4]

DURING THE WAR, CALGARY WAS A MAJOR CENTRE FOR THE BRITISH COMMONWEALTH AIR TRAINING PLAN. HERE, ONE OF THE FIRST GROUPS OF AUSTRALIANS ARRIVE IN CALGARY IN 1940 TO BEGIN AIR FORCE TRAINING. (**HERALD** COLLECTION, GLENBOW, NA-2864-3443)

There was near hysteria as high winds and dust transformed the grounds into utter darkness. Children became terrified as they were separated from their parents, a woman in the stands became hysterical, and a few people tried to stampede towards the exits. Just when officials feared there might be a panic, the lone voice of a man singing "It Had to be You" came echoing through the loudspeakers. It was one of the guest stars, Hollywood actor and dancer George Murphy, who was imitating the familiar voice of Al Jolson. He was dusty and dishevelled but resolutely holding the microphone alone on stage in the face of the driving storm. A few stage lights were turned on as he swung in to "Home on the Range" and called the crowds to sing along. Then there was a chorus of laughter as people began to settle down.

A few minutes later, four members of the Canadian Women's Army Corps—Maxine Grande, Dorothy Trono, Eunice Cockburn, and Olive Tolman—joined him in singing "Me and My Gal."

"The storm was still at its height," said the reporter. "Sgt. Denny Layzell, who produced the army show . . . kept the microphone from blowing away and everyone labored mightily to keep the crowd from thinking too much about its predicament."

The army band picked up its scattered instruments and began to play without sheet music and a little later, Hollywood actress Claire Trevor, with an army blanket wrapped around her, added her voice to those on stage. While this was going on, members of the Provost Corps were conducting an orderly evacuation of the crowds from the aisles and restoring children to their parents.

When it was over, George Murphy commented, "When my grandchildren ask me where I was on May 5, 1945, I'll tell them that I was in Calgary, Alberta, Canada—on the night of the Big Wind."

Two days later, the Germans surrendered unconditionally and the war in Europe was over. V-E Day had arrived after six long years of war.

When the news spread through Calgary, thousands of people dashed into the streets, waving flags and shouting. Office workers dumped papers from downtown buildings while Hudson's Bay staff tossed long red-white-and-blue streamers from the fifth floor windows. Beer parlours, liquor stores, and movie theatres were closed, children were released from school, and all business came to a standstill. One woman, on her way to church, said to a reporter:

I'm going to celebrate, but not by getting drunk. My son's the only person I've got in the world and he's in the air force. He's been trying to get a posting overseas for the last year and a half, and all the time I haven't said a word to hold him back. Now I'm going to say a prayer of thankfulness that he didn't have to go.[5]

The evening was dominated by noisy teenagers and soldiers who paraded through the streets, snake-danced, climbed light posts, beat on tin cans, and piled onto every car that tried to pick its way through the mob. An effigy of Hitler was dragged through the streets where it was kicked and punched as crowds looked on and cheered. Many of the revellers had been drinking but everyone was in good spirits and when the festivities ended about 1 a.m., there had been no damage and no one arrested.

V-E Day actually extended over two days, May 7 and 8. On the second day, a huge thanksgiving service was held on the corner of 1st Street and 7th Avenue SW where people were reminded that there was still a war going on in the Pacific.

Three months later, on August 14, 1945, the Japanese surrendered and V-J Day marked the final con-

CROWDS JAMMED
CALGARY'S DOWNTOWN
AREA ON D-DAY.
(**HERALD** COLLECTION,
GLENBOW, NA-2864-3446)

clusion of the war. The celebrations were a repetition of V-E Day, but this time, the mobs were even more exuberant. Rocks and bottles were thrown into the crowds and fistfights broke out among teenagers and service men.

"Listen, boy," said one of the exasperated soldiers, probably thinking of his buddies who had died overseas, "you don't even know what it's all about. You don't even know why you're yelling and screaming. You don't even know what war was like."[6]

At the height of the celebrations, the downtown area along 8th Avenue and 1st Street West was a "screaming sea of teen-agers," plus scores of service men and women, and a few adults. Before the night was over, bonfires had been lit in the streets, a few cars damaged, and windows broken in a number of stores. But the police took a tolerant view of the holiday and no arrests were made. Celebrations also took place in Chinatown where both whites and Asians joined to cheer the victory over Japan. Chinese flags and bunting decorated many stores to remind everyone of China's part in the war while fireworks added to the din.

"Now that history's most awful war is over," editorialized the *Albertan*, "many will be inclined to sit back and relax. That is permissible, but only for a short time. All mankind's problems are not solved. The future is not a straight, broad downhill avenue without any stop signs or ruts. The next five years may be more difficult and in one way more decisive than the last five. Peace has brought a new problem, one that men and women can evade only at the peril of their lives. It is how to prevent future aggression and with it another war."[7]

Now it was time for the boys to come home and for Calgary, and Canada, to face a new post-war world.

ANOTHER BOOM

INTO A NEW ERA

DURING THE SIX YEARS OF WAR, CALGARIANS HAD GONE WITHOUT MANY NECESSITIES AND LUXURIES. AUTOMOBILES HAD BEEN PATCHED AND REPAIRED, SOME FOODSTUFFS WERE IN SHORT SUPPLY, WOMEN WERE PAINTING THEIR LEGS IN LIEU OF REAL STOCKINGS, AND DECENT HOUSING WAS ALMOST IMPOSSIBLE TO FIND. AS EARLY AS 1941, ACCOMMODATION WAS SO SCARCE THAT A SOLDIER'S WIFE AND FAMILY HAD TO LIVE IN A TENT NEAR ST. GEORGE'S ISLAND WHEN THEY COULDN'T FIND ROOMS TO RENT. AS FOR LUXURIES, WHEN THE FIRST BIG SALE OF NYLON STOCKINGS OCCURRED IN FEBRUARY OF 1946, WOMEN MOBBED THE DOWNTOWN STORES.

Calgarians had a lot of catching up to do. They wanted new cars, new houses, new fridges, new telephones, and new clothes. As the *Calgary Herald* commented in 1945, "Scarcity developed in many lines of manufactured articles. One of the earliest effects of the conversion of industry from war to peace output should be the turning out of products of higher quality than have been available in recent years."[1]

But it could not happen overnight, and shortages continued for a number of years during the period of reconstruction after the war. Rationing was maintained and Wartime Housing Limited was kept busy building standard frame houses to meet the demands. And with price controls removed, the cost of goods began to inch upward. Milk went up two cents a quart to twelve cents; beef up four cents a pound; and gasoline a cent a gallon. At the same time, the government reported that wages in Calgary reached a record high.

The first soldiers to return home were the men of the 1st Canadian Infantry Brigade, RCASC, who marched through Calgary's streets on October 6, 1945, before being demobilized. They were followed by the Calgary Highlanders late in November and the Calgary Tanks two weeks later. There were strong feelings of happiness, relief, and gratitude as men went back to their old jobs or took advantage of the government's offer of getting a college or university education.

Some idea of Calgary's situation in the post-war years can be seen in its growth. At the outbreak of war it had a population of about 85,000. This had increased to 97,000 by the Dominion census of 1944, and passed the magic 100,000-mark two years later. That was an increase of almost 20 per cent in seven years. Much of the business expansion could be absorbed by the overbuilding which had taken place in 1911-12 but a shortage of housing presented a problem which could only be solved by new houses, new subdivisions, and additional basic services. By early 1946, more than 2,000 veterans and their families were on a waiting list for homes in the city.

Calgary was no longer a small town, but neither was it a big city. As journalist Allan Connery wrote:

In 1947, Calgary was a quiet little city of about 100,000 people. Street-cars and horse-drawn milk wagons still contended with cars for space on the narrow streets. The main roads were paved, but some

side-streets were still dirt, graded and oiled every year. The Palliser Hotel and the Robin Hood flour mill loomed over the city skyline. Tuxedo Park, West Hillhurst, Elbow Park and Inglewood were at the edge of the city, with a few scattered houses beyond.[2]

Calgary's progress had been impressive since the outbreak of war but this became a mere blip in its expansion when compared with the events which were to follow in the next four decades. The discovery of oil at Imperial Leduc No.1 well on February 13, 1947, launched the city into a new era of growth and opulence. Even though the well was only eighteen miles south-west of Edmonton, the benefits were most profitably felt by the foothills city to the south. Ever since the discovery of the Turner Valley field in 1914, Calgary had been the centre of the oil industry; its head offices were located there and any corporate planning started in their panelled board rooms.

The Leduc and Redwater fields launched Calgary into the oil age.

Even though agriculture still remained the province's primary industry, oil became the centre of Calgary's existence and the basis for its economy. Effects of the oil boom included the expansion of the city limits to take in Windsor Park in 1951, The Meadows in 1952, Meadowlark Park in 1954, Forest Lawn in 1961, Montgomery in 1963, and Bowness in 1964. The 1950s also saw the construction of the Mewata Bridge, Jubilee Auditorium, General Hospital, and Red Cross Crippled Children's Hospital. In the next decade, the University of Alberta in Calgary (forerunner of the U of C), McMahon Stadium, Heritage Park, and the planetarium were opened. Meanwhile, a few new office buildings, banks, and oil company offices began to replace the older buildings of the 1912 era.

This gave rise to a bold new experiment—Urban Renewal. Launched in 1966, its goal was to "rejuvenate" the downtown area by wiping out entire blocks and

replacing them with modern buildings. The program was particularly aimed at the area east of Centre Street. Over the next few years, houses, stores, and many historic buildings fell beneath the wrecker's ball and were replaced with such structures as the Calgary Convention Centre, Calgary Board of Education, YWCA, and the public library. Only later did many Calgarians realize that they were destroying the very buildings which gave the city its unique flavour and often were replacing them with faceless steel, glass, and concrete monoliths. During this era, the CPR station disappeared, and even a last

THIS 1965 VIEW OF 7TH
AVENUE SHOWS THE
FOLLOWING BUILDINGS,
LEFT TO RIGHT: BRITISH-
AMERICAN BUILDING,
ELVEDEN HOUSE,
GUINNESS HOUSE, AND
(AROUND THE CORNER)
THE FINA BUILDING.
THESE WERE AMONG
CALGARY'S FIRST POST-
WAR "SKYSCRAPERS."
(GLENBOW, NA-4952-12)

A GRIDIRON SPECTACLE

By 1948, Calgary had shrugged off the restraints of the recent war and was heartily embracing the newly revitalized oil industry. It was still a small city by North American standards—little more than 100,000 people—and it was a mere bubble in the sea compared to the big cities of Montreal and Toronto. But it had two things going for it: unbounded optimism and a strong collective outgoing personality.

Calgary was like a kid who wanted to be noticed by his big brothers. It had the Calgary Stampede but that wasn't enough; a budding oil town, it wanted everybody to sit up and take notice. And the chance came in 1948 through the aegis of one of Canada's favourite autumn sports: football.

In professional terms, the Calgary Stampeders were newcomers on the football scene. The city's first team, the Calgary Tigers, had been formed in 1908 when the Calgary Rugby Club decided to change from the English style of association football to the Canadian game of rugby football. Three years later, Calgary won the western title but could not compete for the Grey Cup because it didn't belong to a league that was recognized by eastern Canada.[1]

The Tigers eventually joined the Canadian Rugby Football Union but then disbanded for a few years. They were replaced by the 50th Battalion team in 1923 and then by the Altomahs, but in 1929 they returned to the football wars. The Tigers immediately created a sensation when its quarterback, Gerry Seiberling, threw the first forward pass in Canadian football history. In the early 1930s, the team was replaced by Calgary Bronks but by the onset of World War Two in 1939, none of the Calgary contenders had ever made it to the Canadian finals and the Grey Cup.

The Bronks were disbanded at the beginning of the war but a new team was organized in 1945—the Calgary Stampeders. Their first coach gave a lacklustre performance so in 1948 he was replaced by Les Lear, a thorough professional who was told to put together the best possible team. The rules permitted only four American imports so he took Keith Spaith and John Aguirre from the Honolulu Warriors and Woody Strode and Ezzard "Sugarfoot" Anderson from American teams. He then added a coterie of Canadian stalwarts like Rod Pantages, Normie Hill, Fritz Hanson, Pete Thodos, and Normie Kwong.

ditch attempt on the part of Calgary pioneer Mary Dover to save the city's original court-house failed. For a number of years, the cry was, "Out with the old, in with the new."

As a result of the oil business, Calgary's population mushroomed and by the 1960s, it was growing at the rate of 15,000 a year. Yet these developments were overshadowed by the events of the 1970s. For a few years, it was just like being back in the boom days before the First World War. Only this time the magic word was not real estate, but oil.

A SIGN OF THE FEAR CRE-
ATED BY THE COLD WAR
WAS THE CONSTRUCTION
OF FALLOUT SHELTERS IN
THE EVENT OF A NUCLEAR
ATTACK. HERE, HENRY
VANCE INSPECTS HIS
SUPPLY OF FOOD IN
HIS CALGARY SHELTER
IN 1960. (HERALD
COLLECTION, GLENBOW,
NA-2864-178)

The Calgary Stampeders sailed through the Western Conference without a loss and by the time they got to the western finals, football fever had engulfed the city. The wooden bleachers at Mewata Stadium were jammed with enthusiastic supporters when Calgary beat the Saskatchewan Roughriders 17-6 and won the right to play Ottawa in its first Grey Cup game.

As the team travelled east, a number of Calgarians decided that they didn't want to listen to the classic on the radio; they wanted to be there. Harry McConachie, Bill Herron, and two or three others met at the Petroleum Club to discuss the idea of going as a group. As they talked, their imaginations began to run wild. Why shouldn't they give staid old Toronto a taste of Calgary's hospitality? Why not take a western band! Cowboys! Horses! A chuckwagon! Hell, why not charter a whole train!

Herron said he'd arrange for the horses; R.S. Heberling could supply a chuckwagon from the Buckhorn Ranch; and Art West of the CPR could line up a 13-car passenger train, complete with dance hall and livestock car. And heck, the volunteers at the Calgary Stampede could help to arrange all the details. By the time they finished, the wild dreams had been transformed into an action plan to take Toronto by storm.

McConachie became chairman of the organizing committee and the plans, as Herron recalled, "just snowballed into a hell of a trip."[2] While the football team was already down East practising on the grounds of Appleby College in Oakville, the folks back home were flocking to the special train. There were 250 enthusiastic travellers, many wearing white hats and fancy western gear. There were a dozen horses, a western band headed by Oscar Stonewall, and a mob of well wishers at the station to see them off. "As the train pulled out," said a reporter, "Clint Roenisch leaned from the steps of the train and led the crowd in a cheer for Calgary and as the train left the end of the station the crowd could be heard shouting, 'C-A-L-G-A-R-Y, CALGARY, CALGARY, CALGARY.'"[3]

The three-day trek to Toronto was an epic journey which gained headlines all across the nation. At Medicine Hat, Mayor Harry Viner took part in a leg-wrestling match and at Winnipeg the group put on a square dancing demonstration. They had become so popular that at the tiny station of Schrieber, Ontario, they were given 36 cases of beer in exchange for a half hour's entertainment of music and song.

Not surprisingly, the revellers were inundated by the press on their arrival at Union Station in Toronto. Obligingly, the Calgarians performed reels and square dances, sang the team's victory song, "Put on your Red and White Sweater," and generally hooted and hollered their way to the Royal York Hotel across the street, holding up traffic for half an hour with their antics. While the crowd sang "Calgary, Where the Sun Shines all the Day," City Clerk J.M. Miller told a reporter, "This bunch is certainly letting the east know there is a place in the West called Calgary and a Calgary Stampede."[4] The Ottawa Rough Riders team arrived at the station at almost the same time but they were virtually ignored by the press and the public. Everyone wanted to see the colourful Calgarians.

Meanwhile, two other groups from Calgary, mostly oil men and their wives, decided to fly to Toronto for the game. Both chartered DC-3s from Trans-Canada Air Lines (later Air Canada) and specially painted them for the occasion. Over the doorway of the first one was a yodelling cowboy kicking a football, while more footballs were painted on the cowlings and a bucking broncho on the nose. Slogans such as "Lear's Lambasters" and "Stampeder Special" also adorned the exterior of the aircraft. Two days later, a second DC-3, similarly painted, also flew a load of fans to Toronto.

When the train and aircraft arrived, the visitors were given their tickets but found that only 3,500 had been set aside for Calgary and these were being quickly snapped up. Fans complained that now that Calgary had turned the Grey Cup into a spectacle, the 20,000-seat Varsity Stadium was far too small for such a national event. The Calgary crowd was inundated with people looking for tickets, one man even bringing his birth certificate to prove he'd been born in Calgary. Jack Grogan's phone at the hotel was ringing non-stop from the time he arrived and at 4 a.m., Jim Cross was almost hoarse when he answered, "Grogan's Pool Hall" to yet another ticket seeker.

The next day, November 27, was Grey Cup Day. It started with a street dance in front of the Royal York and with greetings being tendered by two Calgary aldermen,

A.E. Aikenhead and Don Mackay. Jack Miller told the cheering crowd that "the best people in the world came from Calgary and the Eastern trek was just their attempt to prove it."[5]

From there, the jubilant Calgary mob paraded north to the city hall, led by David Crowchild and George Runner of the Sarcee tribe, both on horseback and in full regalia. They were followed by other riders, chuckwagon, and about 500 western fans in trucks and open cars. The mayor of Toronto, Hiram McCallum, was given a white hat, a red kerchief, and invited to ride with the Calgary contingent. When he agreed he was given a sprightly pinto, and although he had trouble keeping his feet in the stirrups, he good-naturedly joined the procession while Don Mackay shouted, "Watch for his bow-legged worship. Yahoo!"[6]

Thousands of curious spectators gathered at the city hall as the Calgary crowd unhooked the chuckwagon and began serving flapjacks. Meanwhile, the square dancers showed their stuff, and at one point, they all broke away and pulled in partners from the Toronto crowd. Then, with spectators and Calgarians cheering and shouting, they moved up Bay Street toward the football stadium. "In all Toronto's years as a sanctuary for tired financiers and business men," said a sports reporter, "its discreet windows had never looked on such a heart-warming show as the pre-game parade staged by the Westerners."[7]

Although everyone seemed to have fallen in love with the Calgary fans, no one gave their football team much of a chance of winning the Grey Cup. Virtually the entire Eastern press corps saw the Stampeders as the underdogs—young, lightweight, and inexperienced. The odds were 8-5 for the Ottawa team. Yet the sentiment was clearly in Calgary's favour as the crowd seemed to have been carried along by their fans' enthusiasm. And as the Toronto team had not made the finals, the locals could be impartial. Rather than choosing East over West, they decided to go along with Calgary's spirit.

Meanwhile, back in the West, local fans were glued to their radios. The beer parlours were deserted, for no entertainment—not even radios—was permitted by provincial government regulations. The only occupants were the waiters, frustrated and angry because they couldn't share in the festivities taking place in private

homes and in stores which had brought in radios specially for the event.

After Governor General Viscount Alexander of Tunis had kicked the ceremonial ball, the confrontation between the two teams became a see-saw affair. Ottawa had more weight and experience but Calgary possessed youth and speed. In the first quarter, Ottawa scored a single point with a kick to the deadline. In the second, the Stampeders launched a 56-yard drive and were on the nine yard line when they fooled Ottawa with the old "sleeper" play. Normie Hill walked to the sidelines as though leaving the field, but then laid down on the ground. He was not noticed by the Rough Riders so Keith Spaith had an easy toss to Hill in the end zone, giving Calgary a 5-point

touchdown, with an extra point for the convert. At half time, Calgary was ahead 6-1.

Coach Les Lear dressed and played in the second half but it didn't stop Ottawa from scoring a touchdown in the third quarter and getting the convert, putting the East ahead, 7-6. In the fourth quarter, Pete Thodos took a handoff on the 10-yard line and ran over for a touchdown. The convert put Calgary ahead 12-7 with nine minutes left to play. The determined Ottawa team fought its

THE CALGARY STAMPEDERS HOLD THE GREY CUP ALOFT AS THEY LEAVE THE CPR STATION TO TAKE PART IN THE 1948 VICTORY PARADE. (**HERALD COLLECTION, GLENBOW, NA-2864-13287A**)

way back deep into Calgary territory but Harry Hood intercepted a Rough Rider pass and ran it out to the 27-yard line. Then, in the dying moments of the game, Ottawa made a 38-yard run and seemed to be on its way for another touchdown. But its attack was diffused on the next play when Spaith intercepted a pass on his own 20-yard line and ran it back 40 yards. He let the time run out on the next play, and Calgary had won its first Grey Cup.

Calgarians, in a sea of red, white, and cowboy attire, swarmed onto the field. They not only ripped down the goalposts, but carried a major part of them back to the hotel and set them up in the lobby. From the time of the win until the tired fans poured on to the westbound train the following day, there was non-stop partying. The Royal York was renamed the Calgary Ranch and was jammed with people. At one point, two guitar-playing westerners had to climb on a table to have enough elbow room to perform. The crowd joined in, dancing and singing everything from "Home on the Range" to the Stampeders' theme song. Torontonians lined the mezzanine balcony, looking down in wonderment at the wild exhibition of gaiety and exuberance. The nearby bars also were crowded with celebrating westerners.[8]

The journey home was a cross-country victory celebration. The entire football team joined their fans on the train and as Woody Strode recalled, "We trained hard and we drank hard."[9] Not only that, but the CPR agreed to alter its schedule so that the train would arrive in Calgary at noon on Wednesday. They had to lose five hours, so they extended most of the stopovers by an extra twenty minutes. This gave the team and fans a chance to greet the crowds which awaited them at every station and to put on a show for them.

When they reached Port Arthur and Fort William (now Thunder Bay) at midnight, thousands turned out with trumpets and horns. At Kenora, the local brass band roused everyone out of the train at 7 a.m., and Winnipeg had a larger turnout than it ever gave its own Blue Bombers when returning home from winning the Grey Cup. Portage la Prairie and Regina both published special editions of their newspapers, one referring to the Stampeders as the "builders of Western morale."[10] And at Brooks and Gleichen, children were let out of school to join the crowds who were greeting the champions. It was,

in every way, a triumphant tour that celebrated a victory for the entire West.

Needless to say, the trip culminated in a massive demonstration in Calgary. A civic half-holiday was declared and a huge banner, "Welcome Home to our Grey Cup Champs," decorated the station entrance. Seven airplanes accompanied the train on its entrance into the city and an Air Force jet streamed over the station and dipped its wings in salute as the train pulled in. Even the weather co-operated, a friendly Chinook arch dominating the western sky.

After speeches and demonstrations at the station, the Stampeders ventured into what was perhaps the biggest crowd ever to attend a parade in its young history. Thousands of people cheered the football players who sat in fifteen open cars, their wives and families following in closed cars. After them came flatbed trucks with the hoarse but happy crowd from Toronto, a Jeep carrying the Grey Cup, a group led by Jimmy Gilkes and George Alexander carrying the goalposts, and then horses, cowboys, local school bands and majorettes, and pipe and military bands. Reporters hesitated to say how many Calgarians lined the parade route but it was equal to any Calgary Stampede. And they were even more exuberant and noisy than they were during the usual summer festival. Ticker tape and paper floated down on the open cars and people waved from windows all along the route.

"Calgary has reason for rejoicing," declared a *Calgary Herald* editorial, "Not just because the Stampeders won the Grey Cup . . . but because both the team and its supporters demonstrated that the old Western spirit isn't dead. Not by a jugful!"[11]

But it was more than that. Until 1948, easterners had seen Calgary as a small city on the main line of the CPR amid the ranches and grain fields of the West. Along with Edmonton, Leduc, and Turner Valley, it was mentioned in newspapers from time to time because of its oil. But that was all.

But with the 1948 Grey Cup, Calgary had proven itself to be a dynamic, aggressive, and exuberant city. It was on the map, and in the eyes and hearts of many Canadians who had never before given the city a second thought.

And after Calgary's spectacle of 1948, the Grey Cup would never be same again.[12]

FINDING THE LOST FORT

By the 1960s, Fort Calgary was little more than a dim memory, a quaint little outpost shown in history books with a few Indians sitting around outside the palisades. It was a relic of the past that had once existed somewhere near the confluence of the Bow and Elbow rivers—nobody quite knew where. Nothing remained and there were no reminders except a stone monument at the corner of 9th Avenue and 6th Street SE.

In its heyday, Fort Calgary had been the judicial, social, and administrative centre of the area. The palisaded fort of 1875 had given way in 1882 to military-type barracks, with wide lawns, and winding pathways. The fort always had enough prisoners to keep the grass mowed, the trees trimmed, and the grounds neat and tidy. It was the showplace of Calgary, the anchor of civilization at the east end of Stephen Avenue. During the 1880s and into the twentieth century, the fort—or "the barracks" as it was called—was a beehive of activity. Men drilled and paraded; constables set out and returned from patrols; dances, banquets, and garden parties brought the townsfolk into the station; and always there was the law to uphold.

The fort housed military troops during the Riel Rebellion, hanged murderers, and was home to such notables as W. M. Herchmer, Cecil Denny, Zachery Wood, and Gilbert E. Sanders. But by far the most interesting occupant was R. Burton Deane, who took over as commanding officer in 1906. One of his first actions was to build a large three-storey house, the finest on any Mounted Police reserve in Canada. However, just as it was finished, his wife died and, as he recalled, "it was a lonely house for me to go into."[1] In later years, the house was moved across the Elbow River where it served variously as a private residence and a rooming house. Today, it is preserved as the Deane House, a tea room and restaurant with all the atmosphere and grandeur of its elegant past.

The Mounted Police barracks came to an inglorious end in 1914 when the federal land was turned over to the Grand Trunk Pacific Railway for use as a station and freight yards. Superintendent Deane noted the police were scheduled to be out of the barracks by April 1. He recalled:

The guard-room was not emptied of its prisoners, nor were the buildings occupied by our men and horses vacated until some days later, but I, personally, did not choose to be under an obligation to the Grand Trunk Pacific Railway, and moved myself and my belongings off their premises on the date stated...[2]

Deane noted that the railway had made a shambles of the Mounted Police grounds. "The once pretty site soon became unrecognisable," he said, "the shrubs and trees were removed, the buildings torn down, and the only house left intact was the one that I had vacated, and that was moved to the opposite end of the enclosure for occupation by the station agent."[3]

When the Grand Trunk and Canadian Northern railways amalgamated to form Canadian National Railways, the site was abandoned as a station and became an industrial area and freight yard. The only on-site acknowledgement to its one-time historical role came in 1917 when the IODE (Independent Order Daughters of the Empire) erected a cairn at the end of 8th Avenue at 6th Street East, paying tribute to the fort. And even this monument suffered indignities in 1946 when it was "torn out of its foundations by the contractor erecting the warehouse for MacCosham Cartage."[4] The stone and plaque were dumped on the side of the road and it took almost two years and the combined efforts of the city and RCMP Veterans Association to have it relocated on the corner of 9th Avenue and 6th Street SE.

By the end of World War Two, the fort had been forgotten and the site was dominated by the huge warehouse of MacCosham's Moving and Storage. Other businesses included a scrap metal dealer, farm equipment supply, and a number of smaller warehouses. Railway tracks crossed the Elbow near its mouth and spread out in sinuous threads throughout entire site.

The original fort and grounds may have remained an industrial jungle had it not been for the efforts of John Ayer, a city alderman. In 1967, when a Bow River beautification plan and suggestions for a four-lane throughway along the south side of the river were presented to City Council, Ayer suggested that the actual site of the original Fort Calgary be marked. He was provided with maps from the Planning Department but when he brought them to the Glenbow Museum, the opinion was expressed that he

THE SITE OF THE ORIGINAL FORT CALGARY WAS DISCOVERED BY GLENBOW CREWS IN 1969-70. HERE, ARCHAEOLOGIST COLIN POOLE CAREFULLY REMOVES A CACHE OF BOTTLES, COINS, AND CLAY PIPE FRAGMENTS FROM THE SITE IN 1970. (GLENBOW, P-903-20)

had been given the wrong location. The city planners had indicated that the fort had been in a low area near the river, among the junk heaps of the scrap metal yard. Based on early photographs, museum staff thought it was several hundred feet farther to the south-east, at the top of a gentle rise.

In order to resolve the question, John Ayer and museum staff set out to see if any signs remained of the old fort. During the summer of 1968, Glenbow engaged the services of a University of Calgary archaeology student, Ron Getty, to search for surface remains. In the first season, his main discoveries were square nails and chinking found in a cutbank along a fence line. However, he believed these were from the later barracks, not the original fort. In the second season, his crews determined that much of the topsoil had been removed during railway and warehouse construction and it seemed that any signs of the original fort had been destroyed. Then, just as the season was ending, Getty discovered indications of the original palisades several inches beneath the ground in a storage yard behind MacCosham's warehouse. Through careful digging, he exposed part of the east wall of the men's barracks. Discoloured earth showed the existence of a trench while in a few places, actual remains of palisades were found still imbedded in the soil. There could be little doubt that this was part of the original Fort Calgary.

The Glenbow archaeological team was back in 1970 for a major excavation. By the time they were finished they had uncovered the remains of three buildings from the 1875 fort and had recovered more than 8,000 artifacts. Among them were Mounted Police buttons, pistol and rifle cartridges, a brass key, clay pipe fragments, metal parts of uniforms, fragments of bottles and jugs, nails, and even a number of early Canadian coins. The fort which had been missing for several decades had been found!

Spurred to action by these discoveries, Alderman Ayer pursued his goal of acquiring the entire thirty-two acres of the Mounted Police reserve. It was a daunting task, for the land encompassed some of the most valuable industrial property in the downtown area and had future potential for highrise development. He got the enthusiastic support of Mayor Jack Leslie and an agreement from the City Council that preserving the Fort Calgary site

should be the number one project for the city's centennial in 1975.

To further the venture, council established a Fort Calgary Steering Committee, consisting of Alderman Ayer, David Coutts of the Historical Society of Alberta, Jim Hornett of the RCMP Veterans Association, John Ballachey of the Heritage Park Board, and the author representing the Glenbow Museum. Later on, Sandra LeBlanc, Cliff Leech, Leo Van Vugt, Vic Burstall, Gilbert Beatson, and a number of others were added to the committee.

With the mayor's support, the city's land department director, Bob Leitch, was given the task of trying to arrange a land swap with the CNR. When Rod Sykes became mayor, he too supported the project but was concerned whether the complicated deal could be accomplished and the site readied in six years. Many of the businesses on the land had leases which would not expire until 1975 or 1976 and they were loathe to move. But Alderman Ayer persisted. He tried to get the federal government to declare Fort Calgary a heritage site of national importance and to provide funds to develop it as a National Historic Park. The government refused. When $22 million of provincial government funds became available for a junior college, he suggested that part of the money be used to acquire the Fort Calgary site and that the college be built on its western edge. This failed to materialize.

However, Alderman Ayer was encouraged when the Alberta government formed the Alberta-RCMP Centennial Committee which ultimately gave $56,000 towards the project. Also, when Century Calgary was established to plan for the city's centennial, it endorsed the idea of saving the Fort Calgary site, both for its historical importance and as part of a Bow River beautification project. In 1973, Rabbi Lewis Ginsburg, executive director of Century Calgary, said, "The interest engendered by the Fort Calgary project far exceeds that relating to any other undertaking by our committee."[5]

The acquisition of the site dragged on for three or four years and as the centennial year drew closer, it appeared that Mayor Sykes had been right. However, late in 1974 an agreement was finally made whereby the CNR swapped the 32 acres for 63.6 acres of city-owned land in the Valleyfield district, plus a cash settlement of $93,000. The city also bought the adjacent CNR right of way for $330,000 with most of the money coming from a federal fund used for railway abandonment purposes.

In addition, the good news was received that the Alberta government had made Fort Calgary its main project for the city's centennial and provided $2.6 million for an interpretive centre and a bridge connecting the site with St. Patrick's Island Park.

Early in 1975—the centennial year—warehouses were torn down, junk hauled away, and the area landscaped in time for the celebrations. The formal dedication of Fort Calgary Park took place near the end of summer, almost to the day when the first policemen had crossed the river to the site a hundred years earlier. More archaeological work was done, the bridge constructed, pathways laid out, and in May, 1978, the interpretive centre was officially opened.

Alderman John Ayer's job was done. His legacy to Calgarians was the original Mounted Police reserve, with gentle slopes and natural grasses, just as it had been in the time of Inspector Brisebois and the gallant men of F Troop. Today, the railway bridge is gone, the fort site marked, and the interpretive centre is a focal point for school groups and the general public who want to learn

about the origins of Calgary. The railway tracks, warehouses, and piles of scrap metal have become a dim memory and the 1875 fort a reality.

THE INCREDIBLE SEVENTIES

Things began to go crazy for Calgary late in 1973, when Libya nationalized a major segment of the foreign oil companies in its country and the Organization of Petroleum Exporting Countries (OPEC)[1] raised the price of oil from $3 to $5 a barrel. Over the winter of 1973-74, oil jumped to $11 a barrel and suddenly the world was facing an economic crisis while Calgary was awash with money.

Until this time, the oil-producing Arab nations had been completely under the thumb of the multinationals and prices had been kept at a modest $1.80 through the 1960s and early 1970s. When power was wrested from them by OPEC, however, prices skyrocketed and at the same time, production was reduced. Until this happened, relations in Canada among the Federal and Alberta governments, and the Calgary-based oil companies had been relatively harmonious. The natural resources were a responsibility of the provincial government which also owned most of the mineral rights. As a result, both royalties and the sale of mineral leases put money directly into the Alberta government's coffers, bringing in some $150 to $200 million a year during the 1960s. Most of the local oil was for export to the United States while some of it went via pipelines to Sarnia, Ontario. On the other hand, most of the oil used by central and eastern Canada came by tankers from the Arab world.

When the prices went wild, Ottawa suddenly saw millions of dollars going to Alberta while it was being left out in the cold. In addition, eastern Canada was being obliged to pay world prices for its imported oil. These events marked the beginning of a bitter conflict between Alberta premier Peter Lougheed and Prime Minister Pierre Trudeau over the division of Alberta's oil windfall.

In spite of the artificially low world prices since the Second World War, Alberta had already reaped a bonanza from royalties and leases since the discovery of oil at Leduc in 1947. And Calgary had been a major beneficiary. Between 1951 and 1961 its population had doubled, then almost doubled again in the next ten years. By 1958, the city had become home to some 275 head offices of oil and gas development, exploration, and producing companies and another 137 branch offices, many of them multinationals. Half of these were strung out along 8th Avenue.

PRIME MINISTER PIERRE TRUDEAU AND PREMIER PETER LOUGHEED WERE AT ODDS DURING MUCH OF THE 1970S OVER THE DIVISION OF ALBERTA'S OIL PROFITS. THEY ARE SEEN HERE WITH JAMES RICHARDSON IN 1973 AT THE WESTERN ECONOMIC OPPORTUNITIES CONFERENCE IN CALGARY. (HERALD COLLECTION, GLENBOW, NA-2864-23502)

But the big building boom had not yet hit Calgary as evidenced by the comments of a visiting journalist in 1958 who thought that 8th Avenue was a depressing sight. "Its tallest structure, the Mobil Oil Building, is only eleven stories," he said. "Its seventeen blocks run through dreary little east-end houses and crowded downtown blocks to a mere smattering of elegance in the west, where new banks strive to outdo each other with potted plants and escalators and the Sun Oil building stands gay and antiseptic in glass, steel and green tile."[2]

While perhaps not yet into a boom period, Calgary in the 1960s nevertheless enjoyed a prosperity unequalled for generations. The decade saw the value of building permits go from $68 million to $172 million, and over half of Calgary's population was either directly or indirectly supported by the oil industry. Its population of American oil men had become a visible part of Calgary's business and social life, and the local Chamber of Commerce liked to brag that the city had more privately owned airplanes and automobiles per capita than any place in Canada.

When the prices skyrocketed in 1973-74, the fight between Alberta and Ottawa began. The first salvo was fired late in 1973 when the federal government approved

a price increase of 40 cents a barrel then promptly took the entire amount via an export tax. In addition, oil company payments made to the Alberta government for leases and royalties would no longer be deductible from income tax. "We do not think," said Trudeau, "that it equitable or fair that surplus profits return solely to the provinces producing oil. In the government's opinion, the whole country should take benefit from any windfall profits."[3] On the other hand, Lougheed described the action as "the biggest ripoff of any province in Canada's history."[4] Little wonder that bumper stickers with the slogan, "Let the Eastern Bastards Freeze in the Dark," began appearing on Calgary automobiles and that Trudeau was jeered outside the Palliser Hotel when he visited the city.

Later in 1974, the two governments were forced into a compromise when oil companies cut back on exploration and began moving their drilling rigs out of the country. In particular, Alberta agreed to make up the oil companies' tax shortfall, to reduce its royalty rate, and to provide incentives for exploration.

The big argument, however, was over the price of oil. Alberta and the oil companies wanted it to reach the world price as quickly as possible while Ottawa demanded that it be kept low for the benefit of non-Albertans, particularly Ontario industries. By 1975, Alberta had been able to push the price up to $8 a barrel but this was still far below the world price. In 1978, it reached $11.75 a barrel but the world price was almost double that amount.

In spite of federal-provincial skirmishes, the money began rolling into the province's treasury at an unprecedented rate and the second boom in Calgary's history had arrived.

By 1977, huge new office buildings were beginning to dominate the city's horizon. Oxford Square and Shell Centre were both opened, adding another half million square feet of office space to the downtown area. Devonian Gardens were under construction and several other buildings, including the gigantic twin Esso Towers and Gulf Canada Square were on the drawing boards. This period gave rise to the comment that Calgary's native bird was the *cranus constructus,* referring to the large construction cranes which cluttered the city's skyline. Connecting the office towers and shopping centres was a new innovation introduced in the late 1960s—

IN 1977, T[...]
TOWER WAS A PROMI-
NENT LANDMARK IN
DOWNTOWN CALGARY.
WITHIN TEN YEARS, IT
WOULD BE LOST IN THE
MAZE OF NEW OFFICE
TOWERS. THIS IS A VIEW
LOOKING NORTH ACROSS
THE ELBOW RIVER NEAR
STAMPEDE PARK.
(GLENBOW, NA-2399-112)

"Plus 15" walkways. These enclosed pedestrian overpasses made it possible for a person to traverse much of the downtown business area in midwinter without ever going outside. For the first time in its history, the city's building permits passed the one-billion-mark in 1978, and the two-billion mark in 1981. This made Calgary the fastest growing city in North America next to Houston, Texas. No wonder the Chamber of Commerce referred to it as the "Boom Town."[5] Companies such as Dome and Husky were also changing the skyline, while the new Petro-Canada building became so dominant that the poor little Husky Tower, once the beacon of downtown Calgary, was almost lost in the plethora of skyscrapers.

Commented a journalist in 1978, "Progress everywhere confronts and confounds us. Take the city centre, for example. One tower after another rises. It seems our cityscape is forever a construction tableau, one vast building project in search of a place."[6]

With this rapid growth came massive changes, both in the city's skyline and in its lifestyle. Many believed that Calgary would become one of Canada's leading financial centres and that its residents should act accordingly. The Calgary Stampede, for example, was seen by some as rustic and *gauche,* not fitting for a cosmopolitan world centre. "When I got there," said a one-time resident,

"Calgary was quite content to be a cowtown, where everybody went nuts for ten days during the Stampede. That was what Calgary was—a cowtown. And it was great. But over a period of seven years or so, it suddenly thought that it had to be sophisticated."[7]

Eventually, it learned to be both. Many people who came to Calgary to make money and leave, ended up staying, putting down roots, and establishing a new culture infrastructure reflective of more cosmopolitan interests. Restaurants like La Chaumiere, Moose Factory, Ambrosia, Prairie Dog Inn, and My Marvin's appealed to a variety of tastes, while some of the city's finest dining was found in the Owl's Nest and the Captain's Table at the Four Seasons Hotel. Even the staid old Palliser went through a facelift, bringing back much of its earlier elegance and serving its unique crusty bread and clam chowder.

Live theatre also blossomed in the seventies. Alberta Theatre Projects began offering plays based on western history, such as the 1974 production about Bob Edwards, while Lunchbox Theatre played to standing room only. Seventeenth Avenue became a mecca for art lovers with galleries such as Masters, Agghazys, Calgary Galleries, and Canadian Art Galleries, while the new Glenbow Museum, which opened in 1976, offered stunning exhibitions from many parts of the world. "Even five years ago," said a reporter, "I'm sure eastern art dealer Mira Godard and the Glenbow Museum could not have staged the Picasso show here and have over two thousand people show up on the opening night."[8]

For those who thought the Calgary Stampede was plebeian, one could always go to Spruce Meadows to see some of the finest jumping horses in the world. International competitions brought the elite from many nations in performances which were at the opposite end of the spectrum from the rough and tumble rodeo contests of the Stampede. Since polo had virtually died out, people could express their love for horses without being common. The events at Spruce Meadows were further proof that Calgary was indeed an international centre with sports and cultural events to appeal to all tastes. And whatever it did, Calgary usually did it with style.

This was demonstrated when the singing and dancing groups who performed at the Stampede grandstand events came together in 1970 as The Young Canadians.

Under the skilful hand of Randy Avery, they became a top notch group which was in demand throughout North America. Although amateurs, they were thoroughly professional in every way, delighting audiences with their enthusiasm, energy, and skill.

Another sign of Calgary's boom was the increasing number of luxury cars on its streets. Where at one time a few Lincolns and Cadillacs were the signs of affluence, now Mercedes, Jaguar, and Porsche cars were seen with increasing frequency and firms such as Cooke Motors, Exclusive Sports Cars, and South Centre Fine Cars specialized in these expensive imports.

On the fringe of the city, subdivisions were springing up seemingly overnight and there was a rush to the suburbs as though people were fleeing from the glass and concrete mayhem in the downtown area. Part of this decentralization included the construction of shopping malls, so that unless you had business downtown, you didn't need to venture into the core area at all. The first of these shopping centres had been North Hill in 1958 and Chinook two years later, but the boom period saw the real growth of shopping malls. During the 1970s, Lake Bonavista, Northland Village, Market Mall, South Centre, Trans Canada, and Marlborough were added to the retail outlets while Chinook undertook a major expansion to make it, at that time, the largest shopping centre in western Canada.

The real estate market also went wild in the boom years, just as it had in 1911-12. A house which could be bought for $12,000 in 1960 was worth three times that amount at the beginning of the boom and continued to escalate through the late seventies. In 1973, for example, the average new home cost $30,300 and was increasing in value about 1 1/2 per cent a month. The price of board lumber doubled, plywood jumped 45 per cent, and chipboard 80 per cent in a single year. Labour costs also escalated as carpenters, electricians, plumbers, and other craftsmen were in short supply and were being enticed to come to Calgary. An economist noted in 1977 that "Thousands of migrants from other parts of Canada flowed into Calgary and Edmonton each month seeking employment and an opportunity to participate in the province's economic well-being."[9]

In 1979, the trouble between Ottawa and Alberta flared up again when an agreed price increase of $1 a

barrel on January 1 was cancelled by the federal authorities. This left a $10 difference between Alberta oil and the world figure at a time when world prices had doubled in a single year. Attempts to establish a new pricing agreement failed. New Brunswick Premier Richard Hatfield summarized the situation by contrasting the positions of Ontario and Alberta, "one side saying oil prices should not be increased and the other saying the sky is the limit. The reality lies somewhere in between."[10]

The standoff continued until October 28, 1980, when the federal government turned its back on provincial claims and unilaterally introduced a National Energy Policy (NEP). This legislation gave the federal government a whopping 25 per cent of all oil revenues and cut so deeply into the earnings of oil companies that their profits

A LIGHT RAIL TRANSIT CAR BREAKS A PAPER BARRIER TO MARK THE OFFICIAL OPENING OF THE NORTHEAST LRT IN SEPTEMBER 1980. (HERALD COLLECTION, GLENBOW, NA-2864-41272/14A)

would actually decline 50 cents a barrel at a time when world prices were still rising. At the same time, the NEP provided for only modest increases in the price of oil for the next three years.

As a result, a number of megaprojects which would mean millions of dollars to the economy were shelved, including the $12 billion Cold Lake oil sands project,

A NEW ERA IN CALGARY'S POLITICS BEGAN IN 1980 WHEN RADIO BROAD-CASTER RALPH KLEIN RAN FOR MAYOR. HE IS SEEN HERE AT CENTRE WITH SUPPORTER WEBSTER MACDONALD, SR. (LEFT), AND MANAGER TED TAKACS, AT THE BEGIN-NING OF HIS CAMPAIGN. (HERALD COLLECTION, GLENBOW, NA-2864-41187)

Judy Creek recovery project, and the $8 billion Alsand oil sands project. In retaliation, the Alberta government cut back production on Crown lands by 10 per cent. As a result, the oil companies said that they were being "squeezed to a point that discouraged future investment and exploration."[11]

According to petroleum journalist Frank Dabbs, the announcement of the NEP marked the end of a "remark-able seven-year economic boom that flared as brightly and briefly as a strip of burning magnesium."[12] During 1980-81, world oil prices began to slump, interest rates reached the double digits, mortgage rates hit 20 per cent,

and the nation's inflation figures shot past the 12 per cent mark. At the same time, the city's unemployment rate jumped by 5 per cent and for the first time in years, the size of the city's work force declined as skilled crafts-men left in search of work. Those who remained suffered a combination of job insecurity, lack of confidence in the country's economy, and a fear of the future.

The final and ultimate proof that the boom was over came at Christmastime in 1981. Optimistic merchants had looked forward to another banner year, but throughout December the mobs of shoppers failed to appear. When the season ended, business had declined by 50 per cent.

Yet the faith and confidence of Calgarians could not be quashed, for the Calgary of 1980 was vastly different from the Calgary a decade earlier. It had become a metropolis, international in influence, and better equipped to cope with the vagaries of the world econo-my. When the dark clouds of recession descended upon the city, its eternal optimism shone through like a bea-con. For example, after painting a grim picture of the 1982 retail trade in Calgary, the Chamber of Commerce suggested that merchants simply sharpen their business skills, carry less inventory, and become more aggressive in their sales. "Hopefully," an official concluded, "the present economy will not continue."[13] Similarly, the Calgary Real Estate Board was sure that "The pendulum may be about to swing back as the laws of supply and demand exert their influence on today's buyers' market."[14] It didn't happen, but the positive thinking was a good indication of Calgary's introduction to the reces-sion of the eighties.

DOWNSIZING

THE UNEASY EIGHTIES

THE FIRST HICCUP IN CALGARY'S BURGEONING ECONOMY IN 1981 HAD BECOME A

FULL-BLOWN EPIDEMIC BY THE FOLLOWING YEAR. CUSTOMERS BECAME MORE CAUTIOUS

ABOUT SPENDING THEIR MONEY AND STARTED SOCKING AWAY THEIR SPARE CASH IN THE

BANK. INTEREST RATES WERE SKYROCKETING OUT OF SIGHT AND PEOPLE BEGAN TO

HAVE PROBLEMS KEEPING UP WITH THEIR RISING MORTGAGE PAYMENTS.

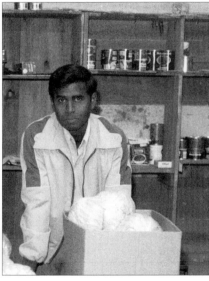

Oil exploration dropped a massive 25 per cent during the year as Trudeau's National Energy Policy began to have a ripple effect through the petroleum industry. Calgary's housing sales dropped, unemployment rose to 9 per cent—its highest in four years—and bankruptcies increased almost 40 per cent over the previous year. In addition, building permits plummeted from their all-time high of $2.5 billion in 1981 to $1 billion in 1982, and $427 million a year later. It was clear that the palmy days of the 1970s were over.

But the decade had its positive features. During the early years, a number of major projects which had been committed before the recession were carried through to completion. One of the most significant was the first leg of the Light Rail Transit line in 1981. This meant that Calgary—like so many other North American cities—was returning to the streetcar. Thirty years earlier, the city had been sold on the efficacy of electric buses and air-polluting diesels but found they ultimately added to downtown traffic jams and proved an expensive alternative to the old reliable streetcar. While the city would never return to the network of car lines which had served it so well in the past, the LRT routes to the south, east, and north became a major part of Calgary's transportation system.

People tried to convince themselves that the recession was only temporary and that soon there would be a return to the wild prosperity of the previous decade. However, the oil companies knew better and soon the euphemistic term "downsizing" became commonplace as staff were dismissed or given early retirements, mergers were concluded, and entire floors of office buildings became empty.

As an ominous indication of things to come, the Calgary Inter-Faith Community Action Association in 1983 asked Joseph Edison to organize a food bank to help the needy. This was reminiscent of the soup kitchens which the city had set up during the depth of the Great Depression. Before the end of the year, Edison had a hundred volunteers busily handing out food to those who had lost their jobs, no longer qualified for Unemployment Insurance benefits, or were otherwise in need.

And in that year, the civic government laid off its first staff since the boom, cut back on maintenance to city parks, and eliminated some of the bus routes. Meanwhile, the bank rates kept getting higher and higher and the value of houses plunged. A house that had sold for $110,000 in 1981 was worth $78,000 by the end of 1984.

Mortgage rates became so prohibitive that people were hard pressed to make their payments. Typical was a man who worked in an office by day and drove a taxi at night. This provided enough money to meet the mortgage payments while his wife's salary covered their other expenses. When his wife became pregnant and had to quit, the value of their house was so low that it was less than their current debt. Finally, he did as many others

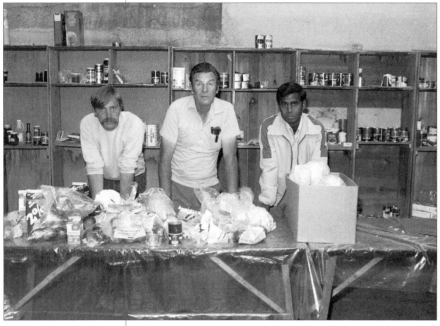

were doing; he simply stopped making payments and lived in the house for another seven months until he was evicted. He still owed a huge amount to the finance company and ultimately filed for personal bankruptcy.

In 1985, there were 4,000 foreclosures in Calgary, another 5,000 home owners were said to be "in difficulty," and foreclosures remained steady at five hundred a month into the following year.[1] But the market finally "bottomed out" and for the first time since 1981, house prices began to rise.

Then, on October 19, 1987, the world experienced "Black Monday" when the value of stocks plunged in their worst fall since the Wall Street Crash of 1929. Within a few hours, Wall Street lost a half trillion dollars while Japan, Britain, Hong Kong, and West Germany suffered similar losses. In less than a month, stocks on the Alberta Stock Exchange had lost as much as two-thirds of the peak values they had reached in mid-September.

"Since then," said a reporter, "prices have hurtled up and down as if they were on a roller-coaster. Companies

have bought back their own stock, and new issues have been reduced to a trickle. Small investors burned in the crash have been avoiding the market in droves."[2] The blame was placed on everything from the massive budget and trade deficits in the United States to a gross overvaluing of stocks.

Yet there were positive signs of stability. The price of houses remained firm during the crash and, when interest rates fell to their lowest levels since the 1950s, many young families began buying their own homes. Meanwhile, events such as the Calgary Stampede, hockey and football games, and other sporting events continued to be well supported while the visual and performing arts attracted faithful crowds. Perhaps money wasn't spent as lavishly as it was in previous decades but there was enough to keep Calgary's economy afloat.

The city's continuing role in the oil industry had also provided an expertise which began to pay dividends. The skills of Calgary consultants were in demand as far away as Saudi Arabia and Indonesia. Many of these people had been laid off by oil companies and had promptly gone into business for themselves. The city also maintained a key role in advanced research in telecommunications, computer science, medicine, and oil-related industries.

During the early years of the recession, Calgary never lost its sense of the Old West. Newcomers perhaps looked askance at the informality of the Stampede when the whole city seemed to go "western" but soon they too were sporting Stetson hats, coloured shirts, and all the other paraphernalia of the week. One of the best lines ever devised by an advertising agency in the early 1980s was, "Quick, what word follows Calgary?" There was only one answer . . . "Stampede," of course.

But there was another word on the horizon— "Olympics." For just as Calgarians had put the city on the map for the rest of Canada at the 1948 Grey Cup, now it was prepared to do the same thing for the rest of the world at the 1988 Winter Olympics.

A BUNCH OF PINHEADS

For several weeks in 1987 and 1988, Calgary was a paradise for pinheads. They walked the malls, invaded shopping centres, made deals at service stations, and guarded their enamelled treasures as if they were pure gold. These were the pin collectors (nicknamed "pinheads") who were part of a short-lived trading frenzy during the XV Olympic Winter Games.

∽

It all started in September, 1981, just as the recession began to clutch the city, when Bob Niven, Frank King, Mayor Ralph Klein, Bill Warren, and a crowd of other civic boosters came home from Baden Baden, Germany, with the news that Calgary had won the right to host the Winter Olympics in 1988. This was their fourth attempt to bring the Games to Calgary and their promises of brand new world-class facilities had finally swung the vote in their favour.

It was a bold enterprise that called for the co-operation of all levels of government as well as support from local industries and the involvement of thousands of volunteers. Funding for the Olympics included $200 million from the federal government, $130 million from the Alberta government, and $43 million from the City of Calgary. Most of these funds were to be used for capital construction work in Calgary, Canmore, and Nakiska. The commitments had been made in the buoyant days of the boom; perhaps if the various agencies could have reconsidered their generosity in light of the recession they may have changed their minds, but this didn't happen. In addition, the American Broadcasting Corporation paid a whopping $309 million for the exclusive television rights to the Games while oil companies and other companies provided significant financial support.

The schedule for the 1980s was a daunting one. The Calgary Olympic Development Association (CODA) had only six years to organize an event which would be watched by the entire world. Much of the initial responsibility fell to Bill Pratt, who had an impressive record in

the construction industry, and to Frank King, one of the original organizers.

Even before Calgary got the Games, the Olympic Saddledome was under construction to house the city's first NHL team, the Calgary Flames. The $98 million facility, funded by the three levels of government, was intended to demonstrate to the International Olympic Committee (IOC) that Calgary was indeed serious about providing first-class accommodations for the Games.

The construction of the ski jumps, skating ovals, housing units, and other facilities during the 1980s gave the city a much-needed boost to its economy and helped to blunt some of the ravages of the recession. The building program was impressive. There was a $72 million development at Paskapoo ski hill, renamed Canada Olympic Park, on the outskirts of Calgary. Funded mostly by the federal government, it included ski jumps, luge and bobsled tracks, visitors' centre, and hall of fame. The Olympic Oval for skating events was a $40 million structure situated at the University of Calgary. In addition, there were media villages at Broadcast Hill and Lincoln Park, a $16 million expansion of McMahon Stadium, improvements to the Max Bell arena, conversion of the Big Four Building to become the International Broadcast Centre, and scores of other projects in the city and west in the Rockies.

Downtown, the Olympic Plaza was constructed near the Stephen Avenue Mall while the rest of the area was spruced up by opening the new Calgary Municipal Building and the Calgary Centre for the Performing Arts. The latter, in particular, would be heavily used for the Olympic Arts Festival.

∽

Long before the start of the Games, the pinheads began to appear; they were a part of the Olympic tradition. The first pins were issued at the 1924 Summer Games but

PEOPLE GATHERED ON THE STEPHEN AVENUE MALL DURING THE 1988 OLYMPICS TO SWAP PINS. (GLENBOW, P-3580-27)

these were just for competitors and were traded among friends. Colourful enamelled pins began to be circulated in the 1930s and, after the Second World War, some of the sponsors started to produce their own pins which were officially sanctioned by the IOC. In 1972, pins began to gain widespread popularity at the Munich Summer Games but the real breakthrough came in 1984 when they became big business at the Summer Games in Los Angeles. A special pin trading tent was set up where as many as 20,000 collectors a day came to buy and trade. A total of 30 million pins were produced for that occasion and they all found a ready sale.

❧

A decision was made early in the planning stages of the Calgary Olympics that the organizers would depend on a small salaried staff and a huge number of volunteers to handle all arrangements. The city had already established an enviable reputation for volunteerism, particularly at the Calgary Stampede, and hundreds of local people from all walks of life were anxious to participate in the Games. The first volunteer committee was set up in January 1983 to create educational material for schools. By fall, forty-five other committees had been formed and three hundred volunteers were at work; as the date drew nearer, the number of volunteers increased dramatically. These enthusiasts were involved with planning such activities as the torch relay, opening ceremonies, public receptions, and the million and one details involved in such a spectacle.

Meanwhile, plans for the Olympic Arts Festival began to take shape. The performing arts included everything from the National Ballet to the Calgary Philharmonic. The visual arts were led by the Glenbow Museum's dramatic exhibition, "The Spirit Sings," which brought together Canadian native artifacts from all over the world. There also were film festivals, art exhibitions, snow sculpting, a rodeo, and a host of other events.

In 1986, some 1.9 million tickets to the Games were put on sale—the most in the history of a Winter Olympics. Yet the overwhelming response soon made it clear that in spite of the quantity, tickets to the favourite events would be in short supply. In fact, the initial rush for tickets was four times greater than the organizers had expected; everyone wanted to see the Olympics.

As the date for the Games approached, Calgarians became more and more excited. Thousands of people offered their services and prepared to open their homes and their hearts to the city's visitors.

❧

From the United States, members of the International Pin Collectors Club and commercial dealers began preparing to invade the city, positive that the pin mania of Los Angeles was going to be revived in Calgary. Actually, pin collecting wasn't really new to the city. The pins produced for volunteers and officials at the Calgary Stampede had been prized objects since they were first issued in the 1920s and curlers were accustomed to wearing outfits festooned with pins from their various competitions. But these were nothing compared to the Olympics.

❧

Calgary was unique in Olympic history in that its construction program remained on schedule during the 1980s and except for the Saddledome it was well within budget. Much of this was due to the unstinting work of the volunteers. By the summer of 1987, fifty-nine countries—an Olympic record—had confirmed they would be participating in the Winter Games. By this time, Calgary's volunteer force had risen to more than 9,000 people and was still growing.

According to the official Olympic history, "Over the next six months, OCO '88 feverishly prepared for the Games. The last of the major sports venues, the Olympic Oval, officially opened in September. The Preview 88 events in figure skating, speed skating, and short track speed skating, were successfully staged in November and December."[1]

❧

The exclusive right to produce and market pins with Olympic symbols went to Laurie Artiss Limited of Regina. As the official licensee, this company made all the pins for the sponsors, suppliers, and other licensees, as well as producing its own commercial sets for sale directly to the public. By early 1987, the firm was already publishing a pin collectors' newsletter for those planning to take part in the Games.

❧

The trans-Canada Olympic torch relay started in November, 1987, when the flame was taken from Athens to Newfoundland and then to Halifax by air. From there it began an eleven-week journey across Canada, the longest in Olympic history, carried by more than 7,000 runners. The torch itself was designed in the shape of the Calgary Tower and decorated with symbols of Olympic events.

The Arts Festival began early in January 1988 with the Glenbow exhibition being one of the highlights. Its opening was marked by demonstrations from native groups supporting the Lubicon land claim but this did not interfere with the formal ceremonies. In addition to the exhibition, there were presentations of dancing and crafts by native groups from all parts of Canada.

❧

As predicted, the pin trading frenzy started late in 1987. By November, the licensee had released pins of Hidy and Howdy, the Olympic mascots, selling at $5 each, while the pins of a number of sponsors and one of the participating nations—Switzerland—began to appear at local flea markets. By December, some of the forty-four oil companies which had banded together as Team Petroleum '88 circulated their pins and Coca-Cola announced they would erect a huge tent beside the Stephen Avenue Mall where pins could be purchased or traded.

❧

The Olympics began on February 13 when 60,000 people streamed into McMahon Stadium for the opening ceremonies. As two billion people across the world watched on television, Calgary provided a stunning two-hour exhibition of RCMP, Indians, and performers. In the procession, 8,000 costumed volunteers led the parade of athletes, each country proudly bearing its flag. Everything went off like clockwork—the flypast, musical events, and lighting the Olympic flame. Thousands of white hats were tossed into the air in celebration.

During the next fifteen days, the eyes of the world were on Calgary and the winter events. The television and radio networks devoted hundreds of hours to hockey, skating, skiing, luge, and other events which made up the international spectacle. The efforts of the Jamaican bobsled team, the trials of English skier Eddie the Eagle, and a dramatic winning of a silver medal in figure skating by Canadian Elizabeth Manley all added to the colour and drama of the Games.

❧

Pin trading swept Calgary like a tidal wave, engulfing even those who had never heard of a lapel pin before. By the time the Olympics began, Calgary was inundated with sponsor pins, team pins, country pins, bid pins, supplier pins, licensee pins, and even quantities of illegal or unauthorized pins. Two days before the opening ceremonies, 200 enthusiasts gathered at the University of Calgary for a symposium on "The Art of Pin Trading" and were given useful advice on all aspects of this "unofficial sport."

The pins from ABC, NOVA, United States customs, and Atco immediately became "rarities," avidly sought by the pinheads. Even before the Coca-Cola tent was raised, collectors gathered in the rotunda of Glenbow, examining the 600 pins the museum had collected and placed on display. Soon stories were circulating about a Russian team pin that sold for $300, an ABC camera pin for $365, and a Glenbow "Spirit Sings" VIP pin for $60. The owner of a Catelli/Karen Percy pin commented, "Two weeks ago it wasn't worth anything. But I was offered $300 after she won the two bronze medals and if she wins another medal I think I can get $1,000 for it."[2]

Calgary Herald reporter Mike Lamb was sent out on the streets on a humorous assignment to see what he could trade for the newly minted *Herald* pins. During his tour he collected eight bottles of beer, a brassiere, a photograph of himself, a tank of gas, a balloon ride, a pair of pink front-yard flamingos, and a used skateboard. Each he got for a pin, except for the balloon ride which cost him two.[3]

ONE OF THE HIGHLIGHTS
OF THE CULTURAL EVENTS
DURING THE 1988 WINTER
OLYMPICS WAS THE
GLENBOW MUSEUM'S
EXHIBITION, "THE SPIRIT
SINGS." HERE, ALEX
SCALPLOCK, OF THE
BLACKFOOT TRIBE,
DANCES DURING ONE
OF THE MUSEUM'S PRO-
GRAMS. (GLENBOW,
P-3543F-27)

By the time the craziness was over, about nine million pins in 1,500 different designs had been produced and circulated in Calgary. More than 150,000 were sold at the Coca-Cola tent and countless others traded through the highways and byways of town. During the peak of the Games more than a thousand people a day were crowding into the Glenbow pin exhibition, with almost 40,000 viewing the show during its time on exhibition.

A Calgarian or visitor not wearing a pin was a rarity during the Olympics. Some had their vests and lapels covered with them while many other bought glass display cases to be mounted with pins and placed proudly in their living rooms. Even after the Coca-Cola tent had been folded away, pin traders gathered on the mall with loose-leaf albums, fabric-covered cardboard sheets, or portable glass cases to display their wares. They sat on benches and dickered with fellow pinheads who wanted to buy, sell, or trade the little bits of metal.

One of the American visitors had a warning for the local enthusiasts during the height of the craze. The pins, he said, were worth what anyone would pay for them. In the excitement of the Games, the market had become greatly overheated and many pins were wildly overpriced. "I would expect everything to crash just like the stock market did," he said.[4] He was right, of course, but everybody had a lot fun while it lasted.

⌒

When the XV Olympics were over, visitors were lavish in their praise of Calgary for the way it had organized the Games. They were overwhelmed both by the friendliness of the people and their devotion to volunteerism. Olympic president Juan Antonio Samaranch echoed the feelings of many when he declared that Calgary had "the best organization of Winter Olympics ever."[5]

The statistics were impressive. The Games involved fifty-nine countries in fifty events, all of which were successfully completed. The Games contributed more than $1.4 billion to Canada's economy, most of it to Calgary and Canmore, including $506 million in capital improvements. There were more than 11,000 volunteers involved in every aspect of the Games. And where other Olympic venues had incurred massive debts, Calgary ended hers with a profit of more than $27 million.

The event also brought Calgarians together in a spirit of camaraderie that would long be remembered. And so would the pinheads recall the crazy, wonderful days when their pins had actually been worth something.

OLD NEIGHBOURS

During periods of boom and bust, in good times and bad, an important segment of Calgary's history has involved the native peoples of southern Alberta. They were neighbours long before there was a Mounted Police fort and they have left their mark in the uniqueness of the city, in everything from the naming of streets and bridges to the economic and social life of the community. Over the years, the relationship has usually been a close and positive one. As recently as 1992, for example, the Tsuu T'ina tribe estimated that it was adding up to $25 million a year to Calgary's economy.

The association is most obvious during the Calgary Exhibition and Stampede where native involvement in the parades and rodeo events has been evident for years. The only Canadian to win a championship at the first Stampede in 1912 was a Blood Indian, Tom Three Persons. The tradition continued when Pete Bruised Head was Canadian calf roping champion in the 1920s; Jim Wells the steer decorating championship in 1942; and the father and son team of Fred and Jim Gladstone from the Blood tribe dominated the calf roping scene several times since the 1940s.

Fred Gladstone won the Canadian championships in 1948 and 1950 and then went on to become a member of the Stampede's Rodeo Committee. Over the years he acted as flagman, gateman, and performed a score of other volunteer duties until his retirement in 1992. His son, Jim, followed in his father's direction and went one step further by becoming the world's champion calf roper in 1977. Today he is a lawyer living on the southern outskirts of Calgary.

Other representatives from the Sarcee, Stoney, Blackfoot, Blood, and Peigan reserves have competed regularly in all the major rodeo events. In 1952, eleven-year-old Linda One Spot from the Sarcee Reserve was so anxious to be a part of the rodeo that she disguised her identity and entered the boys' steer riding competition as Linder

One Spot. She tucked her hair out of sight and rode three steers successfully before she was thrown. When her hat was knocked off the secret was out and she was disqualified. In the field of chuckwagon racing, drivers like Dave Crowchild and Rufus Goodstriker demonstrated a skill which has been carried on by such men as Edgar Baptiste and Rae Mitsuing who are leading drivers today.

E-100 CALGARY STAMPEDE
FRED GLADSTONE - CALF ROPING

FRED GLADSTONE, A MEMBER OF THE BLOOD TRIBE, WON THE CALF ROPING CHAMPIONSHIPS IN 1948 AND 1950 AND WENT ON TO BECOME A LONGTIME MEMBER OF THE STAMPEDE RODEO COMMITTEE. (PHOTO COURTESY P. DEMPSEY)

In addition, the role of southern Alberta natives in the Stampede parades and Indian village is one which has resulted in pride and recognition to all concerned. Many native families are quick to point out that they are the second or third generation of participants, that their parents or grandparents took part in the first Stampede in 1912. They exhibit their skills in beadwork, painted tipis, and crafts, and vie for the trophies which are awarded annually. There is so much prestige attached to being a tipi owner that, according to one leader, "there's a waiting list of 10 people for every teepee spot."[1]

For many years, the Indian village was located at the main entrance to the grounds, beneath the huge Sun Tree. With the expansion of the Stampede in 1974, it was moved to a more secluded place at the south end where tribal members were able to pitch their lodges in a park-like atmosphere beside the Elbow River. The Tsuu T'ina and Siksika have their tipis along the north side, the Peigans to the east, and the Bloods and Stoneys to the south. In the centre of the grounds are flagpoles for opening ceremonies while below the hill is a dancing stage. In addition to competition dancing, the Indian village also features meat cutting competitions, a princess contest, public openings of selected tipis, and Sunday religious services conducted by native elders.

The Indian village is controlled by an Indian Events Committee which at one time was made up entirely of non-Indian Calgarians who supervised the programs, parades, and other activities. Today, however, the committee is a mix of local residents and tipi owners, with the Indians predominating. Bruce Starlight, who has been a member of the committee since 1973, was elected as its first native chairman in 1989.

In 1991 Starlight became the centre of controversy when he was passed over in an election for a seat on the prestigious Stampede Board of Directors. The *Calgary Herald* complained, "For more than 70 years of Stampede history the board has worked with, and the Stampede has benefited from, the presence and participation of native Indians. Yet for all those years the Stampede board has managed to keep any and all aboriginals from joining its ranks."[2]

Outrage was expressed by native leaders, representatives of the City Council, and the press. Initially the Stampede replied by saying that the rodeo cowboys didn't have a seat on the board either and, besides, the Indians would be well represented by a non-native board members who had responsibility for the Indian village. Meanwhile, Starlight remained imperturbable during the controversy and philosophical about his defeat; his main concern was that the rejection should not cause Indians to lose interest in the summer event.

Stung by the criticism, the Stampede in 1992 named Roy Whitney, chief of the Tsuu T'ina tribe, to fill one of the appointed seats on the Board of Directors and later in the year Starlight was finally elected to fill one of the other vacancies.

Controversy between Indians and the Stampede is not new, but the problems were usually resolved without too much rancour. In 1950, there was trouble when the Stampede ended its practice of giving all Indians free admission to the grounds. Instead, it provided the tipi owners with bundles of passes to hand out to members of their tribes. When the angry Stoneys refused to participate, a rumour was started by a reporter that they had held a "rain dance" which resulted in a heavy downpour during Stampede week. It was all nonsense, of course. As patriarch Tom Kaquitts noted, "The rains were not caused by the Indians but came from someone above, far over the blue mountains."[3] Over the winter, the matter was resolved and the tribe was back the following year.

Another problem arose in 1965 when the poor location of the village caused it to be flooded during a heavy rainstorm. This was before it was moved to its present location. Many valuable costumes and personal possessions were damaged or destroyed and when compensation wasn't immediately forthcoming, some of the owners formed a union-like United Indian Committee to deal with their grievances. However, the Stampede would not deal with the group and ultimately settled with individual owners.

A more serious confrontation took place in 1972, when Dave and Daisy Crowchild, two of the most popular people in the village, were suspended for a year and their tipi site given to someone else. The problem arose when the couple was invited to a native ceremony outside of the city and moved out of the village before the Stampede was over. Even though they left their tipi in place, they were told they had broken the rules and were being punished.

There was a great outcry from the general public, for the Crowchilds were among the leading goodwill ambassadors between the native and white communities. The Crowchild Trail, which cuts a swath through the heart of the city, is named in their honour. Even the mayor, Rod Sykes, appealed to the Stampede Board to invite them back and to correct the "slight on a proud and outstanding Indian family."[4] The invitation was extended but the family never returned.

Yet when any outsider complains about the village, the Indians close ranks. On one occasion, a Calgary alderman said the Indians were being exploited and were being used as "tourist gimmicks."[5] Wilfred Mark, of the Stoney tribe, was among the first to jump to the defence of the Stampede. "Nobody forces us to take part," he said. "We do it because we enjoy it and look forward to going every year. While we camp there, we have a chance to see a lot of things and do some visiting. It is especially nice for Indian youngsters."[6] George Runner, from the Tsuu T'ina tribe, agreed. "I hope my children will take

over after me," he said, "and keep up our family participation in the Stampede." Some time later, Bruce Starlight stressed the importance of the Indian village in keeping their culture and traditions alive. "If it wasn't for the Calgary Stampede," he said, "it would be virtually dormant. We would have been assimilated. It's the only place to display our painted teepee designs, show what goes on inside a teepee, and wear our buckskin outfits."[7]

Bruce Starlight is from the Tsuu T'ina Reserve, Calgary's closest neighbour. Today, the city butts against the east end of the reserve and is beginning to surround it. The tribe has changed its name from Sarcee to its native term, the Tsuu T'ina Nation, and has freed itself from the strictures of the Indian Department.

Tired of having its business run ineffectively by bureaucrats, the Tsuu T'ina formulated their own economic development plan. It began in 1972 when the band formed Redwood Development Limited and established Redwood Meadows, a residential subdivision, and an adjoining golf course at the west end of the reserve. The long-term leasing of lots and their maintenance became a significant source of both employment and income for the tribe.

In 1984 the band formed Sarcee Gravel Products, contracting for all road construction and maintenance on the reserve and serving a large number of customers in Calgary and surrounding rural areas. Then, in 1991, after the tribe had reclaimed land which had been on a long-term lease to the Department of National Defence, it formed Wolf's Flat Ordnance Disposal Corporation to sweep the area with metal detectors to clear the land of unexploded shells, grenades, and other metal objects of war. This is expected to take five years, and at the end of that period, tribal members will have the expertise to undertake cleanup projects in other regions of the world.

During these years, the tribe also built the Seven Chiefs Sports-Plex and the Harry Dodging Horse Memorial Agri-Plex, as well as forming the Tsuu T'ina Cattle Company, and Tsuu T'ina Mechanical, together earning about $15 million annually.

In 1992, the Tsuu T'ina Nation took another step forward with a $15 million construction project at the point where Anderson Road enters the reserve. Within a year a small service station and confectionary were in operation. When the expansion is completed, it will include a 27-hole golf course, a large multi-purpose retail and office complex, restaurant, bank, supermarket, motor vehicles office, and an expanded service station. All the funds for the project are being generated by the tribe and through the Canadian Aboriginal Economic Development Strategy Program. Space in the office building has already been leased to the Treaty Seven Tribal Office, Indian Oil and Gas Canada, Indian Health and Welfare Canada, and a number of Indian-owned businesses.

All of these programs have provided a high level of employment for the reserve, making the Tsuu T'ina one of the most progressive and successful in western Canada. To keep pace with the industrial development, the band has opened its own elementary school and is encouraging higher education. Previously, all students were bused to schools in Calgary. In addition to the usual academic courses, children are now receiving lessons in their native language and learning about their history and culture.

Meanwhile, the city of Calgary is home to an increasing number of natives. Today, there are more than 20,000 from all parts of Canada. Some are employed in the oil industry and professional firms while others may be found in all levels of business and society. There are about 250 students attending the University of Calgary, and others at Mount Royal College, SAIT, and Alberta Vocational College. Among the services available to them are the Calgary Indian Friendship Centre, as well as various counselling and employment services.

In recognition of the ongoing relationship between the native and non-native peoples, the City of Calgary established the Chief David Crowchild Memorial Award in 1986. It honours selected citizens for creating a better understanding in the fields of native culture, education, training, employment and self-fulfilment, and for "encouraging cross-cultural experiences between native and non-native communities."[8] The first recipient was Pauline Dempsey, a member of the Blood tribe who has an outstanding record for native community service in the city. Since that time, a permanent record of the annual award winners is being placed on a sculpture at the main entrance to the Municipal Building. This would seem to be a fitting place to recognize old friends and neighbours.

INTO THE TWENTY-FIRST CENTURY

What will Calgary be like in the 21st century? In the 1970s this became a popular topic for city planners, academics, and journalists. In 1972, writer Ken Hull concluded that by 2000, Calgarians would have a Utopian lifestyle. Automobiles would be banned from downtown Calgary; children would be taught at home via television; apes would wait tables in restaurants; and robots would be used in private homes. These conclusions were based upon interviews with scientists at the University of Calgary.

He was told that shopping would be done via closed circuit television; many people would work at home; and that office towers would be filled with machines, rather than people. Many of the downtown streets would be enclosed so they could be heated in winter and air conditioned in summer. In addition, the Elbow River and the air would be free of pollution.[1]

Some of Calgary's senior citizens had different views. In 1974, George McDougall predicted that pollution would destroy drinking water and the air, that the world's oil supply would run out and be replaced by electricity. Ken Meikeljohn expressed his concern for the survival of the nucleur family. "Abortion, divorce . . . these are symptoms of a sick age," he said. "The sacredness that held society together is being lost."[2] In a similar vein, Bill Atkinson was concerned about increasing violence and predicted world conflict over oil. As for Calgary's boom, he made a remarkably accurate prediction that "Calgary will stop expanding in 10 years . . . Again it will be oil causing it." Jack Rix said that "Calgary will get bigger and bigger, and bigger. Miles and miles. There'll be lots of crime."

On the other hand, May Keir, in 1974, was impressed with the dedication of young people, particularly to ecology. "We may be going back to more natural things," she said, "away from cars and planes, back to walking. Because of them, the ecology will become better. Pollution won't be so bad."

In 1977, a reporter was told by planners that the city would remain within its existing boundaries, developing and redeveloping the land it already had, rather than spreading out to the rural areas. (They were wrong, of course, for Calgary continued to annex surrounding regions in 1981 and 1989 to give it 671.8 square kilometres of land.) The planners also predicted a move away from the core area to suburban shopping and business centres, and that a form of rapid transit would be in effect.

Two years later, in 1979, reporter Mark Tait was told there would be a million people in Calgary by 2000. (Not a very likely prospect, considering there were 727,719 by 1993.) As a result, there would be great pressure on the city to provide housing, basic services, recreation facilities, and drinking water—all of which would be in short supply. The housing sprawl would extend northward in an arc around Nose Hill and southward to gobble up Midnapore.[3]

Also in 1979, reporter Oliver Bertin was told that Calgary would include Cochrane, Airdrie, and Okotoks. The 50,000 people going to work in the downtown area each day would be required to park on the outskirts and take a bus or LRT to their jobs. The city would no longer be known as an oil centre because of the scarcity of petroleum but by then it would have become a major energy centre and would maintain its position of leadership. Oil would be so expensive that the family car could be used only occasionally and many people would live in the downtown area to avoid driving. Multi-storey apartments would replace many single family dwellings. The downtown would be lively place after dark, with theatres, restaurants and clubs being the main attractions.

"And, all important, Calgary will be a nice place to live," he optimistically concludes. "By the year 2000, the city will have a stable and prosperous population based on clean industry, services, finance and head offices. In the centre of the new Calgary will be a Civic Centre which, by then, will be located in a thriving part of downtown."[4]

But perhaps the most interesting comments came in 1974 from a number of eight-year-old school children—Calgarians for whom the 21st century would someday be a reality. Here are some of their remarks: "Transportation might be airplanes that won't crash, automobiles that won't give off pollution, trains that will run without a track, and a boat that won't use gas." "I think houses will be made on the moon and under the sea. In the lakes there will be big cities." "There will be enough food for everyone, but not the same food like pork and beans. The food will be seaweed and ducks." And from a little girl who obviously didn't like turnips: "I think there will be enough for everyone to eat. They will plant it. It would be like a rootabaga but it would not taste like a rootabaga."[5]

Whatever Calgary may be in the 21st century, it will still be a city with a heart—one of friendliness and community spirit. It will continue its long history of volunteer service which has ranged from social agencies to the annual Stampede. The white hat will remain a symbol, not of commercialism but of openness of the type that existed in the ranching country of the Canadian prairies.

NOTES

Note: To avoid an excessive use of endnotes, direct quotes are cited when used for the first time. Subsequent quotes are from the same source unless otherwise stated.

A PRISTINE LAND

1. Currently, the Blackfoot tribe uses the term Siksika Nation while the Sarcees refer to themselves as the Tsuu T'ina Nation. We respect these contemporary political designations, but because so much of the historical literature uses the old terms, we will stay with Blackfoot tribe and Sarcee tribe to avoid confusion.
2. Interview with Pat Bad Eagle, Peigan Indian, by the author, 1953. In author's possession.

THE MYSTERY OF FORT LA JONQUIERE

1. *The Morning Albertan,* Calgary, February 28, 1911.
2. Lawrence J. Burpee, *Journals and Letters of Pierre Gaultier de Varennes de la Verendrye and his Sons.* Toronto: The Champlain Society, 1927, 33; also, John P. LeRoux, "La Jonquiere, Alberta's Lost Fort." Essay for Mount Royal College, 1973, 2. Copy in Glenbow Library.
3. Cited in Arthur S. Morton, *A History of the Canadian West to 1870-71.* Toronto: University of Toronto Press, 1973, 237.
4. LeRoux, 1973, 3.
5. Cited in *Calgary Herald,* September 3, 1955.
6. Cecil E. Denny, *The Riders of the Plains; A Reminiscence of the Early and Exciting Days in the North West.* Calgary: The Herald Company, 1905, 81.
7. Ernest Voorhis, *Historic Forts and Trading Posts of the French Regime and of the English Fur Trading Companies.* Ottawa: Department of the Interior, 1930, 96.
8. *The Morning Albertan,* Calgary, February 28, 1911.
9. *Idem.,* March 6, 1911. Presumably McDougall wasn't including American whiskey forts, as they had been built and occupied during his own sojourn in the West.

PEACE TREATY AT NOSE HILL

1. Many Swans name was sometimes translated as Big Swan, Old Swan, or simply The Swan.
2. William Francis Butler, *The Great Lone Land; A Narrative of Travel and Adventure in the North-West of America.* London: Sampson Low, Marston, Low & Searle, 1874, 313.
3. Alex Johnston, *The Battle at Belly River.* Lethbridge: Historical Society of Alberta, 1966, 3.
4. Interview with One Gun, by the author, March 5, 1957.
5. While Sweetgrass is not mentioned by name in accounts of this treaty, evidence would seem to indicate that he was the leader of the Battle River camp and the most likely person to have led the Cree delegation.
6. *Ibid.*

FIRST INTRUSIONS

1. Letter, John McDougall to Richard Hardisty,

October 20, 1874. Alexander Morris Papers, Public Archives of Manitoba.

THE WHISKEY MERCHANTS

1. Today, the Blackfoot tribe prefers to be known as the Siksika Nation.
2. Joel Overholser, *Fort Benton; World's Innermost Port.* Helena: Falcon Press, 1987, 254.
3. This location is based on L.V. Kelly's interview with Kanouse (*The Range Men.* Toronto: Coles Publishing, 1980, 93). Others have placed the location much farther upstream. Cecil Denny, for example, says it was upriver from another whiskey fort which was seven miles above the confluence (*The Riders of the Plains.* Calgary: Herald Company, 1905, 81).
4. John Johnston supposedly received his nickname from eating a Crow Indian's liver after a fight in Montana. However, Johnston claimed, "I didn't eat any; just rubbed it over my mouth to make that man think I was eating it." (*Cutbank (Montana) Pioneer Press,* April 6, 1917.)
5. *Helena Weekly Herald,* April 18, 1872.
6. *Macleod Advertiser,* August 22, 1912.
7. *Calgary Herald,* June 8, 1957.
8. Lewis O. Saum, "From Vermont to Whoop-Up Country; Some Letters of D.W. Davis, 1867-1878," *Montana The Magazine of Western History,* 35:3 (Summer 1985), 67.
9. Hugh A. Dempsey, ed., "Donald Graham's Narrative of 1872-73," *Alberta Historical Review,* 4:1 (Winter 1958), 19.
10. Beverley A. Stacey, "D.W. Davis, Whiskey Trader to Politician," *Alberta History,* 38:3 (Summer 1990), 7.

THE PIOUS MAVERICKS

1. John McDougall, *On Western Trails in the Early Seventies.* Toronto: William Briggs, 1911, 135.
2. A.J. Hetherington, *Our Lady of Peace.* Calgary: North-West Review, 1960, 35.
3. Interview with Father Tardif by the author, March 5, 1955.
4. John McDougall, *In the Days of the Red River Rebellion.* Toronto: William Briggs, 1903, 71.
5. Scollen Papers, Glenbow Archives. This poem was part of a group of papers held by descendants of Scollen's brother, William.
6. Cited in typed manuscript, "Reverend Father Constantine Scollen, O.M.I.," in Scollen Papers, M8038, Glenbow Archives.
7. Interview with Ayoungman, by the author, July 10, 1954.
8. Bernice Venini, "Father Constantine Scollen, Founder of the Calgary Mission," *The Canadian Catholic Historical Association Report,* 1942-43, 80.
9. R.B. Nevitt, *A Winter at Fort Macleod.* Calgary: Glenbow-Alberta Institute and McClelland & Stewart West, 1974, 55.
10. Letter, R.R. Nevitt, to Lizzie, January 16, 1876. Nevitt Papers, M891, Glenbow Archives.
11. Letter, Scollen to Lacombe, December 13, 1881. Scollen Papers, M8038, Glenbow Archives.
12. Letter, Thomas Taylor to Richard Hardisty, July

16, 1885. Hardisty Papers, M5908, Glenbow Archives.

FIRST FAMILY OF CALGARY

1. W.A. Griesbach, ed., "The Narrative of James Gibbons," *Alberta Historical Review,* 6:3 (Summer 1958), 3-4.
2. Lyn Hancock, with Marion Dowler, *Tell Me, Grandmother.* Toronto: McClelland & Stewart, 1985, 110.
3. This and other quotations from his letter are from the Toronto *Globe,* March 6, 1875.
4. Letter, John Bunn to Richard Hardisty, December 1, 1874. Hardisty Papers, Glenbow Archives.
5. *Calgary Herald,* September 5, 1888.
6. Burns and Elliott, *Calgary, Alberta, Her Industries & Resources.* Calgary, 1885, 77.

A FORT IN THE WILDERNESS

1. Cecil Denny, *The Law Marches West.* Toronto: J.M. Dent & Sons, 1939, 89.
2. Letter, A.R. Dyre to "Trevuss," October 6, 1882, in "Letters from the North-West," *Canada West Magazine,* 4:3 (Fall 1972), 37.
3. *Ibid.*

THE POLICEMAN, THE GIRL, AND THE STOVE

1. RCMP Papers, RG 18/A1/v.3/f.48A, NAC.
2. *Calgary Herald,* June 30, 1917.
3. *Ibid.*
4. Letter, Brisebois to A.G. Irvine, n.d. Correspondence book, 1876, RCMP Museum, Regina.
5. Letter, Leslie Wood to Richard Hardisty, December 15, 1875. Hardisty Papers, Glenbow Archives.
6. Letter, Brisebois to Hon. David Mills, December 20, 1875. Macdonald Papers, vol.324, p.301, NAC.
7. Letter, William Leslie Wood to Richard Hardisty, December 15, 1875. Hardisty Papers, Glenbow Archives.
8. Letter, R.R. Nevitt, Fort Brisebois, to Lizzie, January 16, 1876. Nevitt Papers, Glenbow Archives.
9. Letter, Irvine to Deputy Minister of Justice, April 25, 1876. Fort Macleod correspondence book, RCMP Museum, Regina.
10. *Minnedosa Tribune,* September 19, 1889.
11. *Idem.,* July 3, 1885.
12. *Montreal Gazette,* March 10, 1890.

WHAT'S IN A NAME?

1. Letter, A.G. Irvine to the Minister of Justice, February 19, 1876. The original letter is in City of Calgary Archives. All subsequent quotations of the letter are from this source.
2. Letter, Nevitt to Lizzie, January 16, 1876. Nevitt Papers, Glenbow Archives.
3. RCMP Papers, RG 18/A1/v.R4/no.112, NAC.
4. Cecil Denny, *The Law Marches West.* Toronto: J.M. Dent & Sons, 1939, 95.
5. *Calgary Herald,* January 22, 1983.
6. *The Naming of Calgary,* researched by Andrew Young. Calgary: Glenbow Museum, 1976, 6.
7. *Calgary Herald,* December 1, 1930.
8. *The Naming of Calgary, op. cit.,* 4.

THE SARCEES FIND A HOME

1. *Annual Report of the Department of Indian Affairs for the Year 1881.* Ottawa: Queen's Printer, 1882, xxv.
2. Hugh A. Dempsey, ed., "The Starvation Year; Edgar Dewdney's Diary for 1879," *Alberta History,* 31:1 (Winter 1983), 11.
3. *Annual Report for 1880.* Indian Affairs, 85.
4. Letter, Norman Macleod to Edgar Dewdney, December 1, 1880. Blood Reserve letter-book, RG 10, NAC.
5. *Ibid.*
6. Letter, Macleod to Dewdney, December 31, 1881. Blood Reserve letter-book, RG 10, NAC.
7. Letter, Percy G.H. Robinson to Norman Macleod, May 18, 1881. Blood Reserve letter-book, RG 10, NAC.
8. Edgar Dewdney in *Annual Report of the Department of Indian Affairs,* 1881, 40.

AN END TO ISOLATION

1. Charles Aeneas Shaw, *Tales of a Pioneer Surveyor.* Toronto: Longmans Canada Ltd., 1970, 120-21.
2. Letter, A.G. Irvine to Comptroller Fred White, February 27, 1882. RCMP Records, RG 18/B3/v.3/p.436, NAC.

ARRIVAL OF THE RAILWAY

1. *Manitoba Free Press,* March 15, 1883.
2. Letter, Irvine to Hon. Thomas White, February 19, 1883. RCMP Papers, RG 10, vol.4, NAC.
3. *Calgary Tribune,* August 5, 1887.
4. *Ibid.*
5. *Ibid.*
6. *Calgary Herald,* August 31, 1883.
7. P. Turner Bone, *When the Steel Went Through.* Toronto: Macmillan, 1947, 63.
8. Rev. Joshua Dyke in *Calgary Herald,* April 9, 1907.
9. *Winnipeg Daily Times,* September 29, 1884.
10. *Montreal Gazette,* May 7, 1884.

PATRIOTS AND RENEGADES

1. *The Globe,* Toronto, July 31, 1885.
2. Current political correctness demands that the troubles of 1885 be referred to as the "North-West Resistance" but this text uses the traditional term because it is more appropriate to this type of history.
3. Hugh A. Dempsey, ed., "Calgary and the Riel Rebellion," *Alberta History,* 33:2 (Spring 1985), 8.
4. Letter, W. Sherwood to Indian Commissioner, report for March 1885. Blackfoot letter-books, RG 10, NAC.
5. T. Bland Strange, *Gunner Jingo's Jubilee.* London: Remington & Co., 1893, 408.
6. Telegram, C. Shields to J.M. Egan, March 29, 1885. Scrapbook, "Outgoing Telegrams from the North-West." Glenbow Archives.
7. Desmond Morton & Reginald H. Roy, eds., *Telegrams of the North-West Campaign, 1885.* Toronto: The Champlain Society, 1972, 36.
8. *Idem.,* 108.
9. *Idem.,* 34.
10. Dempsey, 1985, 8.
11. David H. Breen, "Plain Talk from Plain Western

Men," *Alberta Historical Review,* 18:3 (Summer 1970), 8.
12. *Idem.,* 12.
13. *Calgary Herald,* September 16, 1885.
14. See "Ripping off the Soldiers in Alberta," by Jack F. Dunn. *Alberta History,* 41:2 (Spring 1993), 12-15.
15. Dunn, 1993, 12.
16. *Idem.,* 13.
17. Dempsey, 1985, 14-16.

JERRY TRAVIS AND THE WHISKEY RING

1. *A Law Treatise on the Constitutional Powers of Parliament, and of the Local Legislatures, under the British North America Act, 1867.* St. John: Sun Publishing Co., 1884.
2. *Calgary Tribune,* June 26, 1886.
3. Report of Commissioner A.G. Irvine in *Report of the Commissioner of the North-West Mounted Police Force, 1884.* Ottawa: Queen's Printer, 1885, 20.
4. *Idem.,* June 27, 1888.
5. *Calgary Tribune,* June 26, 1886.
6. Quite likely his name was Ingraham but he was never identified that way in the press.
7. Letter, Travis to Lieut. Governor Edgar Dewdney, December 3, 1885. Dewdney Papers, A/D515, Glenbow Archives.
8. Cited in *The Daily Sun,* St. John, December 7, 1885.
9. *Calgary Tribune,* November 11, 1885.
10. *Calgary Tribune,* November 11, 1885.
11. *Ibid.*
12. *Ibid.*
13. *Idem.,* December 16, 1885.
14. *Calgary Herald,* December 2, 1885.
15. *Idem.,* December 30, 1885.
16. *Calgary Tribune,* December 30, 1885.
17. *Manitoba Free Press,* January 6, 1886.
18. *Calgary Herald,* November 16, 1955.
19. Letter, Travis to Lieut. Governor Edgar Dewdney, December 3, 1885. Dewdney Papers, M320, Glenbow Archives.
20. For the mayoralty: Murdoch 130, Reilly 18, Dick 10; for council: Soules 151, Bannerman 149, Freeze 136, Lindsay 131, Grant 29, Davidson 27.
21. *Calgary Tribune,* May 15, 1886.
22. Letter, Chrysler to Bleecker, December 23, 1886. Cited in *Calgary Tribune,* June 26, 1886.
23. *Calgary Tribune,* February 13, 1886. However, this wasn't simply a Liberal versus Conservative campaign, for each party was represented on both sides of the question. For example, the *Calgary Herald* was a Conservative paper but while Cayley was in jail it was edited by Davis, a Liberal. And in the 1887 federal election, Davis worked on behalf of the Liberals while Henry Bleecker, a former Liberal, Alderman Millward and Doctor Lindsay actively supported the Conservatives.
24. Letter, Travis to Macdonald, March 15, 1886. Macdonald Papers, no.45826, NAC.
25. *The Daily Sun,* St. John, January 21, 1886.
26. *Calgary Tribune,* July 3, 1886.
27. Interestingly, Bob Edwards made reference to

this incident in the November 21, 1908, issue of the *Calgary Eye Opener,* commenting that "while we have been on many a bat in Calgary we never yet have had to be chopped out of the ice in the Bow River at four o'clock in the morning." In 1912, Edwards made another dig at the drinking habits of Davis, who by this time was head of the prestigious Vancouver law firm of Davis, Marshall & MacNeill. This time, Edwards went too far; he was sued by Davis and was forced to print a front-page retraction.
28. *Ibid.*
29. *Idem.,* June 26, 1886.
30. *The Western World,* Winnipeg, August 1890, 143.
31. *Idem.,* June 24, 1887.
32. *Calgary News-Telegram,* April 28, 1911.
33. *The Daily Sun,* St. John, December 19, 1885.

FIRE AND SANDSTONE

1. *Calgary Nor'Wester,* February 26, 1885.
2. *Calgary Tribune,* September 16, 1885.
3. *Ibid.*
4. *The Commercial,* Winnipeg, November 16, 1886.
5. Cited in *Calgary Herald,* November 13, 1886.
6. *Calgary Tribune,* November 12, 1886.
7. *The Commercial,* Winnipeg, November 16, 1886.
8. Richard Cunniffe, *Calgary – In Sandstone.* Calgary: Historical Society of Alberta, 1969.

GUNFIGHTERS AND KILLERS

1. *Idem.,* February 27, 1886.
2. *Sun River Sun,* June 19, 1884.
3. *Idem.,* September 4, 1886.
4. *Idem.,* April 10, 1889.
5. *Idem.,* July 1, 1884.
6. Williams wrote the book *Manitoba and the North-West; Journal of a Trip from Toronto to the Rocky Mountains.* Toronto: Hunter, Rose & Co., 1882.
7. Her father had been shown on the records as *See-ah-kus-ka* or *See-a-quak,* translated as Green Grass or Growing Grass. He had been #63 in Little Pine's band and #79 in Samson's band.
8. *Calgary Tribune,* March 6, 1889.
9. *Ibid.*
10. *Idem.,* July 17, 1889.
11. *Calgary Eye Opener,* October 23, 1920.

WAITING FOR THE BOOM

1. *The Dominion Illustrated,* June 28, 1890, 418.
2. *Ibid.*
3. *The Globe,* Toronto, July 29, 1893.
4. *The Commercial,* Winnipeg, January 1, 1894, 366.
5. *Idem.,* 369.
6. These figures are based upon Henderson's directories for 1893 and 1894 which indicate business listings for the previous autumn.
7. *Calgary Tribune,* July 6, 1894.

WHEN CALGARY BECAME A CITY

1. *Calgary Tribune,* February 1, 1893.
2. *Idem.,* May 10, 1893.
3. *Idem.,* May 17, 1893.
4. *Idem.,* July 26, 1893.
5. *Calgary Herald,* August 8, 1893.
6. *Idem.,* September 29, 1893.
7. *Calgary Tribune,* October 13, 1893.
8. *Calgary Herald,* October 17, 1893.

9. In 1901, the *Calgary Herald* had a contest to design an official Calgary crest. It was won by J.C. Wilson of Calgary and A.C. Racey of Montreal and was proclaimed in March of 1902. It consisted of a shield showing the Rocky Mountains and the St. George's Cross overlain with a maple leaf and buffalo bull, flanked by a rampant horse and steer, and surmounted by a mural crown and setting sun. Beneath the shield were the thistle, shamrock, rose, and leek, and below that was a scroll with the text "Onward" and the years "1882" and "1894." The 1882 date was an error, the town not having been formed until two years later. In 1975, the date was corrected to "1884" and in 1984 a full colour crest was adopted.

10. *Calgary Herald,* January 12, 1894.

11. *Idem.,* January 9, 1894.

12. *Idem.,* January 16, 1894.

THE RANCHMEN'S CLUB

1. *Calgary Herald,* April 19, 1900.

2. Sherrill MacLaren, *Braehead; Three Founding Families in Nineteenth Century Canada.* Toronto: McClelland and Stewart, 1986, 251.

3. *Officers, Members, Constitutions and Rules of the Ranchmen's Club of the City of Calgary, 1913.* Calgary: McAra Press, 1913, 48.

4. *The Albertan,* Calgary, November 14, 1930.

5. *A Short History of the Ranchmen's Club.* Privately printed, 1975, 5.

6. *Calgary Herald,* December 16, 1984.

7. *Idem.,* October 6, 1982.

8. *Idem.,* October 14, 1992.

9. *Idem.,* September 18, 1992.

THE TERRIBLE FLOODS

1. *Calgary Herald,* June 18, 1897.

2. *Ibid.*

3. *Ibid.*

4. *Idem.,* June 19, 1897.

5. *Ibid.*

6. *Ibid.*

7. Letter, Herbert Bull Calf to R.N. Wilson, July 8, 1902. In author's possession.

8. *The Globe,* Toronto, August 2, 1902; see also "Stranded on the Canadian Pacific," in *Alberta History,* 39:4 (Autumn 1991), 20-24.

OPTIMISM

1. John O. McHugh, "The Reminiscences of H2 Jack," manuscript in Glenbow Archives, M744. All McHugh citations are from this source.

2. *Calgary Weekly Herald,* October 3, 1901.

3. *Sarnia Observer,* February 22, 1901.

4. James Dickenson in the *London News,* reprinted in *Calgary Weekly Herald,* April 10, 1902.

5. The numbered streets and avenues were as follows:
   2nd Avenue – Abbott
   Centre Street – McTavish
   3rd Avenue – Egan
   1st Street W. – Scarth
   4th Avenue – Reinach
   2nd Street W. – Hamilton
   5th Avenue – Northcote
   3rd Street W. – Barclay
   6th Avenue – Angus

4th Street W. – Ross
7th Avenue – McIntyre
1st Street E. – Osler
8th Avenue – Stephen
2nd Street E. – Drinkwater
9th Avenue – Atlantic
3rd Street E. – Hardisty
10th Avenue – Pacific
4th Street E. – Dewdney
11th Avenue – Smith
5th Street E. – Irvine
12th Avenue – Van Horne
7th Street E. – Conrad
13th Avenue – Kennedy
14th Avenue – Grenfell
15th Avenue – Rose
17th Avenue – Notre Dame

A CAPITAL IDEA

1. *Calgary Herald,* January 20, 1905.

2. *The Birth of the Province.* Edmonton: United Western Communications Ltd., 1992, 75.

3. *Calgary Herald,* February 21, 1905.

4. Lewis G. Thomas, *The Liberal Party in Alberta.* Toronto: University of Toronto Press, 1959, 38.

5. *Calgary Herald,* April 9, 1907.

6. Sandra Martin and Roger Hall, eds., *Rupert Brooke in Canada.* Toronto: Peter Martin Associates Ltd., 1978, 98.

THE HUNDRED THOUSAND CLUB

1. *Calgary Herald,* July 24, 1906.

2. *Idem.,* July 3, 1906.

3. *Ibid.*

4. *Idem.,* November 7, 1906.

5. *Idem.,* November 9, 1906.

6. *Ibid.* The subsequent quotations regarding the meeting are from this source.

7. *Calgary Alberta: Commercial Metropolis of Western Canada.* Calgary: Hundred Thousand Club, 1907.

8. *Ibid.*

9. In fact, Sarah Bernhardt did appear in Calgary in January 1913.

10. *Calgary Herald,* December 3, 1906.

11. *Calgary Daily News,* September 26, 1907.

12. *Calgary Eye Opener,* October 18, 1911.

13. *Calgary News-Telegram,* February 24, 1912.

14. Grant McEwan, *Calgary Cavalcade.* Edmonton: The Institute of Applied Art, 1958, 160.

15. Robert Craig Brown and Ramsay Cook, *Canada, 1896-1921: A Nation Transformed.* Toronto: McClelland & Stewart, 1974, 198-99.

16. *Idem.,* June 12, 1915.

THE PRIVATELY OWNED CENTRE STREET BRIDGE

1. *The Morning Albertan,* April 14, 1911.

2. *Calgary News-Telegram,* April 7, 1911.

3. *Idem.,* April 10, 1911.

4. *Idem.,* April 25, 1911.

5. *Idem.,* April 27, 1911.

6. *Idem.,* July 1, 1911.

7. *Idem.,* July 17, 1911.

THE BIRTH OF CHINATOWN

1. See Gunther Baureiss, "The Chinese Community in Calgary," *Alberta Historical Review,* 22:2

(Spring 1974), 1-8; also Baureiss's MA thesis, "The City and the Subcommunity: The Chinese of Calgary," University of Calgary, 1971.

2. John O. McHugh, "The Reminiscences of H2 Jack," p.17. Glenbow Archives, M744.

3. *Calgary Herald,* September 22, 1909.

4. *The Morning Albertan,* July 23, 1907.

5. *Ibid.*

6. *Calgary Herald,* September 10, 1906.

7. *Idem.,* October 4, 1910.

8. *Ibid.* Bylaw 1090, passed in 1904, prohibited the addition of any more Chinese laundries on the business streets of Calgary.

9. *Calgary Herald,* October 6, 1910.

10. *Idem.,* October 7, 1910.

11. *Ibid.*

12. *Calgary News-Telegram,* October 10, 1910.

13. *Calgary Herald,* October 12, 1910.

14. *Idem.,* October 13, 1910.

15. *Ibid.*

16. *Idem.,* October 14, 1910.

17. *Ibid.*

18. *Ibid.*

WOMEN OF CALGARY

1. Irene Love in *Canada Monthly Magazine,* September 1911, reprinted in the *Calgary News-Telegram,* October 5, 1911.

2. *Calgary Herald,* July 17, 1902.

3. Irene Love in *Canada Monthly Magazine,* September 1911, reprinted in the *Calgary News-Telegram,* October 5, 1911. Unless otherwise noted, subsequent quotations about Calgary society women are from this source.

4. *Calgary News-Telegram,* August 21, 1911.

5. *Ibid.*

6. Muriel Holden, "The Normans Come to Calgary," *Alberta History,* 28:3 (Summer 1980), 26.

7. *The Morning Albertan,* July 22, 1907.

8. *Calgary News-Telegram,* April 10, 1912.

9. *Idem.,* April 13, 1912.

10. *Idem.,* July 25, 1911.

11. *Calgary Herald,* September 22, 1906.

12. James H. Gray, *Red Lights on the Prairies.* Toronto: Macmillan of Canada, 1971, 129.

13. *The Morning Albertan,* October 19, 1906.

PRELUDE TO BATTLE

1. *Calgary Herald,* July 31, 1914.

2. *Idem.,* August 5, 1914.

CALGARY GOES TO WAR

1. *The Albertan,* Calgary, August 21, 1959.

2. *Calgary Herald,* August 5, 1914.

3. Fred Kennedy, *Alberta Was My Beat.* Calgary: The Albertan, 1975, 22-23.

4. Kennedy, 1975, 25.

ONE BIG UNION

1. *Calgary Herald,* March 11, 1919.

2. *Idem.,* March 12, 1919.

3. *Idem.,* March 15, 1919.

4. *Idem.,* March 18, 1919.

BOB EDWARDS AND PROHIBITION

1. *Wetaskiwin Free Lance,* reprinted in the *Calgary Herald,* September 20, 1898.

2. *Idem.,* May 31, 1898.

3. *Idem.*, September 20, 1898.
4. Hugh A. Dempsey, ed., *The Best of Bob Edwards.* Edmonton: Hurtig, 1975, 115-16.
5. Grant MacEwan, *Eye Opener Bob.* Edmonton: Institute of Applied Art, 1957, 158.
6. *The Albertan,* Calgary, January 17, 1959.
7. *Calgary Eye Opener,* July 17, 1915.
8. *Idem.,* September 21, 1918.
9. *Idem.,* August 28, 1920.

THE TWENTIES THAT DIDN'T ROAR
1. *Calgary Herald,* December 30, 1922.
2. Margaret Howson, "Entertainment in the Period 1918-1929." Undated manuscript in the clipping file, Glenbow Library.
3. *Calgary Herald,* August 26, 1922. The article went on to describe the rest of the equipment. It stated, "The plate current is supplied at 2,000 volts pressure and the filaments are lighted by a 20-volt generator. The motor generator set is composed of a 2,000 V-D.C. generator on one end of a 5 h.p. motor and 1,000 watt V-D.C. generator on the other end."
4. *Calgary Herald,* July 22, 1922.
5. *Idem.,* July 15, 1922.
6. *Idem.,* July 16, 1923.
7. *Idem.,* June 30, 1923.
8. *Idem.,* July 9, 1923.
9. *The Albertan,* Calgary, July 13, 1923.

DEPRESSION AND WAR
1. *Calgary Herald,* December 27, 1930.
2. *Idem.,* January 16, 1932.

RIOTS OF THE UNEMPLOYED
1. *Calgary Herald,* December 15, 1930.
2. *Calgary Herald,* May 2, 1931.
3. *Calgary Herald,* June 24, 1931.
4. *Calgary Albertan,* June 30, 1931.
5. *Calgary Herald,* April 1, 1933.
6. *Calgary Albertan,* April 25, 1933.
7. *Calgary Herald,* April 25, 1933.
8. Pat Lenihan, one of the strikers, tried to call a meeting of several hundred unemployed just after the riot to demand a royal commission to examine the unrest in Calgary but the gathering was quickly broken up. Lenihan was arrested and commented, "I've been in jail before but I came out redder than ever." In later years, he became one of Calgary's most popular left-wing aldermen and labour leaders.
9. *Calgary Herald,* April 18, 1933.
10. *Calgary Herald,* August 9, 1941.

ANOTHER WAR
1. Other units mobilized at the outbreak of war included the 13th Anti-Aircraft Brigade and Construction Section, Signallers; 13th Army Service Corps; and 8th Field Ambulance, Royal Canadian Army Medical Corps. Later, they were followed by the 14th Army Tank Regiment (The Calgary Regiment (Tank)); 95th Field Battery, RCA; 23rd Anti-Tank Battery; 31st Reconnaissance Regiment; and additional engineer, service, medical, and ordnance units.
2. Lieutenant-Colonel Charles Carrington, quoted in Hugh G. Henry, Jr., *Dieppe Through the Lens of the German War Photographer.* London: Battle of Britain Prints International Ltd., 1993, 60.
3. Bazalgette was the fifth Calgarian to receive the British Empire's highest honour. In World War One, the Victoria Cross had been awarded to Brigadier F.M.W. Harvey, Major Harcus Strachan, Private John Chipman Kerr, and Private John George Pattison.
4. *Calgary Herald,* May 7, 1945.
5. *Ibid.*
6. *Calgary Herald,* August 15, 1945.
7. *Calgary Albertan,* August 16, 1945.

INTO A NEW ERA
1. *Calgary Herald,* August 15, 1945.
2. Allan Connery, *As Reported in The Herald.* Calgary: The Calgary Herald, 1982, 166.

A GRIDIRON SPECTACLE
1. William M. McLennan, *Sport in Early Calgary.* Calgary: Fort Brisebois Publishing, 1983, 158.
2. *Calgary Herald,* June 3, 1984.
3. *Idem.,* November 24, 1948.
4. *Idem.,* November 26, 1948.
5. *Idem.,* November 27, 1948.
6. *Ibid.*
7. *Idem.,* November 29, 1948.
8. There is a tradition that an enthusiastic Calgarian rode a horse through the lobby of the Royal York during the celebrations. The *Calgary Herald* interviewed Bill Herron (June 3, 1984) who stated the following: "'I absolutely did not ride a horse through the lobby of the Royal York Hotel.' And neither did anyone else, he added . . . The hotel manager, Angus McKinnon, was particulary worried. He'd heard stories that Herron planned to ride horse-back into the hotel . . . So McKinnon decided simply to ask Herron not to do it. He did, and Herron didn't. Herron says he's talked to 'at least a hundred people who've heard I did it. Some even say they saw me do it.'"
9. *Idem.,* July 27, 1984.
10. *Idem.,* December 1, 1948.
11. *Idem.,* November 29, 1948.
12. Once they had found their way to the Grey Cup, the Stampeders returned, but not as often as they would have liked. They were back in 1949 but lost to Montreal, and tried again unsuccessfully in 1968 and 1970. Not until 1971 were they again a Grey Cup winner when they defeated Toronto, 14-11. Calgary then suffered another long dry spell, coming back in 1991 and losing, but winning in 1992 when they defeated Winnipeg. In addition, Calgary played host to the Grey Cup for the city's centennial in 1975 and again in 1993, although in neither instance were they one of the competing teams. On both occasions, the West was represented by Calgary's old nemesis, the Edmonton Eskimos.

FINDING THE LOST FORT
1. R. Burton Deane, *Mounted Police Life in Canada.* London: Cassell and Co. Ltd., 1916, 106.
2. *Idem.,* 114.
3. *Idem.,* 130.
4. Letter, City Commissioner V.A. Newhall to CNR Superintendent L.D. Hickey, March 3, 1947.

MacCosham Papers, M1478, Glenbow Archives.
5. *The Albertan,* Calgary, January 11, 1973.

THE INCREDIBLE SEVENTIES
1. When formed in 1960, OPEC consisted of Saudi Arabia, Iran, Iraq, Kuwait, and Venezuela. Libya joined later.
2. Robert Collins, "Eighth Avenue," *Maclean's Magazine,* July 19, 1958, 21-22.
3. Peter Foster, *The Blue-Eyed Sheiks; The Canadian Oil Establishment.* Toronto: Collins, 1979, 42.
4. *The Canadian Annual Review of Politics and Public Affairs, 1974.* Toronto: University of Toronto Press, 1977, 260.
5. *Calgary Commercial,* March/April 1978, 18.
6. *Calgary Magazine,* September 1978, 8.
7. *Idem.,* November 1981, 54.
8. *Ibid.*
9. David K. Elton in *The Canadian Annual Review of Politics and Public Affairs, 1977.* Toronto: University of Toronto Press, 1980, 217.
10. *The Globe and Mail,* Toronto, November 1, 1979.
11. *The Canadian Annual Review of Politics and Public Affairs, 1981.* Toronto: University of Toronto Press, 1984, 440.
12. Frank Wesley Dabbs, "Empires in Conflict," *Calgary Magazine,* January 1981, 36.
13. *Calgary Commerce,* October 1982, 9.
14. *Idem.,* September 1982, 11.

THE UNEASY EIGHTIES
1. *Calgary Herald,* December 29, 1984.
2. *Alberta Report,* December 14, 1987, 19.

A BUNCH OF PINHEADS
1. *XV Olympic Winter Games: Official Report.* Calgary: XV Olympic Winter Games Organizing Committee, 1988, 73.
2. *Lethbridge Herald,* February 24, 1988.
3. *Calgary Herald,* February 19, 1988.
4. *Idem.,* February 28, 1988.
5. *Alberta Report,* March 7, 1988, 41.

OLD NEIGHBOURS
1. *Calgary Herald,* June 17, 1992.
2. *Idem.,* November 21, 1991.
3. *Idem.,* December 8, 1950.
4. *The Albertan,* February 8, 1973.
5. *Calgary Herald,* February 18, 1972.
6. *Idem.,* February 21, 1972.
7. *Idem.,* June 17, 1992.
8. Letter, Mayor Ralph Klein to Pauline Dempsey, October 27, 1986. In recipient's possession.

INTO THE TWENTY-FIRST CENTURY
1. *Calgary Herald,* May 13, 1972.
2. *Calgary Herald Magazine,* December 27, 1974. Unless otherwise stated, all 1974 quotations are from this source.
3. *Calgary Herald,* November 24, 1979.
4. *The Albertan,* Calgary, October 29, 1979.
5. *Calgary Herald Magazine,* December 27, 1974.

INDEX

Aberhart, William, 124
Adams, S.H., 114
Aguirre, John, 133
Aikenhead, A.E., 135
Akers, Dave, 13
Alberta Field Force, 44, 58
Alberta Irrigation Co., 72, 78
Alberta Mounted Rifles, 44
Alexander, George, 136
Alexander, H.B., 69
Alexander Corner, 84, 97
Amyot, Col. Guillaume, 44
Anderson, Ezzard "Sugarfoot," 133
Andrews, D.H., 69
Annas, Baptiste, 57
Antrobus, Cst. W.D., 26
Atkinson, William, 154
Avery, Randy, 143
Ayer, John, 137-39

Bad Eagle, Pat, 5
Baker, I.G., & Co., 15, 23-24, 26, 32, 35, 37-38, 41, 54, 55
Ballachey, John, 138
Balmoral, 93
Bannerman, James, 50, 66, 67, 68
Baptiste, Edgar, 152
Barter, John, 52
Bazalgette, Ian W., 127
Beatson, Gilbert, 138
Beaudoin, John, 47
Bell, Lt. Col. A.H., 104
Bell, Louie, 94
Bennett, Arthur, 91, 93
Bennett, Richard B., 70, 80
Berard, E., 27-28
Bernard, M.C., 70
Berry, Dick, 13
Bertrand, John, 56
Birney, John, 73, 95, 96
Blackfoot Indians, 3, 8-10, 21, 27, 32, 41-42, 152
Blackfoot Trail, 4
Blake, Cst., 56
Bleecker, Henry, 41, 43-45, 47-52
Bonald, Father Etienne, 17
Bone, P. Turner, 41
Bow Bottom, 4
Bowen, J.L., 53
Bowlen, Eddie, 117
Bowness, 73, 90, 100, 116, 132
Braden, T.B., 39, 42
Braithwaite, A.D., 69
Brett, Dr. R.G., 78-79
Brisebois, Ephrem, 7, 23, 25-29
Broatch, A.G., 109-11
Brocklebank, R.A., 84, 96
Broken Arm, 8-10
Brooke, Rupert, 81
Brown, F.H., 95
Bruised Head, Pete, 151
Buchanan, J., 96

Buckskin Shorty, see Reed, William
Buffalo, destruction of, 27
Bull Calf, Herbert, 73
Bull Head, 34-36
Bulyea, George H.V., 80
Bunn, John, 32
Burns, Pat, 97
Burstall, Vic, 138
Butlin, Joseph, 37-38, 55

Calgary, naming of, 30-32
Calgary, population, 41, 48, 61, 75, 81, 83-88, 131, 133, 139-40, 153
Calgary Exhibition & Stampede, 87, 116-18, 142, 146, 151-53
Calgary 400 Club, 71
Calgary Golf & Country Club, 98
Calgary Herald, 40, 48, 50, 66, 71, 73, 79, 95, 101, 115, 152
Calgary Milling Co., 82
Calgary Petroleum Club, 71
Calgary Professional Club, 71
Calgary Stampeders, 133-36
Calgary Winter Olympics, 146-51
Calgary-Edmonton rivalry, 81
Cameron, A.J., 68
Cameron, A.L., 96
Campbell, D.J., 107
Campbell, Neil, 117
Campbell, Thomas, 74
Canadian Pacific Railway, 37, 39-40, 73, 74, 78, 86, 87, 111
Cardinal, Alexis, 16-19
Carey, A., 55
Carney, Augustus, 43, 50
Carrol, James, 38
Cayley, Hugh S., 48-52
Central Park, 116
Centre Street Bridge, 89-93
Chinese in Calgary, 75, 91-95, 100, 130
Chong Kee, 94-96
Chrysler, F.H., 50
Chuckwagon racing, 116
Clarke, Simon John, 47
Clarke, William, 126
Clyde, Cst. T., 26
Co-operative Commonwealth Federation, 112, 124
Cochrane, Fitzgerald, 41
Cockburn, Eunice, 128
Commerce Club, 71
Commonwealth Air Training Plan, 127
Communism, 109-11, 120-24
Constantine, George, 53
Cook, G.B., 95
Cooper, Ken, 117
Costello, J.W., 41
Costigan, J. Frank, 107
Cottingham, John, 38, 43
Coutts, David, 138
Craig, G.W., 93
Crechita, Gregory, 74
Cree Indians, 8-10, 58

Crescent Heights, 89, 90, 91, 92
Crime and criminals, 56-60
Cross, Alfred E., 68-70
Cross, James B., 134
Crowchild, Daisy, 153
Crowchild, David, 135, 152, 153
Crowfoot, 11, 15-16, 18-19
Cuddy, Alfred, 102
Cunnington, Douglas W., 127
Currie Barracks, 103, 125, 127
Cushing, W.H., 66, 67-68, 79, 80, 81, 84

Dabbs, Frank, 144
Dagg, E.A., 96
Davidson, C.N., 50
Davidson, W.M., 79, 117
Davis, Donald W., 14-15, 23, 32
Davis, E.P., 47-52
Davison, Andy, 119-24
Dawson, Dr. Thomas, 96
Daze, Louis, 17-18
de Niverville, Boucher, 5
Deane, R. Burton, 137
Dempsey, Hugh A., 138
Dempsey, Pauline, 154
Denny, Cecil, 7, 24, 31, 35-36, 39, 137
Dewdney, Edgar, 35, 36
Dieppe Raid, 126
Dog Pound (Blood Indian), 17
Doucet, Father Leon, 19, 23
Dover, Mary, 133
Dunne, T.H., 54
Dyke, Rev. Joshua, 42, 51
Dyre, Cst. A.R., 25

Eastborough, 86
Eau Claire mill, 76
Edison, Joseph, 145
Edwards, Henrietta, 108
Edwards, Robert C. "Bob," 60, 86, 88, 112-14, 142
Elbow Park, 13, 86, 115, 132
Emerson, John, 79, 84
Emmerson, John, 96
English, Thomas, 101-102
Estey, Dr., 101

Feehan, J.S., 67-68
Fifteenth Light Horse, 103
Fires, 53-56
Fish Creek, 24, 35-36
Fish Creek Provincial Park, 4
Fisher, (trader), 13
Fisk, William "Jumbo," 51, 58-60
Floods, 71-74
Food bank, 145
Football, 133-36
Forbes, Hank, 56-57
Forest Lawn, 132
Fort Calgary, construction, 23-29; possible abandonment, 38; rediscovery of, 137-39
Fort La Jonquiere, 5-8

Fort Macleod, 18-19, 28, 30
Fourmond, Father Vital, 17
Fraser, A.C., 68
Fraser, Angus, 37
Fraser, Cst. G., 26
Freeze, I.S., 48-50, 54
French, Captain, 37
French, Lafayette, 38
Fullerton, Elmer, 125

Garden, James H., 93
Gardiner, William, 92
George, Joe, 94
Georgeson, William, 96
Getty, Ron, 138
Gibb, J.S., 52
Gibbons, James, 20
Gilkes, James, 136
Ginsburg, Rabbi Lewis, 139
Giough, Joe, 96
Gladstone, Fred, 151
Gladstone, Jim, 151
Glen, John, 24, 40, 43
Glenmore Dam, 20, 119
Godin, Mr., 72
Goodstriker, Rufus, 152
Graham, Donald, 14
Grande, Maxine, 128
Grandin, Bishop Vital, 15
Grant, Alex, 43, 55
Grant, Archibald, 42, 50
Grant, D.M. "Bitsy," 127
Graves, A.G., 96
Great Depression, 119-20
Great West Land Co., 85
Grey Cup, 1948, 133-36
Griffiths, Cst. H.E., 26, 28
Grogan, Jack, 134
Grogan, Thomas, 110

Halpen, Art, 113
Hamilton, Alfred B., 11
Hanson, Fritz, 133
Hardisty, Richard, 42
Harford, Ben, 68
Harrison, E.D. "Buck," 104
Haskins, Henry E., 96
Hatton, Major George, 44
Haultain, Frederick, 78-79
Hawkwood, 4
Healy, John J., 11, 14-15, 20
Heberling, R.S., 134
Henderson, Dr. Andrew, 41
Henderson, J.B., 95
Henry, Alexander, 3
Herchmer, Lawrence, 97
Herchmer, W.M., 137
Herron, William, 134
Hextall, John, 90
Hextall, Leonard, 107
Higgs, F.F., 84
Hill, Normie, 133, 135
Hillhurst, 73, 82, 87, 89, 92, 116, 119, 132

Hing, Charlie, 94
Ho Lem, 96
Holt, Herbert, 40
Hood, Harry, 136
Hooley, J.S., 111
Hornby, Alderman, 91
Hornett, Jim, 138
Howse, Jane Mary, 20, 22
Howson, Margaret, 114
Hudson's Bay Co., 24, 27, 35, 39, 41, 87, 91
Hull, William R., 66, 95, 97
Humble, Harry, 123
Humphries, T., 96
Hundred Thousand Club, 81-83
Hutchings, R.J., 67, 68, 79, 84

Inglewood, 39, 132
Ingraham, John, see Ingram, John
Ingram, John, 43, 46
Irvine, Col. Acheson G., 29, 31, 38, 46, 67

Jacques, George, 38, 51
Jacques, J.E., 68
Jamieson, Alice, 108
Janes, R.A., 67
Jensen, Emil, 121
Jephson, J.P.J., 69
Johnson, E. Pauline, 74
Johnson, James, 126
Johnston, Sgt., 35
Johnston, John "Liver-Eating," 13

Kanouse, H. A. "Fred," 12-14
Kaquitts, Tom, 153
Keir, May, 154
Kelsey, George, 59-60
Kennedy, Fred, 106, 107
King, Ed, 117
King, Frank, 147
King, George Clift, 23-24, 26, 38, 51-52, 54, 66
Kipp, Joe, 20
Klein, Ralph, 147
Knight, Joe, 110, 111
Knight, Pete, 117
Krueger, Scott, 57-58
Kwong, Louie, 94, 96
Kwong, Normie, 133
Kwong Man Yuen, 94
Kwong Wing Kee, 96

Labour relations, 109-12, 120-24
Lacombe, Father Albert, 16-17, 37, 43
Lafferty, Charles, 57-58
Lafferty, Dr. J.D., 76
Lam Kee, 94
Lamb, Mike, 149
Lambert, H.E., 96
Langdon & Shephard, 39-40
Langevin, Sir Hector, 26
Larondel, Alex, 57

Laurier, Wilfrid, 29, 79
La Verendrye, Pierre, 5
Layzell, Denny, 128
Lear, Les, 133, 135
LeBlanc, Sandra, 138
Leduc, Father Hippolyte, 17
Lee, T.S.C., 69
Leech, Cliff, 138
Leitch, Robert, 138
Lenihan, Pat, 125
Leslie, Jack, 138
Lestanc, Father, 66
Levenotsky, Fred, 121
L'Heureux, Jean, 18-19
Lindsay, Dr. Neville, 50, 65
Lineham, John, 54
Linton, James, 51
Liquor traffic, 11, 21, 45-52, 107-8, 112-14
Little Drum, 36
Livingston, Samuel H., 12, 19-22, 36, 38, 43
Livingstone, W., 96
Local Council of Women, 99, 108
Longbaugh, Harry, 56
Lorne, Lord, 22
Lougheed, Lady Isobel, 98
Lougheed, Sir James, 41, 51, 66, 84, 97, 98
Lougheed, Peter, 139, 140
Lowes, Fred C., 84, 86
Lowry, Lt. Col. W.A., 106
Lucas, Alexander, 65, 67-68
Luck, Phillip, 122
Lynn, Nat, 95
Lynne, Fred, 83

McAdams, Roberta, 108
McArthur, A.J., 89
McBride, A., 68
McCarthy, M.S., 70, 84
McClellan, Clifford, 74
McClung, Nellie, 108
McConachie, Harry, 134
Macdonald, John A., 51
McDougall, David, 20, 24
McDougall, Rev. John, 8, 12, 16-17, 20, 24
McDougall, Rev. George, 12
McDougall, George, 154
McDougall & Forester, 95
MacEwan, Grant, 113
McHugh, Jack, 75, 94
McIntyre, Donald, 125
Mackay, Don, 135
MacKenzie, J., 96
Mackie, Thomas, 96, 102
McKinney, Louise, 108
Mackintosh, Lieut.-Gov. Charles H., 67
McKnight, William L., 127
MacLauchlan, Donald H., 127
Maclean, Wendell, 67
McLellan, Thomas, 55

McLeod, Neil, 38
Macleod, Norman, 35-36
Macleod, James F., 26, 29, 30-32, 97
McManus, John, 57
Macpherson, Duncan, 68-69
Maguire, Jack, 56
Many Buffalo Stones Woman, 9-10
Many Swans, 8-10
Mark, Wilfred, 153
Marlin, Cst. J.C., 26
Marsh, George C., 47-48
Martin, James, 50
Maskipitoon, see Broken Arm
Mason, Lt. Col. E.G., 104
Mawer, Charles N., 127
Mawson, Thomas, 87, 93
Meadowlark Park, 132
Meikeljohn, Ken, 154
Mellon, "Irish," 72, 75
Metis, 24, 27, 43-44, 75
Mewata Park, 95, 116, 124
Might, S.H., 95
Miller, Jack M., 134-35
Mills Estate, 82
Millward, Joseph, 47, 50, 67
Mission district, 82
Mitchell, John, 89
Mitsuing, Ray, 152
Mona Lisa Art Gallery, 4
Montgomery, 132
Mortimer's Bakery, 54
Mount Royal, 86, 100
Mount Pleasant, 86, 90
Mountain Spring Brewery, 87, 101
Movie theatres, 114
Munro, Piskan, 27-28
Munroe, Louise, 24
Murdoch, George, 41-45, 45-52, 54, 59
Murphy, Emily, 108
Murphy, George, 128

Nabors, Jim, 13
National Energy Policy, 143-44, 145
Nelson, John, 5
Nevitt, Dr. Richard, 29, 30
New Grass, Rosalie, 58-59
Newall, James, 123
Newbolt, Robert, 70
Newbolt, Mrs. Robert, 98
Niblock, J., 74
Ninth Voltigeurs, 44
Niven, Robert, 147
Nolan, J.A., 68
Nolan, Patrick J., 97
Nolan, Mrs. Patrick J., 98
Norman, Will, 99
North American Constuction Co., 40
Northcote, Sir Stafford, 24
North-West Mounted Police, 21-32, 45-47
North-West Rebellion, 19, 29, 42-45, 59

Nose Hill, 8-10, 37, 155
Nutt, Fred, 123
Nuttall, George E., 127

Ogburn, R.J., 38
Oil development, 88, 114, 119, 132, 139-44, 145
Old Woman's Child, 13
Oliver, Frank, 78-79
Olympics, 146-51
One Big Union, 109-12
One Spot, Linda, 151
Orr, Wesley F., 39, 67-68
Our Lady of Peace mission, 12, 16-20

Pain, Thomas, 95
Palliser Hotel, 87, 132, 142
Pantages, Rod, 133
Parkdale, 4
Parkhill, 99
Parkyn, R.H., 111, 123
Parlby, Irene, 108
Pasedena, 86
Paterson, J.B., 90
Patterson, C., 117
Patterson, John, 54
Pearce, William, 72, 116
Pearson, Bertha, 101
Peel, F.J., 55
Pell, Cst. James, 27
Perrault, Cst. J.S., 27
Peterson, C.W., 40
Phibbs, Robert, 70
Pinkham, Ernest, 107
Pinkham, Jean, 98
Pinkham, W. Cyprian, 97, 98
Plus 15 walkways, 142
Point Mackay, 4
Poole, Eric, 123
Porterfield, W., 96
Potts, Jerry, 9
Power, T.C., & Brother, 24
Pratt, Bill, 147
Price, Harvey, 108
Prince, Peter, 66
Prince of Wales, 70, 109
Prohibition, 45-46, 107-8, 112-14
Prostitution, 40, 46-47, 51, 58-59, 101-2, 106
Pryce-Jones, Rex, 107
Pump Hill, 100

Quarter Million Club, 88

Radio broadcasting, 115
Rainy Chief, 17
Ramsay, S.A., 57
Ranching, 25, 41, 68-71, 76, 116
Ranchmen's Club, 68-71, 76
Red Crow, 14
Redwood Meadows, 153
Reed, William, 57
Rees, David, 109, 110

Regal Terrace, 93
Reilly, James, 48-51, 66, 67, 78
Reservoir Park, 103, 104, 106
Revenge Walker, 14
Richard, Mr., 72
Richardson, E.L., 85, 116
Rideau Park, 86, 119
Riel Rebellion, see North-West Rebellion
Riley, Dan, 117
Riley Park, 115
Ritchie, David, 122
Riverdale, 73
Rix, Jack, 154
Robinson, Cst. Percy, 26
Roenisch, Clint, 134
Rogers, Major A.B., 37-38
Rogers, E.R., 54, 72
Rogers & Grant, 43
Rosedale, 90
Roselle, Louis, 39
Rouleau, Charles B., 51, 58-59
Rouleau, Dr. E.H., 79
Rouleauville, 19, 66, 75
Rowley, C.W., 82
Roxboro Place, 86
Royal Hotel, 54
Runner, George, 135, 153
Rutherford, Alexander, 80, 81

St. George's Island, 115, 131
St. Pierre, Jacques LeGardeur, 5-6
Samis, Adoniram, 91
Samples, Asa, 38
Samson, Herbert, 68
Sanders, Gilbert E., 137
Sangster, G., 111
Sarcee Camp, 106, 125
Sarcee City, 106
Sarcee Indians, 32-36, 41-42, 75, 151-54
Schreiber, W.C., 39
Scollen, Father Constantine, 12, 16-19
Scott, "Clinker," see Krueger, Scott
Scott, J.S., 84
Scovil, W. Henry, 97
Seiberling, Gerry, 133
Selby-Smyth, Edward, 23, 26, 28
Shaganappi Park, 116
Shaw, Charles A., 37
Shaw, Samuel, 54, 97
Shead, Cst., 27
Short, James, 95-96
Sifton, Arthur L., 65, 66, 78
Sifton, Clifford, 79, 81
Siksika Nation, see Blackfoot Indians
Sinew (Cree Indian), 60
Sixty-fifth Mount Royal Rifles, 44
Smallpox Hospital, 101
Smart, James "Cappy," 73
Snake Child, 60
Social Credit, 112, 124
Soules, T.W., 50

Soup kitchen, 123
Spaith, Keith, 133, 135, 136
Sparrow, Angus, 38
Sparrow, Charles, 38, 54
Sparrow, Janet, 98
Sports, 100
Springbank, 12, 16, 20
Springwell, 86
Spruce Meadows, 142
Standerwick, Rev. R.H., 96
Starlight, Bruce, 152, 153
Staube's Gun Shop, 54
Steele, Supt. Samuel B., 44
Steinbrecker, John, 93
Stewart, Charles A., 79
Stewart, John, 39
Stimson, Fred, 69
Stonewall, Oscar, 134
Stoney Indians, 152, 153
Strange, T. Bland, 42, 44
Strathcona Park, 4
Streetcars, 90, 92, 143
Street names, 78
Strikes and lockouts, 109-12, 120-23
Strode, "Woody," 133, 136
Sun Hong Lee, 94
Sundance Kid, see Longbaugh, Harry
Sunnyside, 73, 92
Swain, L.R., 107
Sweetgrass, 9-10
Sykes, Rod, 138, 139, 153

Talbot, Peter, 79
Tallon, R.J., 109-11
Taylor, Ed, 76
Taylor, Harry "Kamoose," 24
Taylor, Judge Thomas, 51-52
Theatres, 142
Thodos, Pete, 133, 135
Thom, Ernest, 107
Thomas, Charlie, 20
Three Persons, Tom, 151
Tolman, Olive, 128
Toole, E.T., 107
Tourism, 116
Travis, Jeremiah, 45-52
Tregillis brick factory, 87
Trench, Hon. Sydney, 68
Trevor, Claire, 128
Trono, Dorothy, 128
Trott, S.W., 54
Trudeau, Pierre Elliott, 139, 140
Tsuu T'ina Nation, see Sarcee Indians
Turner, Harry, 72
Turner Valley, 88, 114, 119, 124, 132
Tuxedo Park, 86, 93, 132

Underwood, Thomas, 68, 94, 96, 97
Universities, 81, 87, 132
Urban Renewal, 132-33

V-E Day, 128
V-J Day, 128
Valleyfield, 139

Van Horne, William, 61
Van Vugt, Leo, 138
Van Wart, Sheriff, 96
Van Wart, J.G., 96
Vandermeer, Pete, 117
Victoria mission, 20
Viner, Harry, 134

Wah Kee, 94
Walker, James, 37, 41-43, 51, 72, 79, 97, 103
Warren, William, 147
Watson, E., 67
Weadick, Guy, 116
Webster, Charles H., 85, 87
Webster, George, 116-17
Wells, Jim, 151
West, Art, 134
Whiskey trade, see Liquor traffic
White Eagle, 13
Whitney, Roy, 152
Williams, Jesse, 57
Williams, W.H., 59
Windsor Park, 132
Wing, W.R., 94, 95
Wing Kee, 94
Winnipeg Light Infantry, 44
Wolves Den, 68
Woman's Canadian Club, 98
Women, 70-71, 97-102, 108, 114-15
Wong Yuen Jan, 96
Wong Chui, 96
Wood, Zachery T., 137
World War One, 104-107
World War Two, 125-28
Wright, Thomas, 35

Yee, Charlie, 96
Young, Andrew, 32
Young, John, 58
Young, Mrs. J.J., 98
Yuen Sun, 96